BACK *to the* LAND

Arthurdale, FDR's New Deal, and the
Costs of Economic Planning

C.J. MALONEY

WILEY

John Wiley & Sons, Inc.

Published by John Wiley & Sons, Inc., Hoboken, New Jersey.
Published simultaneously in Canada.

For general information on our other products and services or for technical support, please contact our Customer Care Department within the United States at (800) 762-2974, outside the United States at (317) 572-3993 or fax (317) 572-4002.

Wiley also publishes its books in a variety of electronic formats. Some content that appears in print may not be available in electronic books. For more information about Wiley products, visit our web site at www.wiley.com.

Library of Congress Cataloging-in-Publication Data

Maloney, C. J., 1969–
    Back to the land : Arthurdale, FDR's New Deal, and the costs of economic planning / C. J. Maloney.
        p. cm.
    Includes bibliographical references and index.
    ISBN 978-0-470-61063-3 (cloth); ISBN 978-1-118-02353-2 (ebk); ISBN 978-1-118-02356-3 (ebk); ISBN 978-1-118-02357-0 (ebk)
    1. Subsistence farming—West Virginia—Arthurdale. 2. Land settlement—West Virginia—Arthurdale. 3. Frontier and pioneer life—West Virginia—Arthurdale. 4. New Deal, 1933–1939. I. Title.
    S451.W4M35 2011
    307.1´4120975482—dc22

                                                                    2010045672

Printed in the United States of America

10 9 8 7 6 5 4 3 2 1

For Moma and Casey

Contents

Chapter 8   At Long Last, Arcadia   **179**

Epilogue: To the Victor, the Spoils   **193**

Arthurdale from 1933 to 1947

Federal Agencies that Administered Arthurdale

Division of Subsistence Homesteads, Department of the Interior	July 1933–May 1935
Division of Subsistence Homesteads, Resettlement Administration	May 1935–December 1936
Resettlement Administration, Department of Agriculture	January 1937–August 1937
Farm Security Administration, Department of Agriculture	September 1937–September 1942
National Housing Agency, Federal Public Housing Authority	October 1942–April 1947

Arthurdale Community Project Managers

Bushrod Grimes	November 1933–April 1934
Ornan B. Smart	April 1934–October 1934
G. M. Flynn	October 1934–February 1937
Glenn Work	March 1937–July 1941
Milford Mott	December 1941–April 1947

Acronyms Used
in the Book

AAA	Agricultural Adjustment Administration
AFSC	American Friends Service Committee
CWA	Civil Works Administration
DSH	Division of Subsistence Homesteads
FDR	Franklin Delano Roosevelt
FERA	Federal Emergency Relief Administration
FSA	Farm Security Administration
MCCA	Mountaineer Craftsmen's Cooperative Association
PWA	Public Works Administration
RA	Resettlement Agency
RFC	Reconstruction Finance Corporation
WPA	Works Progress Administration

Acronyms Used
in the Book

Here we sit in a branchy row, thinking of beautiful things we know,

Dreaming of deeds that we mean to do, all complete in a minute or two—

Something noble and wise and good, done by merely wishing we could!

By the rubbish in our wake, and the noble noise we make,

Be sure, be sure, we're going to do some splendid things!

—Rudyard Kipling, "Road Song of the Bandar-Log,"
The Jungle Book

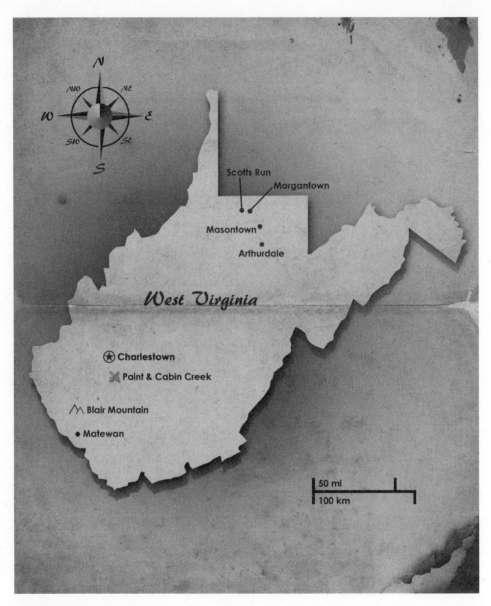

Map of West Virginia.
Source: Thomas Maloney, 2010.

Introduction

Arthurdale today does not, at least on first glance, seem to be much of a place at all.

—Michael Byers, *Preservation*[1]

T he story of Arthurdale begins just outside of Morgantown, West Virginia, in a five-mile long hollow* called Scotts Run. Like almost everything wretched, the tragedy that was visited upon the people who lived in Scotts Run was birthed in the turmoil of war, specifically in this case World War I, fought mostly in Europe from 1914 to 1919. Historian Niall Ferguson wondered aloud in *The*

*Like a valley; just with a notable depth to the bottom and steepness to the mountainside.

1

Pity of War why America does not seem to take much of an interest regarding that conflict's "effect at the time on American society."[2] He is correct; we have yet to take full measure of what President Woodrow Wilson's crusade cost us.

War of a modern scale continues to claim victims long after it ends and far from where it was fought. So it was that on a cold winter day in 1932 America a writer for the *New York Times* witnessed the burial of a little Scotts Run girl—she had died of exposure, a condition brought on in her case through a fatal combination of bitter winter and a lack of warm clothing.[3] Without a doubt, although she was born long after the Guns of August had fallen silent, it would have been entirely accurate for her family to say "She died in the war." If the innumerable contemporary accounts of all that took place in that hollow are to be believed, she was far from the only one.

The immense suffering experienced by the coal-mining peoples of America, a cataclysm that centered on West Virginia, Pennsylvania, and Kentucky, was a direct result of that conflict. The war that at first seemed a blessing for the miners became a biblical plague upon those who could, for the most part, only wonder what in the world had happened. When the Roosevelt administration stumbled across Scotts Run during 1933 and the first lady, Eleanor Roosevelt, saw firsthand the miners' destitution, she demanded of her husband, President Franklin Delano Roosevelt, that something be done for them. The town of Arthurdale, West Virginia, created and sustained expressly on FDR's command, was that something. The town took life as part of one of the New Deal's lesser-known but most influential components—the Division of Subsistence Homesteads.

Arthurdale was the culmination of a long-cherished dream for population resettlement held by FDR and the circle of like-minded men he had gathered about him as he ascended to power. Despite being dressed with the thin veneer of "charity," the town was something else entirely. Through careful planning of the physical environment by the federal authorities and education of the resettled (both young and old), the town was to introduce a "new American way of life," in the vision of its sponsors it was to build a new American man.

Openly touted by Eleanor Roosevelt (the town's most prominent booster) as a "human experiment station,"[4] never before (or in many ways since) have federal politicians ever meddled in the intimate details of the people's everyday lives to such a degree as at Arthurdale. Never have a group of American citizens been subject to such an "experiment." In the vast, discretionary powers allowed to the political class, the Division of Subsistence Homesteads was a battle between the ideals of the Old Republic and those of the New Deal.

The small band of dreamers who brought the town to life—FDR, the land economists Rexford Tugwell and M. L. Wilson, along with their allies—were not the kind to let a crisis go to waste, so to speak, and Arthurdale owes its very existence to Scotts Run. Without the tragedy that took place in the hollow, without all its gun battles and dynamite blasts and hungry children with distended bellies, Arthurdale would have remained just a dream for those who would eventually build it.

It was mostly from the pool of destitute coal miners in Scotts Run that it was populated, all the families resettled as part of a larger federal program that would build around 99 similar colonies across the nation.*

Arthurdale was the first, the most lavish, and the most publicized of the resettlement colonies built by the Division of Subsistence Homesteads. With the maturation of still photography and the growth in the movie industry during the early 1930s, stark images from the Run were broadcast nationally, as was the emergence of Arthurdale. The Run would become the poster child for the horrors of the Great Depression; Arthurdale the poster child for the beneficence of the New Deal and the man, FDR, who made it possible.

The town was massive, readymade, and luxurious, comprised of 165 homes set on multiacre plots laid out around a community center, school complex, factories, and administrative buildings, perched high and isolated in the Appalachian foothills of Preston County just south of Morgantown. The entire project, and the idea behind it, was a radical departure from anything ever before attempted by federal-level politicians. Although now long forgotten, Arthurdale was "one of the most open breaks with the individualistic tradition in American history"[5] as well as "one of the most far-reaching social organization efforts ever attempted by the federal government."[6]

---

*Depending on your definition, that number could rise to a bit less than 200.

I had stumbled across its existence as one trips while walking—by pure accident. It was a passing reference in a history book that sparked my interest,* then I became intrigued and began to dig deeper. Then I became obsessed. What lay before me was not just the story of the town's creation, fascinating in its own right, but the creation of the only America I have ever known.

The town helped serve to "introduce the new frontier of a regulatory welfare state then being blazed by the New Dealers."[7] To read of America before the New Deal is not so much to read of another time but of another country altogether. Arthurdale was the tipping point—every American born after its birth knows nothing of life in a republic.

Look about you today; much of the America you see had its genesis in Arthurdale.

Down the Memory Hole

Arthurdale was never studied, we never talked about the importance of Arthurdale.

—Deanna Hornyak, executive director,
Arthurdale Heritage, Inc. (1993)

America is covered from sea to shining sea with old battlefields, especially throughout its southern part, where one can hardly swing the arms without hitting a display of cannon. Some fields, such as Gettysburg, are visited often and held in reverence while others, such as New York City's Prospect Park, are visited often but no one sunning in the grass knows, or cares to know, that they are lying atop the bones of dead soldiers. And some battlefields, such as Arthurdale, are rarely visited and mostly forgotten. Arthurdale, in fact, is not even considered to have been a battlefield at all.

Admittedly, it looks nothing like an old battlefield; yet there is no better term but "battle" to describe what took place in the small mountain town. Because there were no pile of dead bodies or machine

*Wolfgang Schivelbusch's *Three New Deals*, specifically.

gun nests to be seen some would argue no battle took place, but they are wrong.

It was fought on a plane other than the physical. At Arthurdale one side was led by charging bureaucrats, armed with houses, food, indoor plumbing, and electricity, reinforced with impoverished coal-mining families resettled into the town's world of material plenty. Arrayed in feeble opposition stood the long-decayed remnant of the American republic, armed with warnings against putting expedience over principle and security over liberty. In the midst of a crushing Great Depression, the latter were easily overwhelmed and a new concept of America arose, that of one with a "progressive" government, using the New Deal as its blueprint.

Arthurdale was where the New Deal rubber hit the road, where the self-styled progressive intellectuals who reshaped America put their fondest dreams to the test. The Division of Subsistence Homesteads is one of the lesser-known of the New Deal's myriad projects, despite having had the intimate, deeply personal interest of both FDR and his wife, Eleanor. Animated by the back-to-the-land movement, whose anti-urban disciples called for politically engineered migrations from the city to the countryside, the idea attached itself onto the immense National Industrial Recovery Act of 1933 (through the personal efforts of President Roosevelt) with a treasure chest full of $25 million to get things started.[8]

Construction began in late 1933; the town was built in three stages over a four-year period under the authority of the Division of Subsistence Homesteads. At first Arthurdale was subordinate to the Department of the Interior but spent much of its life passed around repeatedly within the New Deal's swollen belly. From its creation until it faded within a few years to its current obscurity, Arthurdale was deluged by a stream of visitors from every corner of these United States and lay at the fore-front of America's attention. Newspapers, magazines, and newsreels trumpeted or condemned every twist and turn of the town's initial years. For the resettled, it was like living in a fishbowl. Now all is silent and forgotten. This may lead us to try resettlement colonies again, to tout an old idea as new.

During the time of Arthurdale's birth, a Professor R. W. Murchie noted, "In all times of economics stress and industrial disruption the cry of 'back to the land' is certain to be heard."[9] Currently mired in our own depression, the idea that created the town can always resurface, as it has repeatedly throughout our nation's history. We need to tally the costs and benefits of our past endeavors to see if it was worth all the time and trouble—and not only in pure materialistic terms but in something far more valuable: in its effect on our body politic and the rule of law.

As in the New Deal that spawned it, the ideology behind the back-to-the-land movement was "basically conservative, or even reactionary."[10] For all its "progressive" credentials the idea that created the town was centuries old, going back even to the time of Rome's Emperor Tiberius (A.D. 14–37) who instituted a similar project, with similar results.[11] In more recent times, the idea of planned farm communities predates the very birth of the American Republic, when a young Benjamin Franklin authored a land settlement bill for the English province of Pennsylvania,[12] and from 1820 to 1850 scores of settlement colonies, most founded on the socialistic ideologies of Robert Owens and Charles Fournier, were built across the young nation.

The instability engendered by communal ownership hastily destroyed them. From Michigan to New York, they gasped for air a few sickly years before expiring.[13] These settlement colonies (and all that were to follow, including Arthurdale) were animated by the central tenet of the back-to-the-land movement—a strict policy of forced "cooperation," particularly when performing whatever economic activity the colony was to engage in. Charles Fournier's insistence on communal ownership and that "each worker was to be given produce according to his needs"[14] preceded Karl Marx and his *Manifesto* by years.

At first, the federal politicians stayed out of the entire land settlement business, except, of course, for their chosen task of exterminating almost every Indian they came across, herding the survivors onto desolate land that no one else wanted, and giving the now-empty land away under the Homestead Act of 1862.[15] It was not until the 45th Congress of 1877–1878 that legislation was introduced to provide "federal aid to industrial workers, stranded by the depression"[16] in the form of three separate bills, all of which went down to total defeat on constitutional grounds.[17]

One of the sponsors, a Pennsylvania congressman named Hendrick B. Wright, announced after his bill slipped under the waves "that he did not suppose for a moment that the bill would pass, but merely wished to point the way for the future."[18] That future would move closer when the Newlands Reclamation Act was passed in 1902. Then, for the first time, federal authorities "assumed a responsibility for improving the land before sale."[19] It was a small first step toward Arthurdale.

The biggest push to federal involvement in settlement colonies was given by America's entry into World War I. It has always been a tradition, in this country and others, to reward returning soldiers with land, and "from 1916 to 1922 there was always at least one colonization or soldier settlement bill before Congress."[20] Above all it was a trio of men—the irrigation expert Elwood Mead, Franklin K. Lane (head of the United States Department of the Interior), and Senator John Bankhead from Alabama—who eagerly pushed for settlement legislation that would not only help returning soldiers but something more—it would improve and inaugurate "his economic and political life."[21]

Franklin Lane borrowed the specifics of his soldier settlement bill directly from the work Elwood Mead had performed along those lines while in Australia. Funded with taxpayer money and ready built so the new settlers placed therein could get cracking right away, the proposed colonies were not only a significant departure materially from past settlements but ideologically as well. For the first time, the politicians would task themselves with creating a "better world," with the colonists as the test subjects. The idea that would culminate at Arthurdale was now mature.

Their proposal resulted in a full-scale national debate with Mead and Lane the public face of its supporters. Despite the fact that no soldier settlement bill made it out of Congress alive, the ideas the bills expressed were becoming mainstream in America's intellectual parlors as the 1920s came to an end. Even before the onset of the Great Depression brought the idea into the realm of actual policy, it permeated American discourse, and with the hard times beginning in 1929, "never before in the history of the United States had back to the land been so popular, so frequently discussed, and so susceptible to crackpot schemes."[22] The ground was now fertile for Arthurdale's birth.

Wanting to see the town for myself, I first visited in 2009, when the residents were celebrating the 75th anniversary of its creation. I

drove south up the mountain roads of Route 7, past the beauty of a
countryside painted with occasional rows of rundown houses wedged
in between the road and the wall of mountain behind them. Once you
crest the hill that marks the boundary of Reedsville, the town just to
its north, you see Arthurdale before you, pleasant looking and comfortable, and you understand why so many of those resettled there used
"heaven" to describe what it was like to escape Scotts Run, to ascend
1,800 feet higher, 20 miles south, and a world away from the wretched
hollow.

I had expected the town to offer a small museum, a few buildings
maintained to a greater or lesser extent, and, I hoped, an old resident
or two who might remember what took place so many years ago. I
figured my chance of meeting anyone like that was virtually zero; but
I could not have been more wrong. Described by a writer as "one of
several surviving artifacts of the Division of Subsistence Homesteads,"[23]
the town is a "living museum" in every sense of the word. Many
of the current residents are direct descendants of the families that the
New Deal resettled there.

The night I arrived the town was holding its annual reunion dinner
for those who had graduated from its high school, and I had purchased
tickets for my family. Arthurdale is a small Appalachian community
where everyone knows everyone, and we stood out like sore thumbs.
The evening's master of ceremonies asked (in a very kind, polite
manner) if we wished to explain who we were and why we had chosen
to visit them. Taking the microphone, I explained the why (writing a
book) and was stunned by the deluge of offers to provide any information I felt I needed. The people are possessed with the openheartedness
of the country dweller that always takes the city dweller by surprise.
Then and on my future visits and phone calls, they struck me as thor-
oughly decent people, the kind you would not mind having for
neighbors.

Getting "too close" to your subject is something that every writer
strives to avoid, lest it affect your willingness to lay out the cards as you
find them. Much of what my research revealed over the past three years
does not match the happy memories of Arthurdale's later generations;
some of it flies directly in the face of the image the town leaders wish
to project. I have no ax to grind, no agenda to push other than to tell

the story of what happened. Sometimes you are sorry for what you have to say.

The historian Paul Conkin (who wrote the definitive book on the New Deal resettlement program)* spoke at a symposium at Arthurdale in 1994 and directly addressed my dilemma. "Present celebrations may conceal the reasons for such a sense of communal solidarity. A strong sense of community is most often the product of shared adversity . . . it is easy for later generations at Arthurdale to celebrate beginnings that they do not remember. Memory need not deceive, but it is mercifully selective."[24]

A homesteader named Andy Wolfe was interviewed years after the project was closed down and recalled, "Everybody knowed everybody. Everybody was happy. There was no selfishness."[25] Numerous government, private, and even homesteader records from the time tell us otherwise.

Today, Arthurdale has settled nicely into its role not as the gateway to some desired New World but as a bedroom community for Morgantown, the city that holds West Virginia University and most of the area jobs. Over half of the town's current homes were built during the early 1930s and have a unique distinction—they were the ones erected by the Division of Subsistence Homesteads. From the time of Arthurdale's birth, U.S. federal politicians would play an increasingly activist role in promoting American homeownership. Arthurdale was a massive federal housing project—the first in our nation—but it was also something much more, and that is what makes it so unique to our history and so important to understanding what we have become as a nation.

In 1934 a reporter from the *New Republic* said of the town, "Here the 'Roosevelt Revolution' shoots its farthest bolt and changes nothing."[26] He was incorrect; for Americans, both then and now, what happened at Arthurdale changed everything. Rexford Tugwell, who ran the Resettlement Administration responsible for Arthurdale from 1935 to 1936, was more accurate when he declared, "We have already made many commitments which are inconsistent with complete laissez faire and which clearly foreshadow the future."[27] Arthurdale was touted

* *Tomorrow a New World: The New Deal Community Program.*

as not only the Roosevelt administration's answer to the poverty and violence of Scotts Run but also, more important, as the answer to what it saw as a problem with American society as a whole. Again in the words of Rexford Tugwell, it wished to "make America over"[28] and for better or for worse in that it succeeded.

The experiment conducted at Arthurdale during its period of federal control from 1933 to 1947 shaped the world of every American today. It was there the ideas that once limited and dispersed political power in America were put to rest and pushed aside, and the idea that it was possible to make men "better" via politically engineered social experiments replaced them. That concept of government is the one that rules our world; 75 years on we can imagine no other way of life. The seeds that grew into the centralized, monolithic state we live under today were planted at Arthurdale.[29] Even now the constant political efforts to improve the human material of America continue apace.

Yet today, it has slipped into an obscurity so deep that the I-68 Interstate just 10 miles to its north bears no mention that Arthurdale, the Lexington and Concord of the Roosevelt Revolution, lies but 10 miles south. Back in the late 1930s, Bushrod Grimes (the town's first federal project manager) wrote that what had happened there was "a tale that will also be told in good time."[30] This book is about what happened all those years ago high on a West Virginia mountain plateau and how we live with it effects in our everyday lives, eight decades later.

It is time that Americans grant Arthurdale the respect it deserves. Our world is the one erected by Franklin Delano Roosevelt's New Deal, and the dramatic rise of federal power into everyday life was given its purest expression in the resettlement colonies of his subsistence homestead program.

Arthurdale was that program's crown jewel; it is the cradle of modern America.

Scotts Run at the Dawn

Without Scotts Run, Arthurdale would not exist.
—Nancy Hoffman, *Eleanor Roosevelt and the Arthurdale Experiment*[31]

Scotts Run was not always the image of Dante's *Inferno* that Mrs. Roosevelt first saw in 1933 and area missionaries had been seeing from 1924 onward: The hunger, misery, and endemic poverty arrived on the scene long after the coal companies. Scotts Run was a special place because it was laid over some of the richest coalfields in the world,[32] and for a brief burst of time it had enriched many, both owners and miners. The Morgantown and Wheeling Railroad was laid up into Scotts Run specifically to help bring out the coal, and contemporary accounts claim it to have been "the most profitable short run railroad in the country."[33]

It lay just to the west of the city of Morgantown and like that city belongs to Monongalia County, in the northern part of West Virginia that lies just below the southern border of Pennsylvania. The name itself comes from the stream that wanders from the mining town of Cassville in the western part of the hollow, flows down between the steep forested ridges on each side and past the coal camps of Jere, Pursglove, and Osage, to empty into its eastern terminus, the Monongahela River.[34]

The Run morphed from a world of small family farms into a line of endless coal camps with stunning rapidity. According to one source, the area's population rose from 1,173 in 1910 to 3,160 in 1920 then rose again by 1930 to 6,857 people and numerous coal companies crammed into the narrow, five-mile-long hollow. Cass District, of which Scotts Run is a part, "became one of the three most populous districts within Monongalia County."[35] The heavy inflow of miners created a quirk in the age of Jim Crow—an extraordinarily diverse mix of racial and national groups living all mixed up together, mostly in peace.

In the mid-1920s a church group in Osage coal camp recorded a population of 162 families with 322 children, composed of native white and black Americans, Hungarians, Italians, Irish, Lithuanian, Polish, Serbian, Slovak, and Greek.[36] A survey conducted by missionaries in the area during the early 1930s put the population as majority (about 60 percent) foreign born, with native-born whites and blacks splitting the difference at 20 percent each,[37] in an area that as recently as the late nineteenth century had been a patch quilt of small family farms where "immigrants and African-Americans composed barely 1 percent of the population."[38]

Plans were discussed to create subsistence homesteads for blacks in Monongalia County in 1935, but they came to naught.[39] While many contemporaries from that time and place made note of the Run's relative harmony among the various races, that situation was quick to change in the postbubble world, and "with hard economic times came frustration and prejudice against those who were foreign born and African American."[40] Historian Jerry Bruce Thomas makes clear that "the Ku Klux Klan was very active in the state in the 1920s,"[41] and no doubt during that time in history this did not make West Virginia unique among any state in the union. The progressive's insistence that Arthurdale exclude nonwhites was one of the few decisions made by the federal planners that observers found, for the most part, noncontroversial.

The starting gun blast that set in motion the creation of Arthurdale was the bursting of the great coal bubble, pumped into a manic speculative bid by the lethal combination of America's entry into World War I and the easy money policy of the Federal Reserve Bank during the same time. The end game of that frenzy, which landed on America's great coal-mining regions in the early 1920s, established a level of misery and violence in Scotts Run that shocked and frightened outsiders who observed it. The word "revolution" was in the air. Where once President Thomas Jefferson specifically feared a *lack* of revolutions (feeling it foretold the death of liberty), in contrast Arthurdale was born from a pervasive fear *of* revolution within the Roosevelt administration.

The federal government employees who cried alarm at the prospect of revolution from the coal camps of Scotts Run were undoubtedly correct in their worries that violence could explode at any moment. Yet a West Virginian coal camp was, for the most part, always on the verge of violence. The bloodshed of the early 1930s that so horrified Eleanor Roosevelt and others had a long, sad history behind it. What they observed in Scotts Run was just one of the series of battles that came to be known as the Coal Wars.

When it comes to labor violence, absolutely no people in our union can hold a candle to the West Virginians. Those who noticed the coal camps for the first time in the early 1930s were almost without exception stunned by the West Virginian tradition of settling labor disputes by rifle, machine gun, and dynamite blast, not realizing they were looking on what was by then a long-established tradition.

Even to this day the people of West Virginia are some of the most distinctive of our union, but they were far more so in the early part of the last century. Being the land of the Hatfields and the McCoys, memory and blood feuds ran both deep and swift. The mountain people who came down from the hills to mine coal were an independent breed, with little understanding of the modern world, prone to lash out in violent confusion at what they did not understand and to react swiftly to any slight, real or perceived, to family honor. They set the tone for all the miners who would follow. On average, the people of Scotts Run were a volatile bunch.

The men who owned the coal mines were every bit as stubborn, intransient, and prone to violence as the rudest coal miner, and for those outside owners who were smart enough not to get physically involved on their own, armed local men were always available for the right price, eager to pitch into the fray.

Until the Civil War, what is now West Virginia was simply the western part of Virginia, one of the largest and most powerful states of our union. Coal mining has long been a part of the tapestry; even as early as 1861 it "was an important commercial enterprise in many counties"[42] throughout the area. One author described Logan County, which also lay along the Appalachian Mountain zone 150 miles or so south of Scotts Run, as "a land of high mountains, deep gorges, rushing streams, and blood feuds."[43]

Life on the mountain farms was isolation and poverty, and by the time the coal companies began to arrive in the late 1800s, not much had changed since the first settlers had pushed into the area. The introduction of the industry would engender a sea change in the lives of the mountain people—a range of new choices and knowledge were opened up to them. They eagerly flocked to that which promised a better life and, for a time, coal mining made good on that promise.

The average coal mine was usually located in an isolated area far from any modern amenities, so in order to attract workers, the coal operators needed to provide everything, from housing, to stores, to the church. The owner of the mine was employer, landlord, credit agent, and church deacon. This gave the coal operators an unusual degree of control over their workforce, and some took full advantage. Striking miners, or any thought to be troublemakers, faced an unceremonious eviction from company housing. Evictions were often the spark to ignite violence.

The most insidious feature of the camps was the company store system and miners' wages paid not in money but in "company script," redeemable only at the store. While the company store always charged higher prices than that which might have been available in the surrounding area, they also extended credit to mine employees.[44] It was not uncommon for the company store to allow miners "a dollar or two at the end of the week to get along on."[45]

Although this may be seen as a decent gesture on the part of the coal company, as a form of charity to help ameliorate the miners' plight, it also had the effect of sinking them even deeper into debt, and over time it made miners "entirely dependent on the company store for food."[46] The ready road this provided for miners to get themselves into hopeless financial straits was frequently commented on in news reports and firsthand accounts. If competition appeared in the area, some coal companies would institute a firm policy: Shop anywhere other than the company store and you would lose your job.

It was only at the company store where miners could spend at face value the round brass discs or pieces of paper known as company script that they were "paid" with.[47] The script could be traded close around the camps but only at depreciation to its face value. This blatantly illegal and fraudulent "money" was often all that miners would see for years on end, if they were lucky.

Many miners labored for months without receiving any pay at all, so indebted to the company store had they become.[48] Between the higher prices charged for food in the company stores, the payment for labor in "money" that was utterly useless outside the camp, and company policies that would see anyone who shopped elsewhere fired (and evicted), the ability of miners to feed themselves and their families on already inadequate wages was severely compromised.

Most insidious of all, when the mines shut down, the workers, paid (if at all) in money that was worthless outside of the coal camps were left utterly destitute and helpless. While the Joads from Steinbeck's *The Grapes of Wrath* had the U.S. dollars to go seek opportunity elsewhere, all too many families in the coal camps had, at best, worthless company-issued tokens. The term "stranded" came into popular usage to describe the people in such straits. Their suffering is beyond our comprehension—the worst examples that modern America can produce give nothing comparable to the wretched postbubble coal camp.

As always, this fell hardest onto the most vulnerable members of the population—the women and children. The life of a woman in the coal camps could be particularly severe, as custom dictated strict barriers to what she could and could not do. One thing women were encouraged to do was to have children, rapidly and frequently.[49] One news reporter from the time found that "[i]t is quite usual for the girls to marry at 15 and to be having their eighth child at 27. At Crown Mine there is a young woman of 31, but she is already a grandmother."[50]

In a world with so much to despair, the combination of alcohol (available at the company store) and the ubiquitous labor strife left women exposed to physical violence, and relief workers quickly grew used to being greeted at the door by women with bruised faces.[51] The control dominating husbands had over their lives could be extreme; one relief worker noted a young woman, married at 13 and with four children (and one on the way) by age 21, had a husband who had not "let her off the hill for months." The woman could not read. The relief worker added "this [is] a general condition on Scotts Run."[52]

Life in the Run was particularly harsh on the camp children. When a Quaker relief organization entered the Run in 1932, it reported that lack of clothing and food had bred "epidemic numbers of children with bad tonsils and throats, troublesome teeth, weak eyes, and nervous disorders."[53] The typical fare for Scotts Run was dried beans, cornmeal, and fatback. If the surrounding area allowed, the children were sent into the mountains to scrounge for wild berries.[54] The average diet in the camps lowered resistance to a host of preventable diseases and lead to a mortality rate among the younger children of one in five (the average in America at the time was less than six per hundred), according to a report in *The Nation*.[55]

When child-feeding programs were instituted across the Run starting in the 1920s (using schoolhouses as distribution points), the lack of clothing and shoes made it impossible for many of the worst-off children to reach the offered supplies. For the children born into the hardest-hit camps, all the squalor and poverty was their entire world; they knew of no other. The progressive magazine *Christian Century* commented from the Run in 1932, "[T]he children, sweet faced and beautiful seemed to have forgotten how to smile."[56]

As coal companies went bankrupt during the postbubble collapse, the coal camps took on the appearance of towns laid waste by war. Structures sagged, then fell to pieces while refuse collected into whatever catch the wind or a human hand had tossed it, to the utter delight of legions of vermin. Most camps lacked even the most basic of sanitation services.[57] When social workers visited North American and Jew Hill (on the eastern edge of the Run), they found 16 families sharing six outdoor latrines[58] and saw "rats and mice were everywhere."[59] They were joined by swarms of flies and mosquitoes that happily multiplied in the stagnant, garbage-filled creeks.

At one time long before all of this, in what must have seemed a hazy dream, the Gilbert-Davis Mining Company had kept the water supply "carefully guarded" and saw to it that "an abundant and ample supply of pure spring and well water is provided at each camp,"[60] but by the early 1930s in Scotts Run, stagnant pools of water collected the runoff from the mines and outhouses that sat farther upstream, and as for those who live along India's Ganges River, the water supply in the area was a combination toilet, washing machine, bathtub, and drinking fountain.[61] The water in the Run turned predator.

To a greater or lesser extent, the scene in Scotts Run was repeated across America's coal-mining regions. The crushing debt burdens, isolation, endemic poverty, and suffering of the coal camps created frequent strikes and long periods of labor violence between the miners and the coal operators. Two of the better-known episodes took place south of Scotts Run, one at Cabin and Paint Creek and the other culminating in the largest land battle on American soil since the Civil War—the Battle of Blair Mountain. The famous massacre at Matewan was born of the labor strife, and while colorful characters such as Old Mother Jones and Sheriff Sid Hatfield fought for union aims, equally colorful (and violent) men such as "Boss" Don Chafin and the Felts Brothers stood opposite them.

These were just a few of the larger clashes in a story known to the people of West Virginia as the Coal Wars. The conflict would soon enough migrate north to Scotts Run, and by the time Eleanor Roosevelt set foot on stage, the Coal Wars had been a long-simmering conflict in the hollow, the constant skirmishes giving to the area its nickname touted by all the press, "Bloody Run."

It is within the hollow of Scotts Run and how it turned bloody where the story of Arthurdale must begin.

Chapter 1

The Damnedest Cesspool
of Human Misery

Oh, the pity of it.

—Mary Behner, missionary, Scotts Run,
West Virginia (1932)[1]

It was 1933. After nearly a decade, the fighting within Scotts Run had finally petered out. A reporter from the *Christian Century,* Charles R. Joy, had been sent to observe conditions in the area. He watched as a coal train rumbled slowly past a row of derelict cabins, abandoned and silent, like many of the coal mines spread in the hills around and above. The train, its cars piled high with coal, screeched to a halt.

A sudden burst of ragged families rushed out of the cabins and pounced on the immobile train. After climbing up the sides of the cars, they tossed coal out onto the ground as fast as they could. By the time the train left six minutes later (per Mr. Joy's timepiece), the coal in the railcars were no longer piled high, but concave.

"I suppose it is awful for us to be doing this, but if we didn't do it, we'd freeze," explained one woman to the incredulous reporter.[2] What he witnessed must have seemed straight out of a Charles Dickens novel, but by the early 1930s, it was a scene repeated from one end of the hollow to the other. Sidney D. Lee, who grew up in Scotts Run, recalled that "in 1926, purchased coal cost at least $3 a ton" from the local stores,[3] far out of many families' reach. For them, scrounging for coal was a necessary part of surviving West Virginia's harsh winters, and children throughout the Run ran to whatever lumps fell off the passing trains, to bring them home for burning.

The reports of what happened not only in northern West Virginia but also throughout America's coal-mining areas are all the more heart-breaking to read because they become so monotonous. It was a tragedy that, like the world war that caused it, need not have happened at all yet surfed all the way to the sand on a wave breaking beautifully from end to end, powered by ignorance, envy, money, and greed for power. Signed by the miners' union and the coal operators in 1924, the supremely foolish Jacksonville Agreement was the signal for Scotts Run to begin its share in the suffering.

The agreement had within it two fatal flaws and, in retrospect, you wonder how anyone could have missed them. First, it assumed that wage rates from the 1922 contract, set when coal was in high demand and prices were solid, could continue to be used as a rational pay scale in the face of both declining demand and falling prices. Second, the ability of nonunion operators to adjust their labor costs on a dime provided them a distinct pricing advantage that union mines could not hope to match. A man with a family would always, without fail, buy coal that was both lower priced and of better quality; and to him, whether it was mined by union labor or not was beside the point.

With both the demand and the price for coal in decline, it was only a short time, practically before the ink on the contract was dry, that "in a desperate attempt to stay solvent the northern operators abrogated the Jacksonville Agreement,"[4] an act that was the Sarajevo* for Scotts Run. It would trigger hostilities and mark a radical departure from the area's past experience, as this strike would be vastly more violent than anything seen before.[5]

While the fighting that was to erupt in Scotts Run did not provide battles on the scale of Blair Mountain or spectacular shoot-outs like Matewan, it would not finally end until 1932, eight years later, and the United Mine Workers of America (UMWA) strike that ended in 1931 made it the longest labor dispute in West Virginia history.[6] Scotts Run was a low-burning conflict, as the soldier-scholars like to say, a long, drawn-out war of attrition.

As always, history provides us with an expert's glowing report on the state of affairs, uttered the moment before the ship hit the iceberg. This one belongs to noted geologist I. C. White, who wrote during the summer of 1923, "The Scotts Run field has one distinction that is unique in its own way; union and non-union mines have been working peaceably, almost side by side, since the settlement of the strike last summer."[7] The end of this Eden would take the miners and their families into a crushing poverty that would literally remove the clothes from their backs and the very shoes from their children's feet, and throw them "into destitution and misery, and many of the operators into bankruptcy."[8]

But Scotts Run was not always a tragedy.

The Great Coal Bubble

The coal boom was the first and last high mark for the industry on Scotts Run.
—Professor Ronald L. Lewis, West Virginia University (1994)[9]

It had long been common knowledge that the area of Scotts Run was stuffed to bursting with coal underneath. As early as 1836, a geologist named William Barton Rogers led a team into the area, reporting back

---

*The Serbian city where, during 1914, the Austro-Hungarian Army's inspector general, the archduke Franz Ferdinand, had his trip cut short by getting assassinated, thereby triggering World War I.

that it possessed "several fine beds of coal";[10] his words would turn out to be one of history's great understatements. Scotts Run had more than a few fine beds of coal—it was estimated in the early 1920s that it had about 3.7 billion tons underneath[11]—and the field is still being mined to this day.

The area surrounding Morgantown had eight coal seams in the immediate vicinity, giving it, in the opinion of geologist White "the unique distinction of having more coal . . . than any other city in the world."[12] While White did have a bit of an interest in excessive cheerleading, as he himself was invested in those coalfields, it has to be granted how difficult it would have been to exaggerate the riches that Scotts Run seemed to dangle before any would-be businessman.

Scotts Run itself is part of the larger Fairmont Field, and had lying under it five massive coal beds that White designated "the Monongahela series":[13] the Pittsburgh, Redstone, Sewickley, Uniontown, and Waynesburg. Not all of them turned out to be economically viable to extract; as one contemporary recorded, "the Waynesburg seam proved unprofitable to mine."[14] Luckily, two seams in particular, the Pittsburgh and Sewickley, would prove to be mother lodes.

The Pittsburgh seam was "considered by many experts to be the most valuable mineral deposit in the world"[15] and had lying about 90 feet above it the Sewickley, which was for a time the Rolls-Royce of coal. Preferred by many for its characteristics when burned, farmers in particular took to it as it "burned like wood."[16] The Sewickley had "from a fuel viewpoint such marked and extraordinary qualities"[17] as would give Scotts Run coal its premier reputation, and many of the finest, high-end "limited" trains in the world would use nothing but Sewickley to power their engines.[18]

It is said that the first railcar loaded with coal on Scotts Run was at the Maidsville Mine on July 8, 1914, and "the biggest individual factor in building up this great industry was the construction of the railroads."[19] The man who wrote those words was incorrect—more than anything, it was World War I and the war machine's insatiable demand for the coal that built up the industry to its highest highs, before sending it all smashing to the ground.

Historian Ronald L. Lewis stated his opinion that "World War One unleashed the pivotal chain of events,"[20] and doesn't war always? There is no greater way to seemingly stimulate an economy than war, for making everyone get frantic to work, and combined with the easy money provided through America's newly reborn central bank, the industrial development in Scotts Run went into a speculative frenzy.

What happened in the coal fields outside of Morgantown, West Virginia, was nothing more or less than a tragedy, brought on by the artificial stimulus of war. Coal was in heavy demand in wartime America as it was vital to feed a booming weapons sector. The country became manic busy making things that explode, all to be shipped overseas to help the good people of Europe prolong the slaughter. In World War I, this was what allies were for, and come 1917, Woodrow Wilson's fondest wish came true and Congress agreed to send American boys into Europe's charnel house.

From a mere 400,000 tons as late as 1914, the amount of coal extracted annually from the coal fields of Monongalia County exploded upward to 2.9 million tons by 1920.[21] In a rapid transformation that seemed to have taken place overnight, Scotts Run's gradual change from a farming community to an industrialized mining center was put into overdrive, and it "became one of West Virginia's greatest industrial districts."[22] This hyperjump in demand for coal from the hollow overwhelmed the available rail lines, and on the "uneven, poorly ballasted roadbed . . . wrecks were frequent."[23]

The Run took on the physical features that later observers would remark on—it became a five-mile-long, narrow hollow stuffed with homes, people from both near and far, stores, and churches, and, in a long line as if soldiers at parade, the coal tipples* stood from end to end.[24] The war seemed a positive benefit to those in the hollow, providing jobs for many and coal dust for all. Scotts Run was industrialized to an extent unseen in any other hollow in West Virginia, if not in the country.[25]

Chasing after the profits offered by government purchase agents, operators and workers all flocked to the Run. Large and small operators sprouted like mushrooms.[26] While the Lever Act was passed in the summer of 1917, leading to price controls on the industry, coal still could be sold at $2.53 per ton in 1918 and in the spot market (for

---

*Structures from which coal can be loaded onto railcars for shipment.

immediate delivery) at $14 per ton. All this was from a price of 97 cents per ton in 1916.[27]

The coal boom caused the value of land in the Run to skyrocket. There are on record properties whose value rose from $6 in 1913 to around $2,000 during the war.[28] Land was not the only thing to see its price skyrocket—labor enjoyed a munificence that was only a dream during peacetime. Although government price setters had decreed a $5 minimum daily wage for miners, at the height of the coal bubble, "a miner might earn as much as $25 a day."[29]

Wages of $12 to $15 a day were common, and a newly christened coal miner after only a short period of time "received wages far in excess of the modest salaries paid to college professors" at the nearby West Virginia University.[30]

Like many a businessman, the workers who flocked en masse to the Run, lured by high wages, found the entire boom hard to understand yet took it for granted. Although wages far above what they could have earned just a short time earlier should have been a warning that it all could not last, many behaved as if it always would. A few decades later, looking back on it all, a writer for *Harper's Magazine* said of them, "of the majority that peculiarly American observation may be made: they couldn't stand prosperity."[31]

Even the *New York Times* (usually so understanding in these matters) took the miners to task for their profligate behavior toward this bounty, declaring "a coal loader made $20 to $40 a day. He bought silk shirts and wore them underground."[32] As icing on the cake, while 60,000 men were taken from West Virginia and inducted into the war machine, coal miners were specifically exempted from the draft.

Moving now into the picture, during the war the coal miners' union, the UMWA, won recognition from the federal government as the miners' agent.[33] Using as a lever a government concerned above all with maximizing war production and keeping labor quiet, the union forced its way into the coal fields despite an industry traditionally reluctant to accept it.

Union membership, traditionally moribund in West Virginia, exploded from 6,000 in 1914 to 53,000 by the war's end. The southern West Virginian coal fields, though, maintained their long resistance to such measures and remained for the most part free of unionism.

To be a Scotts Run coal miner during the war meant that times were good, yet just over the horizon waited something else, and when it arrived times would never be so good again.

The Hell of Peace

From the end of World War One until the early 1920s, Scotts Run was the marvel of the industry . . . the intensity of its rise was matched by its rapid and extended fall.

—Phil Ross, historian (1994)[34]

For a few years after the armies disbanded and marched home, the boom in Scotts Run continued to sound off loud. The happy miners and coal operators had yet to learn that war demands from all who participate that they, too, share its misery and suffering, but in the early 1920s the signs were easy to ignore.

More important to the long-run health of the coal industry, and therefore to Scotts Run and all who lived and worked in it, was the awakened appetite among federal employees to intervene in the coal industry. Although the early 1920s were still a time when the American people were far less willing to bow before political control than today, the war had introduced the government decree to business owners, and it was only natural that the powerful in Washington, DC, wished to continue to flex their newly found muscle.

It was not until 1922, *three* years after the guns fell silent, that President Warren G. Harding would finally lift federal regulation of the industry, yet before that time others in Washington would look to place their stamp onto how the coal industry was run.

In early 1921, the Republican senator from New York, William M. Calder, charged that the coal industry was making "excessive profits," specifically in the year 1920, and introduced a bill that would have allowed the Department of Commerce (then under President Herbert Hoover) to force the coal operators to reveal any statistical information on prices, production, and profit that a federal employee demanded.[35] As the chairman of the Senate Reconstruction Committee, Senator Calder had previously threatened the entire industry with nationalization as the coal operators had "failed to reduce prices adequately"[36] per his demands.

The coal companies had used the emergency of war to make a deal with the devil, and while that deal guaranteed them easy profit and labor peace, it came at the price of their freedom. In 1921, a great admirer of the wartime industrial codes, Republican senator William S. Kenyon from Iowa, began to agitate for a peacetime industrial code over the entire coal industry. He openly wished for a "code of principles for the determination of industrial disputes."[37]

Neither of these proposals would attain the status of law, but the coal operators were conditioned to walk softly around federal politicians, and this was to have negative consequences for all, especially in the aftermath of Herbert Hoover's disastrous meddling that led to the Jacksonville Agreement of 1924.

For now, although the end of the war did lead to declining demand for coal from other mined fields, Scotts Run continued to expand, bucking the trend due to the superiority of the area's coal as "the Sewickley seam's suitability as a steam fuel"[38] kept business humming. The year 1921 would prove to be a very good one; the violence between the coal operators and miners in the southern West Virginian coal fields pushed production north to Scotts Run, sending annual output in Monongalia County from 2.9 million tons in 1920 to 4.4 million tons in 1921.[39]

Rail freight traffic reflected the continued good times, with the average number of railcars sent out of the Run to shipping points on its east end rising from 175 per day to an average of about 200 per day between 1921 and 1924.[40] The average price received for a ton of Scotts Run coal in 1921 hovered around $4.65; although well below the market price of $14 per ton brought on by the war, it was still above the price ($2.53 per ton) decreed by government fiat during the conflict.[41]

The coal industry publication the Black Diamond from that time notes that, if given steady work, a hand loader in the mines of the Run could earn $168 per two weeks, or more than $4,000 per year, while a machine operator working the same hours could earn over $6,700 per year.[42] (About $50,000 and $84,000, respectively, in 2009 U.S. dollars.) In jarring contrast to what relief workers would encounter when they ventured into the wreckage of all this during the early

1930s, in the early 1920s, you could find "company towns that were clean and well maintained, with sturdy houses, paved streets, bowling alleys, and a theater."[43]

An article from 1923 points specifically to the Gilbert-Davis mines as a fine example of company-provided housing, with "electric lights, water, and modern conveniences."[44] With the price of coal high enough so that workers were able to produce sufficient revenue to pay for such amenities, life in the better coal camps along the Run was good.

At the peak of the coal boom, which reached its plateau in the years from 1922 to 1924, Scotts Run attained the height of its industrialization and had about three dozen or so mines operated by scores of companies large and small, from the well established to the fly by night operators.[45] The total capacity of the area could produce "536 cars, hauling 26,800 tons per day."[46]

Although 1924 was forecast to be another banner year for the Run, it was actually the beginning of the end. Efficiency gains in coal-burning trains and electrical plants combined with the rise of auto travel to lessen demand for coal, while the rising use of mechanization in the mines and its displacement of labor helped spark within Scotts Run the violence so common in the surrounding coal fields. It would knock the hollow from the pinnacle of an all-too-brief golden age. All of Monongalia County would see demand of over 9 million tons in 1926; by 1932, that number would plunge to 5 million tons, and that plunge would take the miners of Scotts Run into an abyss of misery.[47]

The opening ceremony for this plunge was the Jacksonville Agreement signed between the coal operators and UMWA officials in 1924.

The Agreement That Wasn't

The consumers, by their behavior in the market, are the ones who indirectly determine prices and wages.
                    —Ludwig von Mises, economist (1941)[48]

As 1924 approached, no less a person than future President Herbert Hoover, continuing the newly formed habit of political meddling in the coal industry, brokered an agreement on a new contract between the coal operators and the union. Designed to bring a modicum of labor peace to West Virginia, the resulting Jacksonville Agreement, like many a plan throughout history, would have the exact opposite effect of what was intended.

Calvin Coolidge once famously remarked about Herbert Hoover (whom he referred to derisively as "Wonder Boy") "that man has offered me unsolicited advice for six years, all of it bad."[49] If only the men gathered for the coal negotiations at Jacksonville, Florida, had felt the same way as Coolidge, a great deal of violence, bad blood, and trouble could have been prevented. Of his many blunders, the Jacksonville Agreement he brokered between the coal operators and the UMWA in 1924 ranks as one of his most destructive.

During the war, federal politicians granted to the United Mine Workers of America the designation as speaker for all miners and "refereed" the Washington Agreement between the union and the coal operators.* At a minimum of $5-per-day wages, the workers were happy, and despite the fact that government officials declared the power to arbitrarily set coal prices, the owners were satisfied because they did so at a level that "virtually guaranteed operators handsome profits," so much so that "even marginal operators profited handsomely during the war."[50] Everyone was making out like bandits, except for the taxpayer—but this was of no concern to anyone involved. As any reading of history will tell you, when matters such as these are decided, the taxpayer never counts for much.

Unfortunately for the miners, all the inflation engineered by the central bank was eroding the value of their new wages; their cost of living rose at a 64 percent clip within the four-year period of 1914 to 1918.[51] At the annual union convention in September 1918, the membership demanded a wage hike to account for the debasement of the U.S. dollar. Not getting any satisfaction, in November 1919 they began a nationwide strike.[52]

Scotts Run miners refused to join in the strike and continued to work under police protection. Within six weeks, the striking miners

---

*Come to an agreement or we'll "nationalize" your property, they said to the coal operators, and by all accounts this was a very persuasive argument.

grabbed for themselves a 14 percent wage increase, and a federal commission piled on another 27 percent soon thereafter. These actions, combined with aggressive union recruitment in the hollow, convinced many a miner that being union was not such a bad deal after all.[53]

This postwar agreement remained in effect for two years, from April 1920 until April 1922. Although the severe depression of 1920–1921 saw coal prices collapse by half, during negotiations in early 1922, union officials started off by demanding that wages for their members remain unchanged at $7.50 per day.[54] It was going to be a long negotiation process.

The year 1923 did not bring any relief to the industry, as nonunion coal came online with "a lower cost and often higher quality product."[55] Despite a further fall in coal prices to between $1.15 and $2.00 per ton and "the smokeless coals enter[ing] northern markets at even lower prices,"[56] as the year drew to a close, Hoover (Secretary of Commerce at the time) corralled the coal companies into signing the Jacksonville Agreement, which "maintained the 1922 wage scale."[57] Even more inexplicably, the contracts were to last until 1927. Unfortunately for the happy union members, most had just priced themselves out of a job.

According to one historian, "it was something of a tightrope walk for the industry to increase wages and prices but to remain competitive against other energy sources"[58] and it was a walk most could not make. Besides the competition from gas, diesel, and oil, the nonunion coal mines, with wages up to 35 percent lower, could provide consumers with coal at a far lower price.[59]

The Jacksonville Agreement did nothing more than drive union coal operators into bankruptcy and throw thousands of union coal miners out of work. It was a contract based on the same foolish policy— to never allow the price of labor to adjust downward even when necessary—that Hoover would push all over again from 1930 to 1932 with equally disastrous results. It had been lamented in the *Black Diamond* as early as 1922 that "there is no effort to go into the economics of the coal industry" whenever efforts were made to negotiate labor peace.[60] That should be the epitaph carved into Hoover's gravestone. Why the coal operators agreed to it in the first place is beyond rational explanation. They looked to break it before the ink had even dried.

Why UMWA president John L. Lewis happily agreed to the unchanged pay scale is a bit obvious, and it is also telling about the type of man he was that he knew and *hoped* it would throw over 200,000 miners out of work.[61] He was also banking on continued political pressure in favor of his union—for instance, in his push to have the Interstate Commerce Commission revise rail freight scales by political decree to favor union-mined coal.[62]

By its very nature, a union that makes economically irrational demands cannot succeed but by the use of force, and Lewis, a big player in Washington's political salons, was well aware of this. He realized that he was demanding wages out of line with what consumers were willing to pay for coal and that nonunion workers, more than willing to sell their labor for wages in line with prevailing economic conditions, could (and did) price his men right out of their jobs. To meet the goals demanded by the UMWA, lower-priced competition had to be legally forbidden and consumers forced to pay a higher price, things possible only by the use of political force. It was not until the New Deal instituted those very policies that the UMWA could claim victory in the coal fields.

The UMWA was more than willing to use political means to obtain an advantage even over fellow unionists. On July 26, 1926, Van A. Bittner, the union representative in the Scotts Run area, sent a cable to Secretary of Labor James J. Davis urging him to "investigate reports that members of the International Workers of the World (I.W.W.)" were mucking about in the Run, riling up the coal miners with their anarchist, socialist poison. "Our union will not tolerate their interference," he insisted.[63]

When John Brophy ran against Lewis for union president in 1926, he was far less subtle about the necessity of political power to meet their goals than Lewis ever was. Brophy's platform explicitly called for politicians to nationalize all the coal mines.[64] He lost, and Lewis managed to hold onto his position, but the union was rapidly shrinking under the weight of his refusal to acknowledge economic reality.

Lewis's continued demand for real wages that were out of proportion to what the market could bear were causing union mines to shut or severely reduce operations. In four years (from 1924 to 1927), the fields where the UMWA membership was strongest—in Pennsylvania,

Ohio, Indiana, and Illinois—"lost 44 million of yearly production" by consumers flocking to buy coal from nonunion mines in Kentucky, West Virginia, and Virginia, which "picked up 51 million ton."[65]

One of the clearest moments of bluntly spoken truth occurred during 1927 and was delivered by an exasperated southern Ohio coal operator to a group of striking miners. It deserves to be quoted at length. All the words in italics in it are from whatever unknown man once wrote them:

> Your officials say *You Men* instructed them to refuse a competitive scale. That means that *You Men* have forced your mines to cease operations, and have *Given Away Our Trade and Lost Your Own Jobs to Favor West Virginia and the Non-union fields.*[66]

The destruction of the union mine operators, shackled into guaranteed losses by inflexible wage scales, and the flow of miners to nonunion mines that were still open caused UMWA membership rolls to collapse almost into nonexistence by the end of the 1920s. The union had seen its strength fall from 50,000 in 1922 to a microscopic 600 at decade's end.[67] By then the UMWA was virtually unknown "in most of the important fields."[68]

By late 1924, the unionized coal mines were consistently running in the red; during November, coal operator Joseph Pursglove, who had extensive interest in Scotts Run, informed an unmoved John L. Lewis that "all the men who are operating union coal mines are going bankrupt."[69] Early 1925 saw "infinitesimal demand," and in response to coal operators who sold out their interests to other coal operators (who in turn would reopen the same mines as nonunion shops), Van A. Bittner, the UWMA representative in the Scotts Run area, called for a general strike to begin, fittingly, on April Fool's Day "in an effort to force restoration of the Jacksonville wage agreement."[70] Some union operators responded by simply closing their operations entirely. Within a few weeks, 2,240 miners had lost their jobs.[71]

Toward summer, the Gilbert-Davis mines announced they were voiding their contract with the union and withdrawing from the Jacksonville Agreement. Soon after, three of their coal tipples along Scotts Run were destroyed by fire. The company was only partially insured for the loss—which shows how badly its balance sheet was bleeding.

Even worse for all parties involved, "investigators determined that arson was the cause of the fire."[72] By now no one could deny that West Virginia's long history of labor violence in the coal fields had at last made its way into the area. The UMWA strike "triggered another bloody labor conflict."[73] The effects of World War I were now to hit home in Scotts Run, the Jacksonville Agreement marked the bursting of the hollow's coal bubble, later than elsewhere but with just as much suffering. The Run was now to enter a years-long period of misery, want, and labor violence that would earn it the nickname "Bloody Run."

The sad part of it all was that the violence was for nothing and utterly futile; the UMWA was fighting for control of something—a price—that is not tangible and no law can affect. Prices are a derivative of people's opinion as to what something is worth to them at a certain point in time, glimpses of an ever-changing mental state. You can throw all the law books and police at it as you can gather, and all you do is strengthen and delay the inevitable snapback, the time when people start ignoring the powerful and allow their opinions to roam free again.

The kings of any free market, always and everywhere, are the consumers, the ones who decide how much they are willing to pay for whatever you are offering. They determine everything, including how much the people who labor to provide that good get paid. Highlighting the absurdity of all the fighting (and to prove that God has a sense of humor) is the fact that the only ones ever to figure this out was the small communist rump of a union (the National Miners Union, or NMU). They went on strike in 1931 to protest *consumers*, to decry their unwillingness to pay a higher price for coal.[74] That strike was as futile as any other, but at least it showed some understanding on the NMU's part of what it was up against.

The UMWA was fighting for higher wages against the winds of progress, competition, and most of all the sovereign consumer's willingness and ability to be better served elsewhere. The days of frenzied war production and high demand were over, the slack-jawed dumb spendthrift government procurement agent was no longer knocking at their door with fistfuls of Other People's Money—and the union stubbornly refused to see it. The UMWA's insane refusal to acknowledge what was apparent to everyone else—that the coal industry was rapidly contracting in a postbubble period—must be laid at the feet of the men who ran the show, and front and center was most assuredly UMWA president John L. Lewis. Amazingly, and this is truly a testament to the man's political skill, despite his disastrous leadership, he managed to maintain his grip on the union all the way until 1960, and this only after being saved from the consumer by FDR's New Deal and World War II.

The UMWA, in the end, did far more harm than good for the miners of West Virginia. By encouraging the miners under their leadership to fight for wages they knew to be economically unviable, they instantly guaranteed a violent clash between the operators and the miners, with artificially high levels of unemployment thrown into the bargain. The mine operators and the shoddy treatment of their workforce made the situation even more emotionally charged.

Many have asked over the years why the unemployed miners simply did not pack up and leave, to go in search of work elsewhere. More than anything it was the widely noted, fraudulent, and blatantly illegal policy of the coal companies paying their workers not in money but in round brass discs that passed for company script that strongly argues that some operators had their miners in a virtual form of bondage, immobilized by both isolation and company money of no value outside the camp area.

It was here, to right this wrong, that the UMWA should have concentrated its primary effort. A victory would have granted far more miners the ability to leave the camps when things went downhill, freed them from bondage to the company store. Instead, stranded by lack of money and bereft (because of union wage demands) of any job at all, the miners bore the brunt of the bursting bubble; they were, literally, sitting ducks.

Those who were to suffer the most from all this were, at least in the beginning, pulled from their mountainside farms into Scotts Run as they sold out that hardscrabble existence for the relative abundance of coal mining.

Now, their farms a distant, hazy memory, they lived among the foul-smelling, smoking slag piles,* their deteriorating company shacks perched high and wretched, clinging to the sides of the steep hollows. In the mountains all round them empty black holes that once were teeming coal mines sat quiet and cold, while just to the east the gleaming lights of Morgantown, with its office buildings, restaurants, and paved roads, shone bright fewer than 10 miles and an unreachable universe away.

Yet before the trap was snapped closed by the bursting coal bubble, there followed on the heels of the West Virginia mountain folk a wave of foreigners, mostly of Eastern Europe stock, pulled into the local labor pool by high wages and accompanied by a flow of black Americans, fleeing the internal terror of Jim Crow for the relative safety of northern West Virginia.

By the time ink was put to the Jacksonville Agreement, all the victims had been gathered in the hollow for the tragedy of Scotts Run to begin. For Scotts Run, finally, the Coal Wars had arrived.

Scotts Run Turns Bloody

If you haven't got enough to eat go out and take it. There are not enough state police or yellow dogs in West Virginia to stop the army of the United Mine Workers of America.
   —Van A. Bittner, UMWA boss, West Virginia (1932)[75]

It was a busy day for the law officers who worked Scotts Run. The *Washington Post* next day (this was in November 1924) gave a rundown on page two outlining just how busy the Run had become. To start off, in the aftermath of a fight at the Diamond Coal Company mine, eight union and one nonunion miner were charged with attempted homicide and inciting a riot. "Four of the prisoners had bullet wounds,"[76] the paper dutifully noted.

Gunfire had become frequent enough throughout the hollow for the inevitable noncombatant casualties to crop up, and this day's victim

* A slag pile is a collection of refuse from coal mining. The coal in them frequently ignites and burns.

was "five year old Susan Rock, who was struck in the chest by a stray bullet, [and] is in critical condition." The same issue announced that "county authorities" were offering a $2,500 award (about $32,600 in 2009 dollars)[77] for any information leading to the arrest of whoever dynamited one of Shriver Coal Company's tipples to the ground.[78]

The quick death of the Jacksonville Agreement ushered into the Run a time of "evictions, tent colonies and barracks, injunctions, shootings, dynamiting, and arrests of miners and deputies," and it all added up to a "sense of turmoil."[79] One of the most potent and widely used weapons on the union side was dynamite and sabotage rather than widescale open battle. This was an intelligent strategy, as the crushing union defeats at Matewan and Blair Mountain proved that open assault on coal operator property would be met by a far more potent, well-funded force.

In one of many examples to choose from, it was reported that on August 1, 1926, a large dynamite blast erupted in Scotts Run near a barracks holding mostly black nonunion miners.[80] But of all the atrocities one man can visit on another, the most surprising claim from history is that of union-led sabotage against nonunion coal mines—while the nonunion coal miners were still in them. If true, it would highlight the desperate, vicious nature of the Coal Wars. For one group of coal miners to deliberately put another group into danger would seem to be the ultimate taboo, the ultimate breach of trust within a profession.

During the war's early stages, there were suspicious mining disasters on at least three occasions in the northern coal fields. On March 17, 1925, one in Barrackville, Marion County erupted, "completely destroying the mine"[81] and leaving at least 35 men dead. Also in Marion County, 19 died when the mine at Farmington exploded. And in the worst of the three, at a mine owned by the New England Fuel and Transportation Company in Everettville, Monongalia County, 97 men (the majority were African American and nonunion[82]) perished in a horrific blast. For the first two, "circumstances strongly confirmed the suspicions of the operators" that it was union led sabotage.[83]

As for the last, Howard Burton Lee, the Attorney General for West Virginia from 1925 to 1933, arrived on the scene, where he observed "that snarling animal hatred felt by members of the miners' union for non-union miners." He watched as the striking miners and their families openly mocked and cursed the grief and panic-stricken wives and children of the nonunion miners who waited sadly for their man's corpse to be carried to the surface.

Sidney D. Lee, who grew up in Scotts Run, recalled that "one of the sad consequences of a person being accused of being a scab* was that his family could suffer both physically and emotionally. Coal miners often became violent . . . I recall kids of a non-union miner being beaten severely by the children, usually bigger, of a union miner."[84]

All the rage was misdirected and pointless, as the coal companies could pay only what the market could bear, and the market could not bear the demands of the striking union men. During 1927 ongoing wage negotiations in Miami, Florida, came to naught as, "the coal men refused to reinstate the Jacksonville Scale."[85] Eighty million tons of inventory was already stockpiled by coal consumers, demand was forecast to be poor again, and the fact that the coal men were even talking about something so absurd as to pay a wage scale from the boom year of 1922 suggests that the UMWA leadership was actually insane enough to have bought it up.

"Wages fell to less than the 1917 levels for miners as coal dropped well below break even levels for the operators,"[86] and still the UMWA leadership insisted on the 1922 scale. Many union mines had simply closed or sold out to other coal operators, who reopened on a nonunion basis. All of Scotts Run was completely nonunion after 1927, yet another monumental failure on the part of John L. Lewis.

Mines opened and just as quickly closed, companies surfaced and went under like a cork in rough water; the violence ebbed and flowed until want and destitution took up residence in the hollow. Hungry, cold, and despondent, the mining population hunkered down like residents of a city under siege. Years later, the daughter of a famous Scotts Run missionary damned the coal companies, asking "how could they turn away from what they were creating out there?"[87] Yet her anger, like that of the ones blowing up the coal tipples, was misdirected. Why would businessmen deliberately sink their own ship? The endless strikes were a series of "gestures of despair rather than considered attempts to

---

*A nonunion coal miner.

force concessions from those able to grant them,"[88] according to a *New York Times* reporter. It was certainly not the doings of the coal operators who brought the coal industry low and the miners, and the operators too, into such dire economic straits.

The coal operators were no colder or warmer, no more or less human than the lowest hand loader; they were struggling with the same economic forces that the miners were. They could pay their employees only what the market price of coal could cover. During the war in the Run, "the best intentioned employees found it difficult to pay a living wage and remain in business."[89] Even such publications as the *Christian Century*, usually critical of businessmen, granted "the best-meaning employers are unable to pay anything but starvation wages." The striking miners were in a hopeless situation.

As 1926 rolled past, 750,000 men were employed in the coal-mining regions, a region that just a scant time before had supported barely a fraction of that number. By 1927, it is estimated that one-third of them were out of work.[90] Far too many men were chasing after jobs in a postbubble industry. During the 1920s, it was estimated that a quarter million men left the coal industry, "went back to the farm or into other industries."[91] The men who remained behind watched as wages continued to fall along with coal prices, mines closed, and violent action, pointless and irrational, took the place of calm, deliberate thought.

A new term came to be applied to those left behind, "stranded," meaning a group of people whose livelihood depended on one major employer or industry now collapsed. As late as 1934, contemporary writers estimated this "stranded" population to number between 300,000 and 500,000 miners and their families.[92]

By 1932, annual coal production in Monongalia County had dropped to 5 million tons, and come April 1933, approximately 41 percent of the population was on relief with the harder-hit areas spiking to 64 percent. "In some coal camps, virtually the entire population was out of work."[93]

To protest the lowest wage level since 1913,[94] in May 1931, the miners in Scotts Run, for the most part the same ones who had taken jobs as scabs back during the strikes of 1925, themselves went out on strike.[95] In the long line of similarly hopeless strikes, where desperate men made impossible demands, this one would be different. It would finally, seven years after it began, bring the labor strike in Scotts Run to an end. Likely it did not seem that way at the time.

Then John L. Lewis and the UMWA caught two lucky breaks. The miners walked out on their own, without union leadership. That vacuum was soon filled when Van A. Bittner saw his chance and persuaded the former scabs to join the union. Then the coal operators, seeing the local communist-backed NMU stage its own strike, were filled with visions of themselves and their families dangling from hammers and sickles and promptly rushed to the UMWA and officially recognized it as the miners' voice. For the first time in seven years, the operators and the union were dating again.

The union agreement that was signed in June 1931 was notable in that the UMWA, this time, was willing to compromise on the wage scale; the one agreed to, at 30 cents a ton (or $3.60 a day), was less than half of the old Jacksonville Agreement (63 cents a ton). Even more notable, the agreement mandated a union wage scale less than the one prevailing in the area at the time for nonunion mines. Four mines in the area, all nonunion, were paying from 38 to 43 cents a ton.[96] Bittner defended the wage level, explaining that, since the non-union mines did not use union men to weigh the miners' output, they were actually paying about 30 cents a ton after accounting for their cheating.[97]

At first the fighting continued, and "during 1931 Scotts Run experienced sporadic violence, marked by machine gun fire and sniping"[98] with the union targeting mines with nonunion workers. Mine operator James Paisley was a favorite target, and UMWA pickets appeared at his work sites looking to force the mine to be unionized. In June 1932, guards at his mines opened fire on a crowd of strikers, killing one and wounding nine. Charges against all parties from both sides were dropped.[99]

But for the most part, the fighting in the Run dropped off, yet "the end of the seven year coal war did not bring a return of prosperity."[100] The underlying economics of the situation were exactly the same, whether people shot at each other or not, and by 1932, the additional weight of the Great Depression pushed the people of Scotts Run even deeper into misery and hunger.

Although public relief had been provided by local charity organizations for years, "its effect had chiefly been to increase the inertia of the recipients."[101] Where hope had once been there was now nothing, and those who had stayed rather than leave in the late 1920s saw no escape. With no hope, they seemed simply to wait for whatever fate would bring.

The conditions that the larger outside world recorded in the early 1930s when it finally noticed what had been happening in the coal-mining region—and in Scotts Run in particular—were on a par with the worst slums the world could provide, in their time and ours.

Bottom of the Barrel: Life in the Coal Camps

How small one's worries seem in comparison to what so many human beings have been through.

—Eleanor Roosevelt (1933)[102]

For the people jammed into Scotts Run, the Great Depression started years prior to late 1929.[103] Glenna Williams, who grew up in the hollow before her family's resettlement in Arthurdale, remembered that, "we felt the Great Depression long before Wall Street."[104] A young Bob McLaughlin Sr., who moved into Arthurdale at the age of 10 from Harmony Grove (a town right outside of Scotts Run), had never known anything but poverty or imagined anything else: "We thought everybody lived like us."[105]

Some lived a little bit better than others; some lived a little bit worse, many felt pangs of hunger at one time or another. Throughout the country's mining regions thousands of miners and their families could be found huddled together hungry and destitute, living in tattered tents or squatting in abandoned company shacks, the owner having long ago slipped into bankruptcy.[106] The camps themselves, almost without exception, were "ugly, disease-infested slums."[107]

Although contemporary observations of life in those camps are, in this instance, primarily from the Scotts Run area or right outside it, the conditions in the Run can be used to describe those in other, more distant coal camps farther afield. A coal camp during the early 1930s was a depressing thing to observe and a soul-crushing place in which to live. Even the slag piles strewn everywhere on the valley floor seemed designed to accentuate the misery; without fail they ignited and burned, their foul-smelling smoke mixing with the winter fog to create a thick, chill, stinking cloak that smothered the vegetation.[108] "December in the coal mining camp at Osage was rarely pretty,"[109] remembered Sidney D. Lee. The town boasted a slag pile over 50 acres in size.[110]

And everywhere the noise of the tipples[111] and the endless lines of coal cars slowly rumbling up and down the length of the hollow, and the wind spreading coal dust into everything and everywhere. All accounts from the period mention the coal dust, the entire world was painted gray to black with it, and the smallest crack in a wall would see it "come to darken the furniture and walls in the shanty."[112]

Besides the coal dust, the mostly unpaved roads throughout the area exacerbated the task of maintaining a clean household. Osage town in the Run had unpaved, muddy streets and wooden boards for side-walks.[113] Historian Frances Hensley recalls the ubiquitous dirt as "one of the greatest enemies women who lived in the coal camps had."[114] To keep a house clean required an almost superhuman effort, even in a home without cracks between the wallboards and holes in the roof.

The profusion of dirt in the camps was rather common in rural America back in the 1920s. Most of the advances in cleaning tools, such as the vacuum cleaner and washing machine, were useless without electricity. Only one-third of Americans had electricity in their houses at the time,[115] and the majority of them were concentrated in the cities and larger towns. During the 1920s, the difference in cleanliness of the urban versus the rural American was rather wide; in fact you could smell it.[116] While Morgantown and its power company were nearby, even those miners' shacks in Scotts Run wired for electricity made no difference, as the poverty-stricken inhabitants couldn't afford to pay utility bills.

Nor was there any indoor plumbing, and it was usual for multiple families to share a common outdoor latrine.[117] "Camp residences were noteworthy more for the speed with which they were constructed than for comfort."[118] Sidney D. Lee recalls that his family's first home when they moved to Scotts Run was in a row house of completely bare rooms that had once been used to house company pack mules. There were

10 apartments for 10 families, and four outdoor latrines for all of them to share.[119]

It was the housing situation that helped spark much bloodshed between the miners and the operators. Despite the surge in hard-paved roads and private ownership of automobiles, the coal miners of the Run for the most part did not own cars and did not commute to the mine; many lived in company housing.[120]

Evictions were a common complaint of miners, who saw it as being thrown from their home. The coal companies, however, pointed out that the house was not the property of the miner but of the company, and striking miners were no longer employed so they needed to be removed from the house. Arguments like this led to gunfights such as took place at Matewan. Certainly the manner in which the coal operators tended to toss striking miners and their families into the street did not help.[121]

The individual stories of an eviction depict why emotions could get worked up to a fever pitch, however correct the act may have been from a legal and moral point of view. A missionary witnessed one during a cold January in 1932. The Bates family, parents and six children, were thrown out of the Pursglove Mine company house they lived in because he was no longer employed by that firm. With a reputation as a "good for nothing" that was probably reinforced by the fact that Bates made no effort at all to vacate the premises despite repeated demands to do so, the company sent over three agents who "picked up everything and dumped it out of the road,"[122] where it sat in the rain and open air. The youngest of Bates's children was two months old.

As early as 1925, life in many coal camps had deteriorated to the extent that Idaho senator Frank Gooding exclaimed "conditions which exist in the strike torn regions of the Pittsburgh district are a blot upon American civilization."[123] By 1933, investigations by the *Christian Century* (which had the best reports of conditions in the coal fields) still found "cold, bleak, dirty, and forbidding" the best adjectives to describe what its reporters witnessed. "Large families crowded into a few small rooms, grime, destitution, and ugliness everywhere."[124]

There were a few bright spots, an oasis here and there, such as in the Rockefeller-owned mines of the Consolidated Coal Company. It was a nonunion mine, which not only paid higher wages[125] than the UMWA agreement called for but had relatively decent housing and medical care.[126] Overwhelmingly, though, a coal camp offered nothing but crushing poverty and hopelessness.

One writer from that time observed about the residents of Scotts Run: "How can the families manage to live? Mostly by a reduction of living standards to as low a point as not to seem those of humans."[127] Glenna Williams asked, "What can you do when there is nothing? We were on the brink of some kind of catastrophe." Being on the brink was a step up, as there were many who had long ago fallen off it. Entire families slept together on the bare floor of whatever abandoned shack they called home and bedded down with newspapers as mattresses and blankets.[128]

Newspapers served as a crude form of insulation as well. The miners packed it into cracks between the wallboards or, at times, used it for decorative purposes as wallpaper.[129] With no means to purchase clothing, entire families were literally walking around in rags—and it took a heavy toll in sickness, especially among the children, many of whom went about barefoot.[130]

One social worker recorded the housing conditions of a hilltop camp she investigated, and her report gives some hint as to the effect poverty was having on the people of the camps:

In the little section of _____ Hill, there are twelve houses near together. None of them are fit to live in, hardly fit for animals. There are sixteen families in those houses. They all report the place as overrun with rats at times. There are six toilets in the group. Drinking (alcohol) was reported by the people themselves in all the families but two. Ten of the families had one or more members in jail. The doctors warned . . . almost everyone has some sort of social disease.[131]

A journalist came across one moribund camp where the coal miners had for the past 18 months been working two or three days a week at most. Their families were already suffering from the lack of food and clothing. Right before the journalist's arrival, the mine had closed for good. With the steep mountainsides all about like the sides of a coffin, the town had a "general atmosphere of silence—like a funeral."[132]

All the social ills history has recorded as riding hand in hand with poverty put in their appearance. Contemporary accounts from the people who worked among them made no effort to absolve the miners for whatever moral and character failings they may have displayed, and they displayed them all—except for one important difference. I came across but rare mention of promiscuity and none of divorce, single-parent households, or illegitimate children. In fact, it seems that quite the opposite occurred: Families clung even closer to one another, observers reporting "the miner, his wife, and their four to fourteen children have a family solidarity that is very real."[133]

The people who lived in Scotts Run were no saints. Above all, it seems, alcohol was the primary indulgence. Alcohol abuse certainly contributed to another problem that was widely noted in the Run: domestic violence. Passing on stories that her mother had imparted to her, Bettijane Burger, the daughter of Mary Behner, relates that when payday arrived for the miners, some would "go to the store and buy a lot of liquor and they would take that out on their families."[134]

The profligate nature of many in Scotts Run was remarked on as well, and this attitude against frugality and saving for a rainy day stood them in marked contrast to those who had once farmed the area. In 1932, a *New York Times* report for the coal fields thought it notable how, a scant month after a mine would shut down, "every miner [would be] penniless."[135] The installment plan was the undoing for many a mining family, they viewed the salesman "as the personification of the boom," and they resented the one who had formally ridden up with smiles and radios returning later to take it all back.[136]

One account recalled a miner's family living in a "run down" shack yet having a $70 radio that they still owed $50 on. "It's the only pleasure we have," the housewife explained, and there it remained amid the hungry squalor, a musical reminder of better days long gone.[137]

Misery beyond Description: Private Charity in Scotts Run

That thou will do unto the least of thy brothers, thou doest unto me.
—Holy Bible

The Great Depression fell upon the people of West Virginia with a ferocity almost unmatched elsewhere across these United States.[138] Already devastated by the bloody, drawn-out collapse of the coal bubble, the miners were ill prepared for the addition of a countrywide economic calamity.

The miners of Scotts Run were a proud people, ashamed and humiliated to be reduced to beggary. "Often they were literally starving, but they 'hated to ask.'"[139] They had little choice as to whether to turn away the extended helping hand; annual coal production had dropped for all of West Virginia from 145 million tons in 1927 to 83 million in 1932.[140] By that later date, most of the miners in the Run had not known steady employment for years.[141]

Exacerbating the economic disaster in West Virginia was the fallout from the massive fraud put over on the West Virginian people by the state's banking community. In the three years from 1929 to 1932, the number of West Virginian banks fell by 33 percent, taking along with them over $100 million worth of their depositors' money, this from a starting base of $328 million.[142] At that time Americans used gold for money, not pieces of paper, and the West Virginian people were shocked to find that their local bankers had been issuing pieces of paper with absolutely no money (gold) to back up what the paper promised. It was, hands down, the greatest bank robbery in West Virginian history—pulled off by the bankers themselves.

Monongalia County was not immune to the fraud. Every single bank in the county closed down, taking with them all the tax receipts used for poor relief.[143] Tax revenues continued to fall into 1933, straining the system even further. In the early days, long before the better-known and famous Quakers and Eleanor Roosevelt entered the field to help, local charities, religious missionaries, and the coal-mining companies were plowing through the misery, doing whatever they could to help.

Much has been written over the years denigrating the coal companies with a broad brush; much of the criticism is well deserved, as for example the policy of paying the miners in company script. Yet it would be simplistic and incorrect to assume that every coal-mining company and its owners were little more than American versions of

Ebenezer Scrooge. Many, in fact, gave valuable help for the welfare of the destitute miners.

The homage paid to the coal-mining companies by both journalists and social workers was too widely stated to be discounted. Even the *Christian Century*, most damning in its coverage of what was happening in Scotts Run, granted that "many of the coal companies have been as generous as could be with the men, even when they could pay no rent."[144] As an example, it was noted that the Crown Mine owners, despite the fact they had closed down operations, did not evict any of the workers who squatted in the company houses.[145]

The missionary Mary Behner was able to open "The Shack" (the focal point of her relief efforts) because the building was given to her by the Pursglove Mining Company. Clarence Pickett from the American Friends Service Committee and Bushrod Grimes from West Virginia University's garden program singled out the coal operators for providing the operational funds for much good work.[146] It was the locally based company, those with owners who lived in the area and knew firsthand what was happening, who were "especially helpful,"[147] even going so far as to try to find other positions outside the industry for the miners they let go.[148]

Of the 50,000 or so people living in Monongalia County by the early 1930s, it is estimated that around 15,000 lived in the coal-mining sections, which is where the most extreme cases of poverty were concentrated. The resources of the local charitable agencies were crushed by the weight of the indigent coal miners and their children; almost 40 percent of the young were suffering from malnutrition.[149]

The most prominent of the charitable organizations was the Council of Social Agencies, which coordinated and worked with the local American Legion, Salvation Army, American Red Cross, and later the American Friends Service Committee (AFSE). Volunteer workers and "the anonymous generosity of many citizens" funded the entire machine.[150]

Two early prototypes of religious-based private charity in Scotts Run drew their ideas from two sources—on one side the Bible School Movement, on the other the Settlement House Movement. The former would tend to the earthly necessities of the "religiously needy" while turning them to God; the latter would tend to the earthly needs of the newly arrived immigrants while turning them to the American flag. Both did much to help alleviate the suffering.[151]

The Settlement House was established in the Run in 1922, and would offer a program of services that included "naturalization, cooking, motherhood, and other skills."[152] While the Bible School Movement got a relatively late start—1928—it would gain greater fame due to the dogged energy and pluck of a young missionary named Mary Behner, who would oversee the program from its inception until she left in 1937.

A graduate of Ohio's Wooster College and daughter of a Presbyterian minister, she originally had wished to work as a foreign missionary but was persuaded by the Board of Missions of that denomination to work instead in West Virginia's northern coal fields. She would keep a series of diaries, leaving behind an intimate record of the people and events in Scotts Run. A remarkable young woman with courage to spare, she "rebuked the coal industry, the operators, the churches, and the Scotts Run residents themselves."[153]

Originally asked to begin a Sunday school program for the area children, while making her rounds amid the grinding poverty she realized "that there was a community beyond the Sunday school that she had to do something about,"[154] and she would spend the next nine years of her life doing something about it. The most prominent result of her tireless charitable impulse was a building in the town of Pursglove that would be known as The Shack.

Donated to her in 1932 by the Pursglove Mining Company,[155] the building was once a horse stable, a meat storage locker, and now the center of Behner's charitable efforts, the home for her nursery school, child feeding station, library, shower baths, Bible classes, and even the occasional movie.[156] Like everyone who lived in the Run, she found that "because of the coal dust it is very difficult to keep clean."[157] Despite an operating budget that often was nothing at all, she displayed an admirable resourcefulness. She ran up and down the Run gathering discarded powder boxes to use as seats;[158] eventually able to seat 175 people at a time, she offered the UMWA the space for union meetings. (An offer it gratefully accepted). She began feedings for the children six days a week, exulting, "The twenty-four children that have been having these lunches have gained in a marvelous way."[159]

Behner's blunt assessment of the miners and the habits they displayed are of particular interest. She was adamant that she would not make The Shack "a spoon-fed affair," charging the children a nickel each to join the library and to use the shower baths.[160] She derided handouts as "so called charity" and declared them "an outworn method . . . which has already so pauperized these people."[161] She also noted the profligate ways of the spendthrift miners, "rarely is there (one) who plans and saves. They have learned not their lesson from the depression."[162]

Laziness to her was a cardinal sin, and she lamented, "A lot of the men not working are those who choose not to work because they are lazy, or do not work because they cannot get along with 'the boss.'"[163] She found it frustrating that it was a long, laborious process to convince people to "better themselves," and her chagrin at the unwillingness of many unemployed miners to pitch in and help fairly leaps out of her diary.[164]

Despite her private misgivings and disappointments in what she saw of the miners in Scotts Run, she had a fondness for many of them. One entry in her diary is telling when she angrily relates her disgust with a resident of Morgantown who insisted that not all the youth of the Run "should be encouraged to follow higher lives—some should be encouraged to be good maids."[165]

Her daughter recalls that "she never really got any hostility from the people out there,"[166] which is mostly true, except for one moment in August 1937. There would be one final moment, a "nightmare" in her own words, that would close out Behner's time in the Run. A few articles published in the *Wooster Voice* (written by some college students she had invited to work at The Shack) were the catalyst. Seeing the conditions around them, they had written an exposé of the poverty. The residents of the Run somehow got hold of the paper and were outraged, feeling it was a slander.

She wrote to her parents "nine years of giving everything to the people of Scotts Run—to be put on trial—accused—hissed at—slandered, defended by not even my friends." Heartbroken, she had to endure "the petty things brought up. A person can make a lot of mistakes in nine years. What a closing dramatic chapter to my work."[167]

As the 1930s began to age, while she was grateful as other organizations arrived to pitch in to help the miners, she felt that "as so many programs came in, she began to see a sense of dependency. "They would just . . . not really think about living their own lives and being in charge of their own lives."[168] By 1937, it appears that she had grown weary under the load of endless toil, with no end in sight. She had put off her own life for long enough. In the spring of that year, she accepted the marriage proposal of David A. Christopher, an employee of West Virginia University.[169] One year later, she married and was no longer part of the Presbyterian missionary work in Scotts Run.

Now in a new home, The Shack is still standing, and to this day the charitable programs begun long ago by Mary Behner still serve the people of Scotts Run.[170]

American Friends Service Committee

The situation was a depressing one to walk into.
   —Clarence Pickett (AFSC chief) on Scotts Run[171]

Clarence Pickett came into the world the youngest of eight children in 1884, his home part of a Quaker colony in the farmland about 80 miles south of Chicago. His family was part of the Friends since his youth, he records that a sister was sent to Tokyo as a teacher in 1892, and the religiosity of his surroundings was "deep and genuine."[172] After meeting his future wife at college, they delayed marriage until his graduation from Hartford Theological Seminary, after which he taught biblical literature from 1922 to 1929.

In that latter year, he "was astonished to receive an invitation to become executive secretary"[173] of the Quaker's charitable organization, the American Friends Service Committee, an enterprise justly famous for its relief work in war-torn Europe in the period right after World War I.[174] He accepted the position, and it would soon enough have him working with other victims of that same war.

The series of events that would lead the AFSC into the Scotts Run coal fields (and the surrounding areas) was put into motion by the Council of Social Agencies, which had appealed for help to the federal United States Children's Bureau. That bureau had already (in early 1931) been tasked by President Hoover to investigate the conditions of the children in the coal-mining camps of the Allegheny and Blue Ridge mountains.[175] The initial reports began to filter back—horrific.

Soon thereafter Grace Abbott, chief of the Children's Bureau, was the distinguished speaker for a gala reception at Bryn Mawr College.[176] By chance (or maybe not), Rufus Jones, part of the AFSC's leadership, was seated right next to her. During a friendly chat, she said, "Dr. Jones, I wish your service committee could do something to save the lives of my children"[177]—meaning that "President Hoover had suggested that . . . the AFSC might undertake to feed the children."[178]

This was quickly followed up by a visit to the AFSC's Philadelphia headquarters from Fred Croxton, acting chairman of the President's Emergency Committee on Employment. Accompanied by Abbott, they pleaded with the AFSC's board of directors to enter the coal fields. This made sense on a number of levels, as the AFSC had on its roster people with extensive experience in large-scale charitable operations and had undertaken exactly this sort of work in the South Wales coal fields of Great Britain.[179] Even more to the point, as reported from the minutes of an AFSC meeting held not too long after, "there is no one else to do it."[180]

The leadership of the AFSC did not immediately jump at the chance to accede to President Hoover's request. This would be an immense undertaking, and Pickett admitted, "I knew little about the bituminous coalfields of this country."[181] The AFSC tentatively agreed to move into the coal camps for a two-year period, yet it knew from experience the ease to take on a project was often exceeded by the difficulty in ending it.[182] The organization needed to husband its scarce resources.

On June 4, 1931, a Coal Committee was created to study what areas would be the main focus of relief efforts, with Clarence Pickett picking Monongalia County for "the possibility of a clear-cut piece of child feeding."[183] The AFSC admitted in all candor that many other areas could have been chosen besides Scotts Run; for example, nearby Marion County "had some isolated mines as bad as those in Scotts Run."[184]

Although conditions in Scotts Run were vile, it was known that "there are in some cases more intense stories to be told about other communities. Conditions in Kentucky were particularly grim and challenging."[185] In Kanawha County south of Scotts Run, the devastation in the coal fields was exacerbated by severe flooding and, in the county's northern area, drought.[186] The AFSC leadership could have thrown a dart at a map of West Virginia, chosen the area hit, and doubtless would have found plenty of hungry mouths to feed.

Drawing on its deeply experienced roster, the AFSC appointed Professor Homer L. Morris of Fisk University field director of the coal field operations, a good choice as he had served with the committee in Germany, Poland, and Russia.[187] The project was almost stillborn as it was hoped the Red Cross would grant a large sum of money to fund it, but that organization "did not feel this particular service lay within their province." Hoover rode to the rescue, giving the AFSC $225,000 in taxpayer money, payable in 10 monthly installments.[188]

With the organizational structure in place and money in hand, the AFSC began yet another foray into its specialty: helping to clean up the sad aftermath of World War I.

In the Thick of It All

Brave attempts at relief are being made in many places.
—From *The Christian Century* (1932)[189]

The AFSC program officially opened on September 30, 1931,[190] when the AFSC, after a careful study of the situation in Monongalia County, opened 24 feeding stations therein, fully half of them in Scotts Run.[191] With barely 10 percent or so of the county's population in the Run, that fact alone highlights the depths to which the coal camp residents had sunk. The private charities were a godsend for the people, as the public welfare till was empty.

Investigators for the Friends had collected their observations of the camps, and the results were mind numbing. Almost all the children had "remediable illnesses, including malnutrition, enlarged tonsils, defective vision, and decayed teeth."[192] When given toothbrushes, many of the children had not the slightest idea how to use them and had to be taught.[193]

The feeding program, which due to financial constraints and the vast size of the destitute population was offered only to children and pregnant women, quickly ramped up, and "within five months 40,000 children a day were being fed in 563 communities."[194] Besides Monongalia County, feeding stations were established in the southern coal fields of West Virginia, in Kanawha, Mingo, and Logan counties, as well as areas of Kentucky, Pennsylvania, Ohio, and Illinois.[195] Fifty-five men and women drove their secondhand cars across 35 counties (into areas poorly served by roads) to deliver the food.[196]

During the first phase of its time in the fields, the AFSC held fast to a "10 percent standard," meaning that for children to qualify, they had to weigh in at least 10 percent below the average standard for age and height. The overwhelming majority of children in Scotts Run had no problem passing that benchmark. In the town of Cassville, 70 percent of the children qualified; in Bertha Hill, 80 percent did so.[197]

The peak number fed daily was reached in April 1932, with 40,000 children per day on average using the feeding stations throughout the multistate area. A program to dispense milk to preschoolers and expectant mothers was instituted as well.[198] It was a large-scale operational undertaking, and the fact that it was pulled off at all is a testament to the professionalism and goodwill of all those who took part in it.

During a two-month stretch in the summer of 1932, the AFSC shut down its operations in the fields. West Virginian state officials were very anxious to have the Friends return for the coming winter and offered "funds which [they] could borrow from the Reconstruction Finance Corporation" for the purpose.[199] The AFSC agreed to return, and during the 1932–1933 school year in Monongalia County, "over 5,000 children were fed daily through the Friend's feeding program."[200]

Relief workers in the coal fields had to be aware at all times that the people of the camps, although desperate for help, would not accept it "unless the helpers stepped gingerly around the sensitive spots of pride and independence."[201] One contemporary noted of the coal miners: "Fairy tales and feuds occupy the minds of these people. The stranger must walk warily if he is to live among them."[202] The miners could react strongly to slights to manhood or what they believed to be underhanded dealing on the part of others, especially outsiders. That feeling of pride extended even to the local charity workers, one of whom admitted, "I am ashamed to see outside people like the Quakers, nice as they are, come into West Virginia to help the needy miners; it hurts my state pride."[203]

The AFSC encountered the same problem that other, earlier charities faced when working in the Run—the lack of clothing that kept too many children at home. Ironically, it was those very children, bound to their homes by a lack of shoes and dressed in rags, that most needed to reach the feeding stations.[204] Seeing this, the AFSC collected over 150 tons of used clothing from donors, refurbished and issued it to the miners' children.[205]

Working in tandem was the West Virginia University's garden program (run by Bushrod Grimes), and AFSC canning facilities were set up in church basements where professors' and miners' wives worked to preserve the surplus fruit and vegetables that the program provided.[206] Grimes, who would go on to play a large part in the initial stages of Arthurdale, ran "the best organized subsistence garden program," and he credited the AFSC for providing valuable help in making it such a success.[207] In 1933 alone, the surplus food was estimated to be worth almost $60,000, and Grimes's work, and similar efforts by the other 33 garden clubs in Monongalia County, did much to fight hunger.[208]

One of the more interesting programs begun by the Friends involved the hiring of a furniture maker named Isaac Samuel Godlove to supervise a cooperative shop. Funded by a donation of $10,000 from the Elmhirst Fund,[209] it allowed a select group of miners to be taught the trade and, it was hoped, turn a profit. Initially located at Crown Mine in a building donated for the purpose by the coal company, although the cooperative never turned a profit,[210] it would eventually grow to fame as the Mountaineer Craftsmen's Cooperative Association (MCCA) and be relocated to Arthurdale. The Godlove chair it made would become renowned throughout the eastern seaboard, and it had a well-earned reputation for quality craftsmanship.

As massive as the AFSC effort was, everything added together—the feeding, the co-ops, the clothing drives, and the garden programs— were like a drop of water in a desert. The need was so great, so many of a tightly packed population was destitute that "to feed a child and let his parents go hungry [was] a harsh reality which the Quakers [had to] face."[211] Pickett compared it all to "trying to sweep back the ocean."[212] While one could, and did, see "children eagerly eat their porridge or drink their allowance of milk, or become silent with ecstasy over a pair of second-hand shoes,"[213] standing behind that one was a crowd of other children, hungry and shoeless.

To those involved, the solution seemed to rest in one place— with the federal government. As Pickett despaired at coping with the flood of misery that made the AFSC's huge operation seem feeble in comparison to the need, "the social application of religious faith was beginning to be the focus of much of [his] attention."[214] Or, as the investigative journalist James Myer called out in the pages of the *Christian Century*, "only federal government action can save it now."[215]

And somewhere to the north, that very federal government was motoring toward them by auto in the form of a relief investigator named Lorena Hickok. Following close behind, descending from Washington like the Good Witch from *The Wizard of Oz*, would be none other than Eleanor Roosevelt, wife of America's new president, FDR.

The federal government would soon arrive in Scotts Run, bringing in its wake consequences felt to this day.

Chapter 2

The Angel of
Arthurdale Arrives

"Got a lot of sinful idears—but they seem kinda sensible."
—From John Steinbeck's *The Grapes of Wrath* (1939)

L orena Hickok was only in that car headed toward the Run because her close friend and confidante Eleanor Roosevelt had asked Harry Hopkins (head of the Federal Emergency Relief Administration) to put her on the payroll, and when the president's wife asks you to do something, well, you know.[1] Being no fool, Hopkins hired Hickok as an investigator and defined her role as "What I want you to do is go out around the country and look this thing over. I just want your own reaction."[2] Her "going around" the country saw her in Scotts Run during the summer of 1933, and American Friends

Service Committee (AFSC) worker Alice Davis gave her a tour of the coal camps. Needless to say, Hickok was appalled.

Eleanor Roosevelt first visited Scotts Run on August 18, 1933, driving herself without escort into Morgantown.[3] How exactly that visit was set up and by whom depends on the source you consult. Some say she had purchased a piece of furniture from Godlove's workshop and, having her own little furniture shop on the Roosevelt estate in upstate New York, asked about the co-op and became interested to see the Friends work in the area.[4] Another says Lorena Hickok urged her to visit,[5] but whatever the reason, on August 18, there she was.

She was escorted through the camps and at that time in her life, no one had any idea as to who she was. She saw "American babies with their bellies distended . . . prematurely old miner's wives . . . and shacks, [where] every night children went to sleep hungry on piles of bug infested rags spread on the floor."[6] As appalled as Hickok had been, from that day forward and for the rest of her life "Eleanor Roosevelt [would be] shameless about asking for donations in time and money,"[7] and the AFSC would become "the main recipient of her private charity over the next several decades."[8]

To help raise funds, she began to take people on tours of the Scotts Run town of Jere, for to her "it was a good example of what absentee ownership could do as far as human beings were concerned."[9] Even more important for those who wished to see federal efforts in poor relief, the value of Eleanor Roosevelt was magnified as the movie newsreel and radio made her increasingly famous, so much so that a gaggle of journalists and photographers followed in her wake wherever she ventured, and when she visited Scotts Run so did they. It was this that would make Scotts Run the poster child for the Great Depression.[10]

As Morgantown lay right next to it and the Morgantown and Wheeling Railway ran a trolley line right through the middle of it all, its easy accessibility helped promote the story of Scotts Run.[11] By the time Eleanor arrived to shine the spotlight on the area, "it had become a gruesome caricature of the blight the depression has spread over the country."[12] The phrase "the damnedest cesspool of human misery I have ever seen," coined by a journalist, became "synonymous with Scotts Run."[13]

It was without a doubt the photographers who did more than anything to bring Scotts Run to the nation's attention. "Their images captured the human face of poverty . . . making it much easier for social workers . . . to raise scarce resources for the relief effort."[14] During the 1930s, photography saw new technological advances that made it the "central instrument of [the] times."[15] Small 35mm format, flash bulbs, and high-speed film allowed millions of Americans to become amateur photographers, and their craving for this new field extended to buying the "picture magazine."

Newly born magazines such as *Life, Look, Chic, Focus,* and a multitude of competitors fed American consumers' demand for photographs, and the pictures did not need to be exclusively of movie starlets, although having one between the pages never hurt sales. The practice of accompanying news stories with photographs could make a report hit hard, and the pictures from Scotts Run were as stark and hard hitting as you could hope for.

Demands that federal authorities do something to alleviate the poverty of the coal fields were trumpeted in newspapers, journals, and interviews from all corners of the union, despite the fact those authorities lacked any legal power to do so. Yet the idea of federal government action outside the bounds of the Constitution had long been simmering, and it reached a boiling point in the economic crisis of the Great Depression. Expediency, especially when accompanied by pictures of suffering children, easily knocked aside warnings of those who pointed out the importance of the rule of law. AFSC chief Clarence Pickett later wrote of "the practice which the country had during the depression in throwing off traditional patterns in order to meet unprecedented emergencies"[16] or, as Eleanor Roosevelt put it, "breaking rules or even laws saved a good many lives."[17] Such attitudes quickly gained the upper hand.

President Hoover, the habitual meddler, had begun many of the programs and policies that his successor FDR would claim credit for (and be granted, all because he pasted on it the catchy label "New Deal"). Hoover "actually did respond to the resulting problems of unemployment and underemployment," as with his establishment in July 1932 of the Reconstruction Finance Corporation (RFC) that was to prove so instrumental in funding the activities of the AFSC.[18]

Although the first year of the AFSC's work in Scotts Run was funded with private donations and from the federal Children's Welfare Bureau, the final two years (before the AFSC left the Run in 1934) were funded with RFC money. And like most intellectuals of his time, Pickett welcomed this change in federal activity, believing that "relief efforts of this sort on a widescale basis should be a public responsibility" as "the chief function of the state should be the welfare of its whole citizenry."[19]

Even Mary Behner, who so feared the dependency and corruption of spirit that long-term relief can engender in its recipients, lauded the rise of FDR, writing "surely religion has not been in vain—we are on the threshold of a new era—when some leaders who are at the helm are striving for 'life abundant' for all."[20] Upon her return from Scotts Run, Eleanor Roosevelt wrote a column in the *Women's Democratic News* stating "in this country the day is past when we will continue to live under any governmental system which will produce conditions such as exist in certain industries and in certain parts of the country."[21]

During the summer of 1932 it was reported that Professor Homer L. Morris (the field director of the coal field operations for the AFSC) was planning a "detailed sociological survey . . . as a basis for intelligent placement of surplus miners." "One can but hope," the journalist went on, "that a similar statesmanship may appear among political leaders."[22]

That hope would soon enough come true, for within a year Bushrod Grimes, project leader for the West Virginia University's subsistence garden program, would ask a visiting Eleanor Roosevelt if federal funds might not be used to purchase land to expand his operations.[23] Pickett would later give his opinion that "this visit [of Eleanor Roosevelt] would have some bearing on the fact that the first subsistence homestead was located on the Arthur farm."[24]

In fact, that question from Grimes would find fertile ground in Eleanor's head, for it was soon to be filled with the exact idea that drove Morris to conduct his survey. That idea—which was to birth Arthurdale—was embodied by the phrase "back to the land."

Getting Down with the Sickness

A nation does not take a new direction overnight.
> —Rexford Tugwell, Resettlement
> Administration chief (1933)[25]

All 28 families had assembled in front of Brooklyn's Borough Hall for the gala send-off, their $3,000 payment fee enough to make them the center of New York City's attention, if only for a day. That day was July 28, 1921. The newspapers made note that the families had been brought together by the leadership of William D. Scott, a Brooklyn store manager who had "found himself inevitably moving in the direction of a belief in the necessity of organized rural life."[26] Now long forgotten, they were modern-day (for their time) pioneers, off to the West not in covered wagons, rifles at the ready to fend off Indians, but in automobiles towing pop-up campers, to be feted by American towns as they motored across the continent toward a better life.

A good part of the attendant publicity was no doubt worked up by the newly born American Automobile Association, which, seeing a readymade publicity stunt to tout the automobiles it hoped to mass produce, helped Scott plan the route. That was not the only assistance Scott had received; his enthusiasm for "organized rural life," popularly referred to as the back-to-the-land movement, had brought him into the circle of Franklin Lane, onetime head of the United States Department of the Interior and himself a diehard back-to-the-land advocate. Provided with notable references, Scott felt comfortable to purchase for his new world over 5,000 acres of Idaho land—sight unseen—and name it "Roseworth."

In the glowing reports that followed his caravan's departure, it was said of Scott that he was "wise enough to select his associates with great care"[27]—unfortunately, the same could not be said about his selection of the land. After a months-long journey across an America devoid of interstate highways, the weary pioneer families arrived at their destination to be greeted by Roseworth, "a desolate region of sagebrush," with nothing more than a few forlorn shacks to provide comfort. Twenty-four of the pioneer families sold off their equipment and headed back home. Scott's venture to go back to the land, like so many before and since, collapsed into a heap.[28]

It is hoped that the departed (and Scott) were wiser for the lesson, but judging by the history of this country, it is to be doubted. For whatever reason, one inexplicable to most city folk, Americans have from the time of our founding harbored a feeling for "the land" of such a quasi–religious fanaticism that they block out any rational thought about what they are about to embark on.

Although communally organized land settlements have been part of the American tapestry since the first Europeans arrived from the Old World, it was not until the time of the Panic of 1907 that the idea moved out of the fringes and started to gain widespread acceptance. Bolton Hall, a proponent of the idea, published his influential *3 Acres and Liberty* and *A Little Land and a Living* in 1908. Both expounded on the virtues of country life and the evils bred by city living.[29]

For the next three decades, articles praising the wholesome joy of an autarkic farm life appeared in numerous magazines, such as *BusinessWeek, Saturday Evening Post, Survey Graphic*, and *The Nation*, along with the added weight of friendly newspaper editorials from coast to coast.[30] The steady stream turned into a flood as the Great Depression deepened; the *Wall Street Journal* carried ads urging its readers to "buy an abandoned farm and live on trout and applejack until the upturn!"[31]

Organizations such as the Catholic Rural Life Conference and the National Forward to the Land League arose to promote the idea, and the movement as a whole would present an oddball, diverse mix as everyone from the journalist Stuart Chase, to strange religious sects, to the rabid Southern Agrarians (Distributionists, a socialist sect based out of Vanderbilt University) took up the torch and fell into lockstep with one another.

It all looked so nice while still just a fluffy dream. Ralph Borsodi, who had started his own subsistence farm just outside New York City in 1920 and would do much to help promote land settlements, declared that such colonies would be "little islands of intelligence and beauty amidst the chaotic seas of human stupidity and ugliness."[32] The *Literary Digest* featured a poem called "Back to the Land" wherein a contented farmer was "quenching [his] thirst for a smell of the soil" and insisting he "croon[s] with joy at my toil."[33]

The activist William Borsodi (father of Ralph) opined, "The drudgery of the farm is not like the drudgery of the city, which has a twin—suffering."[34] It all was a yearning for an imagined past, a vision that believed a simple farm life (with a nearby factory sometimes thrown into utopia for good measure) was the panacea for all the changes a modern, industrial society had brought. The deeply conservative nature of the movement was given clear play by Hilaire Belloc (author of *The Servile State*) who "romantically praised the Catholic, agrarian society of the late Middle Ages."[35]

On occasion one would come across a fish that swam against the tide, as in a 1933 piece from the *New Republic,* which referred to the movement as "almost a cult" and stated that while it might be a hoot "to think of a former bond salesman" plodding in dirty overalls behind a plow team, the days of the small yeoman American farmer were dead and gone—large-scale industrial farming had long settled that question.[36] Nevertheless, as the early 1930s arrived, multitudes of desperate men were flowing back to the land, many of them "tragically deceived" into buying land that was not worth dirt, so to speak.[37] It was a spontaneous movement "comparable to that of pioneer days,"[38] men flooding back to the farms that they had once fled, the overwhelming majority to barely make a go of it.

This gave ample opportunity for the self-styled "Progressives" to agitate for a new policy as a response to all this. Always deeply rooted in the country soil,[39] the Progressive movement believed that land colonization, of a type funded by taxes and planned by government-employed experts, could show America a new, better way of life. And it would be far less risky, too, because with a bevy of experts always standing ready to provide advice, "men need not have any previous knowledge of agriculture," insisted Franklin Lane.[40]

Everyone involved had fallen for what Alexander Hamilton warned against in *The Federalist Papers*, the "deceitful dream of a golden age."[41] A follow-on study conducted by the Department of Agriculture in 1942 noted, "the [back-to-the-land] movement was attracting even more than the usual share of cultists, faddists, and crackpots."[42] Crackpots are attracted to crackpot schemes.

The actual implementation of federal subsistence homestead communities would be strongly influenced by ideas that had first been put forward in obscure academic journals decades prior, and the confusion and strife displayed by the federal program was a direct result of trying to implement an idea that was an incomprehensible mishmash of thoughtless contradictions, of Catholics, Protestants, Jeffersonians, capitalist decentralizers, distributionist centralizers, decentralizing distributionists, and the disciples of Rousseau and Thoreau, all bouncing off each other along college corridors.[43]

In all fairness to the back-to-the-landers, even a quick perusal of the early part of the twentieth century is confirmation that nutty theories were rampant; it was a time of great change and confusion in America's intellectual atmosphere. From the moment that FDR's distant cousin Teddy galloped up that hill and into the presidency, "the modern, collective reaction against individualism . . . was to grow rapidly,"[44] and the back-to-the-land movement was at the forefront of that reaction.

Naturally, before magazines and newspapers began to popularize the idea, they first had to be turned onto it by men of ideas and vision. The back-to-the-land movement was birthed neither in the press nor on the farm but in the universities. Those who agitated for the idea were almost without exception a small group of urban-dwelling academics.

Although men such as the publisher Bernarr Macfadden and the industrialist Henry Ford doubtless did much to popularize the idea (helped along by a coterie of others, such as Bolton Hall and Sir Ebenezer Howard, authors who called for back-to-the-land colonies), it would take men of action to make the dream a reality. Above all, the small core who actually got to put these ideas into practice must stand highest in any retelling of the story.

The leading man of this core, without whose influence Arthurdale and its kind would likely not exist, was Richard Ely, a University of Wisconsin professor who created and popularized the study of "land economics."[45] Born in 1854 and raised pious on an upstate New York farm, he used his father's extensive home library to excellent effect and bolted to college at the first opportunity. Discovering early a deep admiration for the reformer Horace Greeley, Ely would forever display the attributes of the thin-skinned self-righteousness innate to the species. According to one biographer, "[H]e frequently saw himself as a martyr and compared himself to the Hebrew prophets."[46]

Coming home from Bismarck's Germany where he undertook graduate studies at the feet of "German masters [who] explained that no ironclad principles of economics existed,"[47] he would proclaim upon his 1885 creation of the German-modeled American Economics

Association that "we hold that the doctrine of laissez-faire is unsafe in politics and unsound in morals."[48] His mind was ripe plucking for the back-to-the-land movement.

Almost every prominent land economist of the time would pass through Ely's hands, and his prodigious output of academic papers provided the ideological rationale used for the subsistence homestead projects.[49] Through him and his close friend Simon Patten (whom he had met while both were students in Germany) passed Rexford Tugwell (head of the Resettlement Administration from 1935 to 1936), M. L. Wilson (director of the Division of Subsistence Homesteads from 1933 to 1934), and his most outstanding student, Henry C. Taylor (who made "rural sociology" a recognized study and through whom Ely would meet Elwood Mead and Cornell's George F. Warren).

His life's work would culminate at a 1931 event sponsored by the National Conference on Land Utilization in Chicago. With an audience hall full of former students, many now ensconced in government positions and eager to implement Ely's teachings, he gushed, "I feel that I am in the Promised Land."[50] He would pass away in Connecticut in October 1943, after ample time to see just how his promised land turned out.

Another prominent influence on Arthurdale would be Elwood Mead, whose government-run farm colonies in Australia and California would provide the blueprint for its practical application.[51] Never in any way officially connected to the Subsistence Homestead Division, nonetheless "his influence was unmistakable (and) he was mentioned as a possible head of the new agency"[52] when it was formed in 1933.

Born and raised on a farm about 40 miles south of Cincinnati, like Ely he used his family's well-stocked home library to launch himself away from a life of farming, earning degrees from Purdue and Iowa State in civil engineering, with a specific focus on irrigation.[53] An immensely hard worker with a cavalier attitude toward roadblocks, when he severed his arm by slipping under a trolley car, he brushed it off by saying "If I understand my field, I can do well without any hands as well as both." While recuperating from his injuries, he taught himself to write left-handed.[54]

It was during his time in Australia, where he worked as head of the State Rivers and Water Supply Commission of Victoria, that he came into his own.[55] With taxpayer funds at his disposal, he was able to put his ideas of farm colonization (on land reclaimed by irrigation) into effect. His plan of prebuilt houses, experts on hand for advice, land prepared for immediate use, cooperatives, and (as always in the tax-payer-funded variants) lots of credit on easy terms would provide the operational blueprint for both his California colonies and Arthurdale. Like so many such schemes, it turned into a financial disaster, yet he returned from Australia convinced of its success and a firm believer that "government paternalism . . . awakens hope, arouses ambition, and strengthens belief in the brotherhood of man, it is altogether good."[56]

His writings reflected a wish for a level of political control over farms not seen even today, all of it infused with a particular hatred reserved for "speculators," absentee landlords,[57] and, above all, an almost comically obsessive racism toward Asians and Mexicans. After returning to America, he would be appointed in 1924 to head the Bureau of Reclamation.[58] Franklin Lane admired Mead for his work, and Mead's ideas were to influence land settlement advocates in Congress, in particular the Bankhead brothers, sibling congressmen from Alabama, one of whom (Senator John Bankhead) would become the legislative father of the Division of Subsistence Homesteads that built Arthurdale.

Mead would remain at the Reclamation Bureau until his death in 1936. One of his last (and most famous) projects was the Hoover Dam, and the body of water impounded by that dam, all 112 artificial miles of it, is named Lake Mead in his honor.

At the top of the New Deal power structure was Franklin Delano Roosevelt, and our 32nd president needs no introduction except to add that he himself was an early, diehard convert to the back-to-the-land movement. One historian noted that FDR had "a kinship with the more romantic agrarians,"[59] and Rexford Tugwell remembered he "always did, and always would, think people better off in the country and would regard the cities as rather hopeless."[60]

As early as 1912, FDR was introduced to the idea of planning through the influence of his uncle, Frederic Delano (who was an active member of both Chicago's and New York City's planning commis-sions),[61] and within a year he was introducing legislation in New York State for resettlement of the city poor onto rural farms.[62] His urge to use political power to reorder the countryside became a lifelong desire. Decades later, in 1932 he wrote in the progressive magazine *Survey*

Graphic that America needed to "adopt some kind of experimental work based on a distribution of population."[63]

And he laid out in a 1931 speech exactly what the experiment should look like; it was to be "wholly new rural communities of homes for workers on good agricultural land with . . . the establishment of new industries aimed primarily to give cash wages on a co-operative basis during the non-agricultural season."[64] That describes the idea behind Arthurdale rather nicely, and when a distraught Eleanor returned from Scotts Run demanding that FDR do something, that idea is the one he pulled out of his head and handed to her.

And that was how Eleanor Roosevelt became the Angel of Arthurdale, the one whose memory the settlers' descendants honor above any other. The publicity that Arthurdale generated did much to make Mrs. Roosevelt, its most visible champion, a recognized national figure in her own right. She once wrote to her friend Lorena Hickok "someday I'll be back in obscurity again."[65] Three-quarters of a century later, obscurity has yet to find her.

M. L. Wilson, who was (along with FDR) considered "among the more conservative elements,"[66] was a rarity within the leadership —he had been an actual farmer at one time,[67] and a rather successful one. Educated at Iowa State College before studying under Richard Ely,[68] he had once been an "advisor to the Soviet government in connection with experimental farming,"[69] and that about sums up his political views.

His domestic allocation plan called for consumers to be parceled out among a farm cartel. It would also create a countryside where neighbor would be set against neighbor, "each farmer would be policing his neighbors and, on the other hand, his neighbors would be policing him,"[70] all to enforce centrally mandated restrictions on production.

Additionally, he knew his plan would result in "surplus farm families," their land taken from them and now forbidden to compete in the only business they had ever known. "What is to be done?" with those homeless, hungry people he worried, because he did have a heart, after all. His solution was resettlement colonies, and having been influenced by Elwood Mead,[71] he was long "an active behind the scenes worker" to get the subsistence homestead idea into reality.[72] He would head the Division of Subsistence Homesteads responsible for Arthurdale from its creation in 1933 until his resignation in June 1934.

Gracing the cover of *Time* magazine on June 25, 1934, but now largely forgotten, Rexford Tugwell was considered the most radical of the group. A faithful student of Simon Patten,[73] he was radical, just not any more than anyone else involved. He, too, dreamed big, and his pet project was taking farmland out of production, by force if necessary, to save Earth from human error. He publicly declared, "Much of the land now in use—east of the Mississippi, at least—must be abandoned . . . devoted immediately to forests again."[74] His ambitions were big, if rather vague.

In 1927, he visited Soviet Russia on an intellectual pilgrimage, and his reaction to Stalin's handiwork was a gushing "I knew from then on how determined dictators come to manage a people!"[75] And that about sums up his political views.

He would be responsible for Arthurdale as head of the Resettlement Administration from 1935 to 1936.

Interpreting a Dream

I shall keep out of the slavery of modern city existence, and live in God's sunshine.
—Philip Hubert, *Liberty and a Living* (1889)[76]

In 1908, long before the New Deal codified the idea, Bolton Hall had been calling for taxpayer funds to be used as "special inducements" to get the poor out of the cities and back to the land,[77] an opinion echoed in 1921 by the influential journal *Review of Reviews,* which believed "every state in the union . . . should create for itself a new and aggressive policy for the reconstruction of rural industry and country life."[78] In 1902, Sir Ebenezer Howard, whose English garden city movement so influenced the New Deal's greenbelt communities, declared that "there is no longer any housing problem, only a willingness is needed."[79] He was speaking toward private, voluntary efforts to provide that willingness, but voluntary action did not animate the New Deal.

The willingness Howard desired would instead be supplied through the political agitation of America's intellectual set. As the working masses in their great number actually were going back to the land, the intellectuals gathered in their natural habitat (nicely appointed hotels) and held conferences to discuss how to make all those workers go back to the land in a manner more to their liking. The Smart Set insisted that "this exodus from the cities [is] crying for guidance and control,"[80] and they were just the men to provide it. They were products of their time, perfectly situated to take advantage as America sailed ever closer to the age of planning that they had all long dreamed about. And they dreamed big. The colonies that would leap off their drawing boards were not merely to promote successful farming but "were largely conceived of as experiments to lead a new way of life."[81]

The reasons behind this insistence to plan a wholesale migration back to the land were many, yet in the main consisted of a desire to alleviate the suffering of the unemployed, a fear of revolution, a hatred of city life, a desire to stop people from moving about so much, and, most romantically, a dream to create a better way of life, that last exemplified by FDR "Brain Truster" Rex Tugwell's oft-quoted college poem "I shall roll up my sleeves—make America over!"[82]

Moving about was and still is a distinct characteristic of American life; we crossed a continent in no time flat with little particular direction at all, each man a king following his own plans. That was no longer acceptable, according to the same Rex Tugwell in the *New York Times*, circa 1935. Having not lost an ounce of his youthful fire he declared, "As a nation we have been wantonly profligate in dissipating our real wealth—the land."[83] And with America now settled coast to coast (the joke "Buy land, they ain't making it any more" to become standard investment advice), leaving farmers be to do what they pleased with their own property was just too dangerous to contemplate.

Americans tend to move for a multitude of reasons. We have seen constant self-directed migrations of people throughout our history, the most memorable being the waves of black Americans relocating from the lawlessness of the Jim Crow South to the relative safety of the North during the early 1900s. (Yes, at the same time as our story. But their troubles were theirs alone, as back to the land was an overwhelmingly whites-only gig.)

The reason that so many were fleeing the land was simply that small family farms were going the way of the dodo bird. Especially during the 1920s and 1930s, "the farm . . . economically speaking, was the problem child of the nation."[84] As in coal mining, large-scale mechanization was the wave of the future and quickly supplanted any producer using manual methods. There was no way a man with a team of mules on 20 acres could come close to the productivity—and hence offer the lower prices—of a machine-run farm on 20,000 acres. Small family farms were simply no longer a viable economic species in early 1900s America, depression or no.

For a time, World War I hid the dire straits many small-scale farmers were in. With Europeans plowing their fields under with corpses and artillery shells, a voracious appetite arose for American food exports, and this combined with the easy money of the Federal Reserve to keep farm prices buoyed up and credit freely and easily offered to borrowers. With the end of the war farm prices collapsed, leaving many farmers foolishly overextended. The foreclosure men throughout the Farm Belt were busy.

From 1910 to 1930, the farm population of America fell from around 32 million to 30 million[85]—during a time when America's population overall rose from 92 million to over 123 million[86]—and the stream toward the cities only accelerated during the 1920s.[87] President Hoover, his addiction to meddle now burning like a sore, sent out his Committee on Social Trends to study the matter, and before you knew it, "most sociologists were agreed that the great problem of our day is to stop the drift of population toward the cities."[88]

Then, in three scant years starting in 1930, the situation reversed itself; net internal migration raised the farm population back to 32 million.[89] These numbers all depend on the usual guesses and estimates and especially on how the census takers described "a farm," as many people did not move very far, only "to small semi-rural holdings on the outskirts of cities."[90] Whatever the actual number, there was undoubtedly a noticeable flow back to the countryside. Even farther out, beyond the city outskirts, farms long unoccupied were taken back into cultivation.

Despite the fact that this flow back toward the land was in the direction intellectuals desired, their cherished idea of controlled population movement was still considered necessary, as it was taken as gospel America was still afflicted with "a poor national distribution of population and of industry,"[91] as shown by the shocking level of urban unemployed. According to many of America's leading economic thinkers, these workers would never again be absorbed by industry.[92] They needed to be moved out of the city, which even in the best of times was a way of life inferior to the country. A core belief of the movement held that urban living deprives people "of what is an elemental need of mankind: the inner discipline which comes from communion with the land."[93]

The solution was to be offered by welding the factory system onto the family farm, a "third way" that would allow the workers factory employment when times were good and yet, when times were bad, to always have land to fall back on so they would not starve. "Even a few acres of land can reduce . . . our dependency upon this factory-dominated civilization," promised Ralph Borsodi.[94] These semi-autarkic farm colonies would be, according to M. L. Wilson, "a revolt against the crass materialism and the shallowness of the Jazz Age."[95] Once the material promise of the Roaring Twenties collapsed into years of incessant worry, back-to-the-land was a soothing lullaby to an America that yearned for security above all.

And the future would not see the children of those resettled flee to the city's evil lures at the first chance.[96] By planning the communities and making them as enticing as any city, the people would grow attached to their small community and stay put, "not be a part of a general, floating population."[97] Homesteaders, safe and secure from true privation because of their plots of land, would become "the real foundation of America," an America forever free of revolution as "patriotism has its roots in the soil."[98]

Elwood Mead proclaimed that "political danger comes mainly from the unrest of the industrial worker . . . no such danger confronts the government from the unrest of the farmer."[99] When their dream became a reality, America would see itself transformed, laid over with small-scale farming villages full of contented citizens all collectively working the fields in harmony, the political authorities forever free from the threat of revolution.

Thomas Jefferson, whose musings on farm life were often quoted by the same back-to-the-landers who ignored his musings on power, would have been horrified at the very thought.

Chapter 3

The Definition of Insanity

The history of ideas is the history of man.
—Professor Richard Ely, economist (1938)[1]

T he historian Paul Conkin once wrote that to understand all that happened at Arthurdale, "we need to recapture the unique outlook of 1933, one that made subsistence farming so appealing."[2] The economist Ludwig von Mises argued that the ideas that caused men to act was the be-all and end-all of historical research, calling them "the ultimate data of history beyond which no historical research can go."[3] Essentially, history boils down to the question: What were they thinking?

Sometimes after a particularly boneheaded disaster, people will say of those involved, "They weren't thinking," but they are incorrect.

71

Being human, thinking is what defines us; it is in our very nature. All men think, without exception, it's just that some aren't very good at it.

The core set of beliefs that all back-to-the-land acolytes needed to hold in their heart were decidedly reactionary—it was a blunt wish to crawl back into an imagined past, only with electric lights, tractors, and indoor plumbing taken along for the ride.

The highest ideal of the back-to-the-land movement was not freedom but material things. For its proponents, the very definition of freedom was a materialistic one. The belief "real freedom is economic"[4] was gospel, and resettlement colonies were the road to that Promised Land, since owning your own homestead was the first step toward that freedom.[5] For all their self-righteous condemnations of the Jazz Age, they were themselves pure materialists.

Their ideological outlook produced legislative hybrids consisting of sugarplum dreams mixed with a fearful love of an all-powerful parent figure, as defined by "the state." When FDR became governor of New York in 1928, he asked the legislature for a "declaration by law that the labor of a human being is not a commodity or an article of commerce."[6] And in their world it would not be privately owned, either, since all property was to be at the mercy of political authorities. Richard Ely put into his students' heads a belief that property was a creation of "the state"; therefore, the political class has a right to take whatever portion of the workers' product as was to its liking.[7] One sad result of this attitude fell on any poor slob whose home was in the way of a colony, as invoking eminent domain was considered perfectly acceptable.[8]

The danger inherent in the concentration of power their plans called for was dismissed, as it was assumed that only good people would descend from heaven to run things[9] and the political class would always use its immense power to grant all the material wishes of the workers in a just, fair manner. On the flip side of this deal, the individual must submit at all times—"the individual cannot be considered in a matter of national development," declaimed Elwood Mead. "The individual must give way in the interest of the state."[10] In fact, there was no "private" or "public" for Rexford Tugwell, as "it was false to set up dividing lines between the two."[11] It was a philosophy that had a vision of government as a sort of parental figure above all; even at the federal level, government would be "father and mother for all the 48 states," in the words of FDR.[12]

It was through the political power that FDR inherited and expanded that the basic tenet of the German Historical School was applied to America—"the dogma of laissez-faire should be abandoned by our leaders."[13] Their collectivist ideas reflected larger currents around them. The first three decades of the twentieth century were, for America, one when "ideas such as free enterprise, private property, equality of opportunity, and competition became almost meaningless to many men."[14] The laws that had once protected were not changed—they were simply ignored.

With the shackles of law removed, the political class could apply various levels of force to restrict or encourage the people's activities as they wished. The removal of settlers' freedom to choose for themselves was always a part of the back-to-the-land philosophy; the idea of it infested the movement. It was seen as early as 1885, when a Senate Committee on Education and Labor invited the Reverend Heber Newton, a Christian Socialist and resettlement convert, to express his belief that the type of people who needed to be put onto settlement colonies were, "also the ones who most needed guidance and supervision."[15] Even their off-work hours were to be arranged for them. M. L. Wilson, who would run the DSH during its initial years, worried that with all the free time on their hands homesteaders would doubtless enjoy, "the question as to the problem of this leisure time is worthy of careful consideration."[16]

The disciples of back-to-the-land displayed a burning fervor worthy of any religious cult and an intolerance of contrary opinions typical of the same.[17] Wilson looked disgustedly on the people whom his plan would displace, those "hillbillies," and excused himself because "such a way of life in the scientific and machine age is intolerable."[18] Bolton Hall's *A Little Land and a Living* openly called for those urban poor chosen for rural resettlement to be forced into the countryside should they not voluntarily move.[19] In a particularly creepy moment, Ralph Borsodi's 1929 offering *This Ugly Civilization* pities the nonbeliever: "[Y]ou are indeed unfortunate . . . you are in need of a transvaluation of values."[20]

After the "transvaluation" was complete (assuming "transvaluation" is a real word) and the convert attained rapture, he would "raise more than vegetables in your garden, you raise your expectation of life."[21] FDR after his conversion realized that "it [the land] is also the source of all human happiness."[22] Wilson, ever the dry academic, recorded that "proponents of the subsistence homestead movement are quite generally agreed that there are some psychological and philosophical values which attach to the soil."[23]

It was felt necessary to enhance the lure of rural life through the planned nature of the communities, as it was believed that people left to their own devices did not develop any community pride or freely cooperate.[24] Therefore, according to Mead, "The rural community of the future must be organized."[25] Communal activities would banish isolation, the "dreaded ghost" of the rural dweller and a prime reason people fled to the cities.[26] This belief spawned an emphasis on getting settlers to engage in all manner of group activities, and clubs and interest groups would proliferate on the federal homesteads.[27]

It was to be a life happy in its simplicity. Franklin Howe demanded that "we must think more of man and less of wealth,"[28] and the colonies were designed "to change a society in which emphasis is placed upon money into a society in which emphasis would be placed upon ideals."[29] For Tugwell, though, it was not material things he wished Americans to turn away from but something deeper—their right to decide for themselves.

"The important thing, in the long run, is the conscious striving for new national directions,"[30] he wrote in 1935. His was a call to keep the federal legislative pipeline bursting with new plans and new encroachments into everyday life.

Man Plans, God Laughs

It sounded an excellent plan, no doubt, and very neatly and simply arranged; the only difficulty was, that she had not the smallest idea how to set about it.

—Lewis Carroll, *Alice's Adventures in Wonderland* (1865)

The subsistence homesteads project was "a nebulous idea, meaning all things to all men,"[31] which made it a rather difficult theory to put into practice. There was never at any time agreement on what exactly the plan should look like,[32] but there was complete agreement that a plan should be written and implemented nonetheless. Otherwise, things would be left to laissez-faire, which was believed to bring nothing but chaos.[33] FDR opined that "we have grown up like Topsy; we must grow up by planning."[34] They set themselves up to an impossible task, to improve upon God's creation—man. Franklin Lane puffing up his pride with "[W]e've got to put our shoulders to the wheel, help nature along—speed her up"[35] expressed their attitude perfectly. The movement was powered by the mind-set of a planner, utterly convinced of its own superiority on both a practical and a moral level.

Wilson envisioned a "new frontier" that would open "opportunities and more satisfying community life and wage employment."[36] What was certain was that the adoption of such a policy would be a radical departure from past actions.[37] Arthurdale was "probably the first attempt by direct and deliberate governmental action to make a complex, abstract, social idea into a working, concrete social reality."[38] It was understood and accepted that the plans—both hoped for and actually implemented—would require a heavy dose of coercion.[39] All the future cries of "dictatorship" from the colonists resulted from this deal with the devil.

Some, Wilson among them, urged that the homesteads be locally directed, as this was the purer expression of democracy and "the federal government is distant" and slow on its feet.[40] Each colony plan, though, without fail had within it government-employed farm managers, there to dispense advice and to keep an eye on things.[41] Taking a bit from both rural and urban plans,[42] the subsistence homesteads were to be a combination of small, semi-autarkic farm villages with a nationally planned industrial policy that, through intelligent central planning, would decentralize America's industrial base, ever at the ready to dispense small-scale factories on each colony as needed.[43]

It was all so simple: "A home, a few acres of land, machines, and equipment eliminate drudgery, and no more skill and application than most human beings possess, makes all this possible."[44] Not everyone agreed; Tugwell, having been infected with a fetish for The Big from his admiring glance at Stalinism, wished for large-scale reclamation and resettlement policies. His plan, once implemented, promised that all "the remaining problems would be solved with ease."[45] Equally stuffed with pride, under FDR Tugwell's plan, too, would get its chance.

From the earliest time on, it was realized that these schemes would cost a small fortune, and across the board, proponents either openly called for or strongly hinted at the nationalization of banks, for the political authorities to force bank owners to "provide a new kind of credit" and become "agencies of social welfare."[46] This was deemed expedient and necessary because "successful colonization depends on a low interest rate for money."[47] On all the federal resettlement projects cheap, abundant credit would inundate the colonists and the colonies, with the (seemingly unforeseen) result of crushing them under heavy debt.

And it would all be lent so the colonists could "buy" homes that they could never truly own. At issue was the homeowners turning into "speculators," and "speculation is likely to develop under absolute ownership."[48] Between the insistence that the colonists work and own their businesses collectively and the refusal to sell them actual title to their homes, the plans offered for successful resettlement colonies were shot through with an inherent contradiction. People were expected to behave as if they owned something that they had no clearly defined stake in.

Despite superficial appearances, the creation of Arthurdale and its kind had nothing to do with charity, as it is commonly understood. The homesteads were "only secondarily a relief measure";[49] its proponents had bigger fish to fry: the creation of a better way of life. The men who pushed the idea placed emphasis on a colony that would "exalt the man and minimize the labor," where once people had full stomachs and the basics, they "need not concern themselves about amassing more. We think of such a life as wasted."[50]

These men were not prophets of plenty—quite the opposite. Theirs was a mind-set given great example by Wilson, who praised the Agricultural Adjustment Act of 1933 (a deliberate policy to restrict production) for being "the end of a long standing policy of unlimited agricultural expansion and development."[51]

Subsistence homesteads were promoted and championed by the type of men who praised the same act for, in the midst of hunger, plowing under tons of food and slaughtering and wasting millions of hogs, and applauded New York State politicians for threatening to shut down any dairy farmer who dared drop the price of his product.[52] Stuart Chase, the man who popularized the term "New Deal" and was much the Thomas Friedman of his times, "suggested imposing a ten year moratorium on technological and organizational innovation."[53]

This urge to keep production down, all to buoy up the market price of farm products, took the form of forbidding colonists on any subsistence homestead from entering into competition with local farmers—their small plots and community gardens were for home consumption only—and, of course, the homesteaders were expected to become one with the soil.[54] Even the factories within the colonies were expected to be of the small, handicraft kind—the same sort that had "fallen away in competition."[55] It all took on a strange air, with the colonies urged to be a success, but not too much of one as that would "kick out the factory system at the front door to re-introduce it at the back."[56]

Despite the vagueness and contradictions of the plans, with laissez-faire believed to offer nothing but waste and confusion, any type of plan was still sure to be a winner by comparison.[57] Franklin Lane insisted the Mead settlement idea "will not, in the long run, cost Uncle Sam anything,"[58] while Tugwell promised "this method [specifically, his] will save money to the federal Treasury and to the taxpayers."[59] FDR breezily declared to Senator George Norris of Nebraska that "we would get most of the money [from Arthurdale] back in due time."[60]

The dream when it was all up and running would transport America back in time and across an ocean, as "the farm colony is a return to the village type of farming which prevailed for centuries all over Europe."[61] It would be a new, better life, all done to "socialize agriculture . . . [and] the underlying idea is group organization."[62] This, a distinctly European, collectivist form of living, was designed to promote American citizenship.[63]

FDR wrote an article for the *New York Globe* in 1911 in which he praised country living because men who lived on farms "have more time to think and study for themselves"[64] and called them the "political salvation" of America. Those were the words of a gentleman farmer whose hands, should they ever have touched dirt, were quickly cleaned by a legion of servants. For all the complexity of their plans and for all their educational attainments, the proponents of resettlement were completely out of touch with those whose lives they wished to experiment with.

For a group of men who defined themselves by their educational credentials they should have known better. Although a Department of Agriculture study in 1942 concluded that the subsistence homesteads were such a dismal failure partly because "there was no experience in such matters that could be taken for a guide,"[65] American history as it stood in 1933 provided plenty of experiences to choose from. In fact, Elwood Mead himself had created and seen slip under the waves two politically run resettlement colonies not very long before Arthurdale.

Yet instead of studying either of them to determine what went wrong, the Division of Subsistence Homesteads would retain their basic assumptions and replicate their operational characteristics, all to the exact same sad effect.

Lather, Rise, Repeat: Previous Farm Colonies

The dream of a communistic or cooperative commonwealth has found expression from the remotest time in the formation of colonies upon the land, with communal ownership. These colonies have furnished also a demonstration of their futility.

—Professor R. W. Murchie (1933)[66]

In a 1934 edition of *Survey* magazine, Eleanor Roosevelt was quoted as saying "[W]e shall know more about subsistence farming when the first new projects have been working for a number of years."[67] Her husband, the president, seconded that notion in the same year, declaring that "we are starting something absolutely new, something in which we have very little to fall back on."[68] FDR, a longtime advocate of resettlement colonies, most certainly knew that he was telling a bold-faced lie. There were a multitude of examples to fall back on.

For starters, there were the Mormon communities that, due to Wilson's admiration of their community spirit and economic success, "were to influence directly the government sponsored subsistence homesteads."[69] Although the physical layout of the Mormon towns could be used as a benchmark, unfortunately, because Arthurdale was a federal project, the separation of church and state precluded forced mass conversions to Mormonism. There were other communities to study, besides. California, as always, led the nation, and it saw both private and public funds used for a number of colonies in the years preceding Arthurdale. The later colonies, publicly funded schemes at Durham and Delhi, were overseen by Mead and would heavily influence Arthurdale.

One early project began its run in 1908; it was a private venture led by a successful California publisher and irrigation expert named William E. Smythe. He called his fellow travelers "Little Landers," in homage to Bolton Hall's book of the same name,[70] and he would create three separate colonies, all in California, during 1908, 1912, and 1916. All activities were based on the principle of cooperation and the Little Landers' creed: "[T]he spirit of fellowship . . . makes the good of one the concern of all."[71]

The first colony was located a little south of San Diego on 550 acres of marginally productive land and named San Ysidro, to honor the Spanish patron saint of agriculture. After a 1916 flood carried away a number of homesteads and the colony's irrigation system, the settlers, who had already fallen to internal squabbles over the division of co-op revenues, began to abandon the colony. By March 1925, four people were all who remained of the original 500.

Smythe had been busy in the meantime, opening another colony in 1912 named Los Terrenitos (Spanish for "Little Lands") about 17 miles from the center of Los Angeles. Taking no lessons with him from his first effort, he purchased land that was even less productive than that at San Ysidro and laid out farms of far too small a size to be economically viable.

Luckily for him and all he had convinced to invest in Los Terrenitos, San Ysidro paid back Smythe for the compliment. Although the colony's land was useless to farm, by pure luck it was a prime location for suburban homes, being but a short trip from a major city and boasting exceptional mountain views. Finding their lots—for which they had paid $800 (about $17,600 in 2010) an acre—now worth many times more, the colonists dropped their farm tools, morphed into dreaded "speculators," and sold their plots to go away happy and content, if ideologically impure.[72]

The final Little Lander colony was completed in 1916 and was a fiasco, a total financial loss for all involved. Located in Alameda County and named Hayward in honor of the town of Hayward Heath in England's fertile Sussex Downs region, this project would prove for once and all that while Smythe doubtless had a talent for dreaming up snappy names for his colonies, he was utterly incapable of spotting viable farmland on which to place them.

Once again located on infertile soil, the colony had collapsed by 1920. The land was found to be worthless at any price and was simply abandoned.[73] Despite it all, Smythe was brought to Washington, D.C., in February of 1919 by Franklin Lane, who tasked him with choosing land fit to be reclaimed for farming.[74] Smythe would pass away on October 27, 1922, in New York.

Besides the Little Landers' example, there were other homestead colonies that those who created Arthurdale could have fallen back on—even ones they themselves had managed: the disaster at Fairway Farms in Montana, for example. Conceived by Richard Ely's student Henry C. Taylor and funded with a $100,000 loan from John D. Rockefeller at 5 percent interest per annum, the project was the brainchild of a star-studded group that featured Wilson as project manager and board member, along with Taylor and Ely.[75]

The objective was to help tenant farmers to become farm owners[76] while proving that "scientific management" could make even an area where "abandoned or rundown farms . . . were everywhere" into viable farms.[77] In 1924, Wilson purchased nine farms, some as large as 2,500 acres, and moved in the "carefully selected tenants." Despite the best available "proper educational guidance and financial backing,"[78] drought and a continued slide in prices for farm goods had the project habitually in the red. In 1932, the Rockefellers refused to continue funding a money-losing venture. (Rockefeller's people were also particularly exasperated by having "to do business with people who . . . do not look upon a promissory note as a business arrangement.")[79] Soon afterward the project collapsed.

Fairway Farms would also contribute its errors to Arthurdale, as "these farms were . . . early precedents for the tenant-rehabilitation and purchase programs of the New Deal. The experimentation indicated many of the policies that Wilson would adapt to his Division of Subsistence Homesteads."[80] The lessons that could have been learned were left behind in Montana, abandoned with the farms.

Another homestead project was available for study, this one a taxpayer-funded venture in California designed, built, sailed, and sunk by Elwood Mead after his return from establishing (and seeing collapse) taxpayer-funded homesteads in Australia. It consisted of two locations. The first, built in 1917 on about 6,200 acres in Butte County, took its name, Durham, from the railroad station that lay not half a mile from the settlement headquarters. Mead divided the land into 125 farms and 28 farm laborer allotments.[81] The second, built in 1919 in Delhi County on about 8,700 acres amid "even greater enthusiasm,"[82] would prove soon enough to be, like its fellow colony, a financial and social disaster.

As in his Australian farm colonies (and like all subsidized entities) at the beginning, things seemed a rousing success, and commissions and dignitaries from both America and around the globe visited California to study the projects.*[83] By 1923, Mead was an increasingly public figure, his views on his homestead colonies given prominent place in the *New Republic, Review of Reviews, Survey,* and *Ladies' Home Journal.* Despite the glowing articles and public acclaim, taxpayer subsidies were masking the colonies' dire straits, especially at Delhi.[84]

They had started out with much fanfare and high hopes. Mead had "a great compulsion" to take all the methods he had used on the Australian colonies and apply them in the United States.[85] In 1914, Mead visited with California governor Hiram W. Johnson. The governor, though much taken by Mead's settlement proposal, felt it politically impossible to do anything "until public opinion was educated to accept what was so radical a change in policy."[86]

Using the influential Commonwealth Club of California as his education campaign's launching pad, Mead was chosen in 1915 to head a state-appointed Commission on Colonization and Rural Credits to "study" the problem and make a recommendation to the legislature.[87]

---

*Similar colonies were created in Washington, Arizona, Minnesota, and South Dakota, all to suffer the same result.

Mead would years later relate to the readers of *Survey* that "the commission recommended that the state take a leaf from the experience of Australia"[88] without bothering to mention that the commission, far from a bastion of disinterestedness, was run by himself. The most basic problem holding back rural development in California, according to Mead's findings, was that "private companies focused on . . . profit, not on social planning."[89] That statement right there should have given the California legislature pause.

But it did not, and with State Senator Arthur H. Breed leading the charge, the 1917 passage of the State Land Settlement Act[90] saw the California legislature introduce the first-ever land settlement act in U.S. history. Even the fact that "many believed" the act was a "violation of the State Constitution"[91] was brushed aside by the thrill of progress unleashed. The specifics legislated into law would include "almost all of Mead's treasured ideas"[92] and, more important, $260,000 in taxpayer funds to start out with.

Mead gloated as the act specifically targeted two groups of people he harbored a particular distaste for—absentee landlords and nonwhites. "Speculation in land . . . will be eliminated," he wrote of the legislation in 1918, and the colonies would "make it less necessary to import people who are politically undesirable to till our idle fields."[93]

The colonies had a threefold purpose in his mind. He felt that "planned" communities were required to check political unrest by means of increasing land ownership, to keep the rural areas white, and to reverse the population flow to the cities by offering enticing farm colonies. The "enticing" element would be introduced by combining "social reclamation with land reclamation, social engineering with irrigation engineering,"[94] creating a rich social life that combined the excitement of the city with pure, wholesome country living.

Only landless people were allowed to become settlers, and all but those chosen to occupy the farm laborer allotments needed to put capital into the venture ($1,500—about $22,000 in 2010—for a farm allotment).[95] Settlers were carefully chosen, based on "character, industry, and a past record which promises success."[96] A rural credit system was established to allow the settlers to borrow money on easy terms.

Tenants would "own" the farms with a bevy of restrictions: They had to live on and actually farm the land (to prevent absentee ownership), could not sell to anyone not approved by the colony's board, and could sell only to someone who would also farm the land. This was designed to prevent "speculation," as Mead firmly believed that "buying a farm simply to sell it again at a profit was an economic evil" that prevents a colony from "build[ing] up an attractive social life."[97] Anyone who wished to stay had to become a member of the various cooperative associations the colonies would implement.

Of the two, Durham was by far the more "successful," as it was established before World War I boosted food prices (and farmland) into a bubble. The College of Agriculture of the University of California provided assistance, and Mead brought one of his favorite students from his time teaching at Colorado State Agricultural College, George Kreutzer, and appointed him Durham's superintendent. (Kreutzer had worked under Mead in Australia and would one day follow him to Washington, DC).[98]

The profligate waste began immediately. The purchase price of the land, at $500,000, easily consumed the original budget of $260,000 and then some, with the settlement taking on further debt to fund the shortfall. Experts walked approved buyers about their plots, helping the settlers "plan their buildings and lay out their gardens and fields."[99] Durham filled up quickly, a pleased Mead pointing out that even the farm laborer allotments were 100 percent white residents only.[100] It was unlike anything ever seen before in America, a taxpayer-funded farm colony staffed with helpful experts and debt offered on easy terms. Each home offered what at the time was an almost unheard of rural luxury— electricity and indoor plumbing.[101]

On the bare surface all looked well, and in 1919, the California legislature approved an additional $1 million to create another colony, this one at Delhi ($125,000 out of those funds were diverted to keep Durham afloat).[102] Specifically planned for soldiers returned from the trenches of France,[103] it would be a far larger disaster than Durham. Although the land was located in the midst of "one of the most highly improved agricultural sections of that state,"[104] it was not a very good part and was known by locals to be the kind "over which the jack rabbits carried their lunch."[105] The added costs per acre—required because concrete pipes had to be made and laid out to irrigate the fields—scared off many a would-be purchaser.[106] Even with taxpayer subsidies and easy lending terms, Delhi would never sell all its available lots, and by late 1928, over 50 percent of the land still remained unsold.[107]

In financial discipline, Mead and his fellows were decidedly lacking. Although everyone involved pledged from the get-go to "make this settlement a going concern with the least waste of effort, money, and time," Durham itself would boast a 22-acre compound with a dance pavilion, fairgrounds, tennis courts, baseball field, with a swimming pool promised to come.[108] Up in Delhi, a $10,000 community hall was completed (the first settlers placed a portrait of Mead above the fireplace), and the concrete pipe factory (built to provide the colony's irrigation system) came in at $35,000 by itself.[109] In 1921, the California state legislature allocated an additional $1 million to keep the colonies solvent.[110]

It was obvious to anyone that the colonies were living in a manner far beyond the means that their co-op farms and dairies could support. Mead himself admitted that "the settlers could not have raised all the capital needed to build" the infrastructure provided.[111] It was all created on the back of debt; the "ability to carry out this improvement was due to the rural credit feature of the Land Act."[112] This heavy debt burden on the settlers made them extremely vulnerable, since Mead was the one who had designed the credit system and controlled to whom it was made available. This gave him a great power over the lives of those in the colonies. He acted through colony managers, and they were tasked to "report [any settler] to the authorities [Mead] who displayed poor behavior."[113]

Mead had an odd way of looking at the money settlers borrowed; he would allow them to borrow it but felt "the borrowed money could be used to better advantage if the government directed its outlay."[114] He "watched the affairs of the two colonies closely—in fact, in a manner that often veered on being dictatorial," and life in the colonies saw a "minute monitoring of the settlers' lives" that was resented.[115]

A 1922 article in the *Review of Reviews* praised Mead, saying "he succeeded in making it the business of the state itself to do with scientific precision things which had hitherto been left to real estate operators."[116] Those words were written too soon. The fall in farm prices brought on by the end of World War I was already working to destroy the colonies, far too overleveraged to handle a drop in demand or prices. Conditions worsened, particularly at Delhi, and Mead began a desperate attempt to keep it solvent by lending even more money to the settlers, almost all of them seriously behind on their debt payments. Many simply used the new loans to catch up on their delinquent debts.[117]

The "cooperation" that the settlers had been encouraged to display in their everyday lives took an unexpected form, as they organized and agitated for debt relief. Mead angrily denounced those involved as "anarchists" and pleaded with the governor to have them evicted. When this request was refused Mead resigned, and by late 1923 his involvement with the colonies was over.[118]

Things continued to go downhill, and in February 1924, the settlers at Delhi made some time during their day to take down Mead's portrait from the community center hall and "lynch" it.[119] A little over one year later, the state legislature declared that public funds should not be used for homestead settlements in the future and wrote off over $800,000 of Delhi's mortgage debt.[120] The settlers at Durham, also drowning in a sea of debt, demanded the same.

By 1930, the California legislature had extricated itself from Mead's disaster, writing off over $2.5 million in taxpayer funds.[121] Mead insisted that the plan was nonetheless sound, and it was "irresponsible colonists" who were to blame.[122]

Durham and Delhi had been a fatal mix of bad advice, bad land, and bad ideas. Years later his biographer James R. Kluger would state that "Mead was attempting the dichotomy of creating a hearty, independent yeoman by regimented, dictatorial means."[123] Yet regimentation of people's lives and the planning involved in seeing it through were the wave of America's future. So despite the failures of his colonies, both foreign and domestic, the ideas Elwood Mead implemented at Durham and Delhi spread to Washington,[124] while the past results of those very same ideas were completely ignored.

M. L. Wilson, he of Fairway Farms fame, would write in 1934 that "if we really take the subsistence homestead community idea seriously . . . [it] must be forged through trial and error, through success and failure."[125] For all their supposed love of book learning, the people involved were willfully blind to the litany of failures all past efforts had produced (even those they had personally been involved with), instead blindly doing the exact same thing over and over while expecting a different result. Besides the Mormons', there was another example of successful farm colonies that they could have studied—the Salvation Army's efforts at Fort Romie, California. Those involved even left behind their thoughts on the matter.

Fort Romie was begun in 1898 and was completely—and profit-ably—debt-free by 1910 (after which the Army exited the colony). Commander Booth Tucker outlined in a 1903 report for the Department of Commerce and Labor the lessons he felt needed to be learned to enable success.[126] The first lesson above all was "the sense of ownership is from the first cultivated, with excellent results," followed closely by advice to disdain cooperative effort as "a premium is placed upon idleness" under such systems. A rigid ideological orthodoxy would preclude Arthurdale's planners from implementing either piece of advice, and another nugget that they might have used from the report, that it was "deemed wise to pay the best prices for good soil," was something all those responsible never showed any talent for.

A writer in the *New Republic*, in a rare moment of clarity during the early 1930s push to establish more homestead communities, looked at the waves of individuals already flowing back to the land—for the most part with little to show for it—and asked: "Why propose as a remedy a thing that is being tried with such ill success by literally millions of our people?"[127] The answer to that question was provided years before when Dr. Ebenezer Howard wrote in 1902 that "long-continued effort, in spite of failure and defeat, is the fore-runner of complete success."[128]

In every beating heart, hope springs eternal.

Slipping By in the Crowd—Legislating Arthurdale

We are already a semi-socialist state.
> —Dr. Frederic C. Howe, author (1919)[129]

In retrospect, by the time the Division of Subsistence Homesteads (DSH) was created on June 16, 1933, it was a foregone conclusion.

With the ascension of FDR to the presidency, the age of planning had matured, and when Congress passed the National Industrial Recovery Act, Arthurdale simply rode in on its coattails, a tiny rider attached to a gigantic piece of legislation that nobody even read. Unlike previous settlement legislation, which all saw debate in Congress (the last of which, the "McFadden" bills, were defeated in 1932), and despite FDR's stated opinion that it "had implications worth serious consideration,"[130] the actual creation of a federal subsistence homestead program was given no consideration at all; it was merely passed into law.

No one was reading much of anything during FDR's famous first 100 Days, when a torrent of new laws and edicts rained down from Washington on a thankful American people. Everything done then and afterward, all the half-baked measures, were passed unread with a simple shrug and the excuse that "the emergency (of the Depression) demanded immediate action."[131] A premium was placed on acting over thinking.

By that time, Ely's intellectual children were entrenched deeply enough in government, universities, and planning boards throughout the land to take full advantage. To top it off, the back-to-the-landers had a fast friend and fellow traveler in the person of FDR. Rexford Tugwell noted in 1929 that "any group which is determined, under our legislative system, can make itself politically formidable,"[132] and the men who created Arthurdale after years of endless agitation were by 1933 nothing if not politically formidable.

There can be no doubt that they meant well, completely assured they would see things through to a successful conclusion this time and thereby introduce a grateful America to a better world in the process. These were not evil men, nor were they saints. Not to be ignored, however, is the self-interest involved for all those who championed the idea. The fact that a federal subsistence homestead program would be not only a patronage bonanza for the politicians (FDR gloated in 1934 of the "great advantage" of the program, in that it "affects every Congressional district"[133]), but also a steady feeder of well-paid, exciting jobs for those with the proper academic credentials and political connections is too obvious to ignore.

In their speeches and writings they chatted excitedly to each other about what graduate college students now refer to as "job opportunities." Wilson praised the creation of a "national planning board to be

continuously at work,"[134] stuffed to the gills with academic scribblers
putting their dreams into actual application. The New Deal in its first
years, when a flood of PhDs were drawn into Roosevelt's orbit, seemed
the realization of Ralph Borsodi's call for "a new social order—an order
in which the philosopher, the teacher, and the student shall be first."[135]
For a young professor embarked on a career within the New Deal's
rapidly expanding domain, it was an exciting time, gratifying both intel-
lectually and financially.

Of all the people in Washington who made Arthurdale possible, it
was Senator John Bankhead of Alabama, long an ardent believer in
subsistence homestead colonies, who was most responsible for the
endless legwork, effort, and backroom dealings that made the Division
of Subsistence Homesteads a reality. It was on his third try to attach
the amendment in committee that he finally succeeded, and it was
successful in that instance only due to the strong backing of the White
House.[136]

The legislation consisted of a vague, simple paragraph; Section 208
of Title II of the National Industrial Recovery Act was its name. It
read as follows:

> *To provide for aiding in the redistribution of the overbalance of population in
> industrial centers $25,000,000 is hereby made available to the President, to
> be used by him through such agencies as he may establish and under such
> regulations as he may make, for making loans for and otherwise aiding in the
> purchase of subsistence homesteads. The money collected as repayment of said
> loans shall constitute a revolving fund to be administered as directed by the
> President for the purposes of this section.*[137]

That was it, 83 words long. Holly Cowen's thesis on Arthurdale
claimed the legislation was not "well planned," and she was correct;
yet her assertion that it was not "far-ranging" was off the mark.[138] It
was a groundbreaking piece of legislation, a program that tasked the
federal authorities with making a "better world." The creation of
the Division of Subsistence Homesteads represented a complete break
with all past political practice, it was a sea change in the philosophy
behind what form of government Americans live under, and it was
passed with "no hearing and no debates."[139]

It was a blank check for the president to do what he pleased. Five days after its passage, Roosevelt issued a simple executive order (numbered 6209) that transferred responsibility to carry out subsistence homesteads to the secretary of the Interior.[140] After years of dreams, repeated folly, and endless political agitation, the fondest wish of the back-to-the-landers was now a reality; all their stars were aligned. The man at the very top of the nation's power structure was not only a fellow true believer but also a sugar daddy without peer. Through his political power, the purse of the federal government would finally be opened up to them.

They had reached the major leagues, and stuffed to bursting with excitement, they confidently set off to improve on God's design.

Chapter 4

We Lucky Few

It was just like moving into heaven.
—Robert McLaughlin Sr., Arthurdale homesteader (2009)

Moving day for a young Glenna Williams and her family was June 30, 1934. After much delay, one of the most cherished memories of their lives dawned on Glenna and her sister June—the day that they no longer called Scotts Run home. Both set out together ahead of their family, carefully hand-escorting two heirlooms they would be taking with them out of the smoking hollow. A clock and "a relic of her childhood," a cabinet with glass doors, were the pieces of distinction.[1]

Also working their way toward Arthurdale were all nine members of the Mayor family. One daughter, Dorothy, 15 at the time and just about to enter high school, still remembered her wonder at the "beautiful brand new, four bedroom house with a bath" that they were relocated to. She, her parents, and six siblings would find Arthurdale "a wonderful place to live."[2]

The Mayor and Williams families were part of a hugely expensive, massive relocation and construction project that dwarfed anything America's federal government had ever before attempted in peacetime. That it was all undertaken in the midst of a most crushing, extended period of economic depression makes perfect sense, because the idea to build a fully functional town 1,800 feet above sea level on a remote West Virginia plateau would never have been allowed during more placid times.

At first known as the Reedsville Experimental Community but soon enough named Arthurdale after the gentlemen farmer who once owned the land, when completed, the town would boast 165 houses equipped with outbuildings such as barns and root cellars, all on lots that averaged four acres. Included was a town square that featured "a community building, forge, cooperative store, barbershop, weaving room, furniture display room, administrative building, craft rooms, and a filling station." Thirteen miles of road were laid out, paved with red-dog (a by-product of slag)[3] and, at Eleanor Roosevelt's suggestion, designated alphabetically.[4] A multibuilding school complex, inn, three small factories, gristmill, and health center rounded it all out.[5]

It was the blossoming of a new America; no previous president had the political power to pull it off. Lavish, immensely wasteful, and geographically isolated, Arthurdale was America's first pyramid. This one is now dedicated to the memory of Eleanor Roosevelt, and that is as it should be because despite being but 1 of about 99 back-to-the-land colonies the federal government created during the New Deal (that number could rise to about 200, depending on your definition),[6] by all accounts Arthurdale was Mrs. Roosevelt's pet project, the one she poured all her heart, soul, and money into.

Yet for one teenaged girl who was moved into the town, the earth-shaking historic moment she was part of and the immense size of it all did not make much of an impression. Instead, for Glenna Williams, leaving the ubiquitous coal dust of Scott's Run, leaving a world always being painted in light gray for the fresh air of Arthurdale, put one fond memory above all in her head.

"All the walls were so white. That's what I remember most."[7]

Rotting from the Head

Arthurdale is . . . a direct venture in planned economy by an administration sympathetic to planned economy. [It] has been judged on its intentions.

—Wesley Stout, *Saturday Evening Post* (1934)[8]

Arthurdale was snowed in, the blizzard having made auto travel impossible along the unpaved roads. The town was cut off, except to the horse-drawn sleigh, bells singing, racing toward it through the high drifts. Sitting aboard was a party of federal officials and one English guest, Henry Morris, at the time director of education for that country's Cambridge county, over for a visit and along for the ride. Leading man for the federal employees was Dr. M. L. Wilson, representing the Department of the Interior, Division of Subsistence Homesteads. He was to give the dedicatory address and present the town of Arthurdale to the people who were to live in it.[9]

During the ceremony, a fresh storm dumped two more feet atop the waist-high snow already on the ground. Accepting the gift of Arthurdale on behalf of the homesteaders, though the town was still incomplete and three months behind schedule, was Congressman Jennings Randolph, then in the early days of his long attachment to the job.* Still a little wet behind the ears, he let slip a bit of truth to the assembled reporters: "Many changes in the original plan already have been found necessary and more may be made."[10] Where once Thanksgiving had been forecast as the day of Arthurdale's birth, April 1 was, for now, the new move-in date.[11]

It was February 26, 1934. After gestating within a womb of endless conferences, policy proposals, fiction novels, speeches, misfires, and

---

*He would live long enough to become the sole surviving member of Congress during FDR's 100 Days, then the oldest living former congressman. He passed away in 1998, at the age of 96.

hopeful dreams for over 100 years, the idea defined by the term "back to the land" birthed Arthurdale. It was not to be an easy delivery. It would be months later until finally, by July, the first wave of settlers had been moved in and Arthurdale could be declared squalling and kicking alive.

Though the town was delivered late and way over budget, it would be too easy, and unfair, to laugh with superior feeling at our ancestors of the 1930s for their willingness to squander millions' worth of resources on Arthurdale's construction. Although politically directed leaps into the realm of running a business have never been known to go with even a sliver of fiscal discipline, unlike today's Americans, those of 1933 were relative virgins to the whole concept of bureaucratic dreamers running amok.

For the people of the 1930s, "planning" of economic life by the political class seemed a new type of idea to put into action, and in the midst of a great economic depression, most agreed that its time had come. While the seeds of political intervention into daily life had been planted in every mind long before Arthurdale, the New Deal was a radical departure from the past; it seemed chock full of new, bold, and exciting policies because for 1933 America, it was.

Only four of the 99 federal resettlement projects were even desig-nated for the truly needy; the entire program would quickly morph into more of a lower-middle-class entitlement.[12] Besides Arthurdale, the three others designed to accept the destitute were Tygart Valley in West Virginia and the Cumberland and Westmoreland homesteads in Tennessee and Pennsylvania, respectively.[13]

The oft-told story of the colossal waste that resulted from Arthurdale's building is a necessary part of the tale; to not talk about it because those who commanded the town to be built had "good inten-tions" ignores the fact that, with very few exceptions, people *always* have good intentions. It is results that matter. George Washington, who is rumored to have surveyed the land on which Arthurdale stands, once said of government, "[N]ever for a moment should it be left to irre-sponsible action," and the federal employees involved in the fiasco of Arthurdale's birth were nothing if not irresponsible, regardless of their good intentions.

As a self-sustainable project, Arthurdale was doomed from the start. The Russians have a saying, "A fish rots from the head," and the individuals who were the main driving force behind Arthurdale's creation showed themselves to be utterly incompetent home builders and extremely careless with money. The blame for all the squandered wealth rests firmly on their shoulders, the charge made worse by the fact it was Other People's Money they were throwing down a pit, and this at a time when every penny was precious to every family.

From the beginning to the very end, the intellectuals, politicians, and bureaucrats who made Arthurdale a reality showed little ability to do much right. At the top, and coming off as the most culpable must be the team of Eleanor Roosevelt, the driving force behind the project, and her husband, Franklin, the president. When Harold Ickes (Secretary of the Interior at the time) told FDR of the cost overruns the president's blasé reaction, simply shrugging it off with a "my missus, unlike most women, hasn't any sense about money at all,"[14] resulted in a complete disregard to hold down costs at all levels involved with Arthurdale.

Eleanor Roosevelt's lack of concern about costs piled on to her husband's attitude, and she chided Louis Howe "not to be too stingy when it came to the new houses."[15] Combined with FDR's willingness to grant her great leeway with taxpayer money, this allowed and encouraged a devil-may-care attitude toward what the cost of it all would be—waste and inefficiency pervaded the building of the town.

The elite set the tone. Their mind-set had a deleterious effect, and it infected the entire organization. One recorded example had five workmen taking 12 days to dig up and move a "small maple tree"[16]* and the workforce that did the grunt work was bloated beyond any rational measure. Although Arthurdale's hemorrhaging of money was something that any modern American can feel right at home reading about, in 1933 it still retained a newness that caused a scandal, and the newspapers reacted accordingly.

The only bureaucrat involved who seemed appalled by the inefficiency was Ickes, top man at the Department of the Interior under which the Division of Subsistence Homesteads fell. The division was

---

*The tree was destroyed in the process, and who says history isn't funny?

headed by M. L. Wilson, formerly employed as an economist in the wheat section of the Agricultural Adjustment Administration (AAA). He sold Ickes on the idea of experimental communities like Arthurdale.[17] Others appointed to top positions included Clarence E. Pickett, formerly of the American Friends Service Committee and now special assistant to Wilson concerning anything that involved Scotts Run and its environs.

Carl C. Taylor was brought on board from North Carolina State, where he was a noted rural sociologist. Another sociologist joined him, Bruce L. Melvin, who specialized in the study of "youth problems." An Iowa newspaper reporter named Roy Hendrickson was brought in as well.[18] No one had any experience at all in home building, especially on the vast scale of what Arthurdale would become.

In addition, Bushrod Grimes, who had been supervising local garden clubs for the University of West Virginia's extension division, was appointed the local representative for the Department of the Interior.[19] Soon to be transferred over to project manager, he was to play a large part in the building and formation of Arthurdale, including the initial land purchase. Everyone involved failed to take into account the most important aspect of real estate investing: Location is everything. Isolated high on a mountain plateau, Arthurdale was a poor site for a subsistence homestead, to say the least.

Under the top layers of organization was an executive committee that every homestead community was required to have, and Arthurdale's glittered with the heavy-hitting roster of Wilson, Grimes, Louis Howe, and Eleanor Roosevelt. There were also committees on admissions, industry, and population.[20] For the people who worked and lived in the town these layers would add up to a daunting mountain of red tape—by all accounts the paperwork was endless.

Eleanor Roosevelt had taken a direct interest in Arthurdale, and she was to have a profound impact on its history. Described by biographer Blaine Wiesen Cook as "annoyed by petty accounting," Mrs. Roosevelt considered any attempt to hold down costs as "mean-spirited trimming."[21] Although her constant presence and determined sponsorship of Arthurdale was a boon to the settlers (and made their relationship with the bureaucracy far easier and more humane), it created a particular thorn in the side of Harold Ickes.

Although Ickes was a politically powerful man, he had never walked down the aisle with FDR or shared his bed. Even though Eleanor lacked any formal office, her proximity to power made her a very big shaker in 1930s America. Amity Shlaes's history of the Great Depression, *The Forgotten Man,* quotes a contemporary of hers as saying, "It would be impossible to say how often and to what extent government processes have been turned in a new direction because of her determination."[22] Bushrod Grimes noted the same during a dinner meeting in the White House; he wrote that "I noticed the president was very attentive to anything Mrs. Roosevelt had to say and listened to her with interest."[23]

Eleanor's thoughts on financial matters, again according to Cook, was "in matters of such simple dignity and decency one should not be able to tell the rich from the poor,"[24] and good luck arguing frugality into a brain that, good intentions or not, displays such a deeply materialistic outlook on things.

So even though Ickes may have been appalled and outraged at the expense, the inclusion of indoor toilets in the homes making him ask why "While over 80% of rural America had no modern conveniences, why should the rural poor have indoor privies?" His pleas fell on barren soil; his attempt at "mean-spirited trimming" came to naught.

Eleanor and Ickes were a bad personal match (and not the last one Arthurdale would see) among the top people responsible for the project. The most detrimental effect of Mrs. Roosevelt's intense personal interest was the organizational dysfunction it introduced, the direct result of which was to be repeated public embarrassments. "Impatient with Ickes's methods, with government red tape and endless conferences, Eleanor Roosevelt enlisted Louis Howe's support for immediate action."[25] For her troubles in breaking the chain of command and ignoring procedure, Eleanor would blunder Arthurdale right into the biggest, most public fiasco the town was to know: Howe's impulsive purchase of the infamous prefabricated houses that started things off.

Power is too much for some more than others, and Howe was going through a bit of a Napoleonic stage. Despite, like Eleanor, having no official status at all in the Department of the Interior, Howe had been asked by the president's wife to cut through Ickes and all the red tape, and as FDR's right-hand man he had the ability to do much in that regard. The American taxpayer would pay the cost in millions of dollars' worth of their workdays because of Howe's Waterloo moment, particularly for the prefabricated houses—but they first would have to pay for another of his blunders, the actual purchase of the land.

Following the recommendation of Clarence Pickett,[26] Howe ordered Grimes, the government's purchasing agent and project manager, to negotiate with the owners of three parcels, the most prominent being Richard Arthur and his 1,018 acres.[27] The two other small parcels purchased brought the total acreage up to about 1,200.[28] Arthur, a once-prosperous Pittsburgh hotelier, had fallen behind on his taxes, and his bargaining position was a bad one. $48,500 was taken from the taxpayers and given to him; this granted title of his land and the 23-room mansion he'd built on it to the government. On September 29, 1933, the project was announced in the press.[29]

Set amid the pleasantly rolling hill country of Preston County, Arthurdale's location looked feasible for a settlement if one ignored the fact of its isolated locale, which Howe most certainly did, and if one was unaware of the stratum of porous rock underneath that made the water supply unsafe, which Howe most certainly was.[30] These problems caused substantial additional costs to make Arthurdale livable.

The land itself lays a claim to history, noting that none other than George Washington once surveyed it. Before being purchased by Richard Arthur in 1903, the land had been owned from the time of the Revolution by the Fairfax family, and since George Washington had once been a surveyor for a Lord Fairfax, who owned a massive swath of Virginian land (West Virginia was part of Virginia itself until cleaved away in 1861), it was assumed that George had trodden the hills about, taking careful notes.

It is true that George Washington once was a surveyor for Lord Fairfax and that Lord Fairfax was a substantial property owner. A John Fairfax, of no known relation to Lord Fairfax, though, owned the area of Arthurdale itself. Although George Washington knew both men on a personal level, John worked *for* George and was 31 years his junior,[31] so as with many such claims about where Washington visited, this one, too, is likely false.[32]

With the land itself now chosen and purchased, there arose a disagreement among local and federal boosters of the project over how the houses were to be situated on it. "The best thought of some of the local welfare people who were familiar with the terrain, the soil, and the climate" called for the homes to be built together on the higher ground, while reserving the lower ground for one large community plot, to be efficiently farmed with machinery.[33]

The local welfare people also called for the town to be "hooked into" the nearby community of Reedsville, to use funds for Arthurdale to expand and complete the Reedsville School's addition, which lay half finished due to lack of money.[34] It was hoped that sharing a school building would develop a rapport between the settlers and the people who already lived in the area. But the higher-ups in D.C. had other plans, and since they were footing the bills, their plan was to be instituted.

The new plan, redrawn over a single weekend,[35] called for the houses to be scattered over the high and low ground, each autonomous with its very own well instead of all hooking into one central reservoir. The town was not to share any school building with anyone; Eleanor Roosevelt had a dream to build a "progressive" school complex that required an independent stand-alone system. Costs would rise accordingly.

It was said that "here was a planned economy in action, but there was no plan,"[36] but such accusations were unfair and incorrect. There most certainly was a plan; it was simply poorly thought out and ever changing. Arthurdale was not conceived and constructed in a calm, rational manner; it was put into action with much haste, amid confusion and heightened emotions, all funded with $25 million of Other People's Money and a legislative mandate that "contained almost no guide" as to how that money was to be spent, all of it given over to a group of academics and political dreamers who believed that "profit" was a curse word.

It was bound to be a financial disaster, and it was. Costs were simply disregarded, and it was impossible to plan, when even as late as the construction phase "the method by which the homesteaders are going to buy their homes and land [had] not been fully settled."[37] It was a fiasco propelled by the urge to do something quickly, cost and consequences be damned. Arthurdale was the product of frightened people lashing out in the dark. Eleanor Roosevelt herself warned her husband of impending revolution—that without immediate action, "anything could happen."[38]

It would be easy from a safe comfortable vantage point of 75 years later to mock the fear that created hasty, ill-conceived legislation like the National Industrial Recovery Act and the subsistence homesteads, but at the time Mrs. Roosevelt was far from alone. With a national unemployment rate estimated to be over 23 percent[39] (far higher in perpetually depressed Scott's Run), an economy that to many was (inexplicably) unable to recover, and rising concerns of communist-led insurrection, fear was widespread.

Lorena Hickok returned from the poverty of Scotts Run in a panic, calling for FDR to become an "absolute dictator" as the only way to solve the problem.[40] She was joined in chorus by Congressman Earnest W. Marland of Oklahoma, who called for not $25 million but $4 billion to fund colonies such as Arthurdale, as it "must succeed or we are all lost."[41] Ironically, for an administration that came to be defined by the slogan "The only thing we have to fear is fear itself," Arthurdale and all the other resettlement colonies were created due to a pervasive fear within the Roosevelt administration.

It was in this perfect storm of haste, fright, endless available funds, organizational dysfunction, poor planning, and high hopes that Louis Howe, in his shining moment on the Arthurdale stage, committed the biggest blunder it would know: his inexplicable purchase of 50 prefabricated houses to start with, and what followed was even more inexplicable—what was done with those houses after they arrived.

Yet before the houses were ordered, arrived, and built, people to put in them had to be chosen, and the selection process used to fill Arthurdale has, especially with changing times, come under far more criticism than it ever did in its day.

Choosing the Lucky

The New Deal . . . could absolutely ignore lines of race and color, but we know perfectly well it does not and will not, and with the present American opinion, it cannot.

—Professor W. E. B. DuBois (1934)[42]

In 1933, the fact that blacks and foreign-born Americans were deliberately excluded from any consideration at all to people Arthurdale
was seen as perfectly normal and desirable; this policy was one of
the rare things about the town that the press by and large actually
condoned. With the notable exception of Eleanor Roosevelt—who
sweetly, if naively, urged all races and creeds to put in for a chance at
a homestead—it was Elwood Mead's racist views rather than her more
progressive one that shaped the policies not just of Arthurdale but of
all the FDR administration's New Deal resettlement colonies. It was
overwhelmingly a whites-only deal. Out of the 99 built, only one—
Newport News (Aberdeen Gardens) in Virginia—ever allowed a black
family to call it home. (Lake Dick, Arkansas, after its abandonment by
the initial white homesteaders, was opened to black Americans on a
sharecropper basis.)

Homesteaders for the town were chosen from November 1, 1933,
until March 21, 1935.[43] Faculty members from West Virginia University
put together a detailed questionnaire to add a little levity to the pro-
ceedings, and "by mid-October 1933 over 600 applications had been
received."[44] By the following December, M. L. Wilson was informing
Bushrod Grimes that "in the case of the Arthurdale Project the list of
applications registered is already all out of hand."[45]

The eight-page questionnaire was followed by extensive interviews[46] and intimate personal questions[47] of those who applied.
Applicants even traced their hands so the selection committee could
look for signs of deformity and manual labor.[48] Elma Martin (who
arrived at Arthurdale on the second of the three waves of settlers)
recalled, "You had to fill out all kinds of applications and a lot of red
tape you had to go through, but we was really happy when we got this
place."[49] After looking at all the answers, the selection committee converted them "into numerical form, and the applicants were tested
against each other."[50] If it sounds scientific, it was not. How do you
put a numerical value on someone's "ambitions"? The selection process
by its very nature had a healthy dose of the subjective and arbitrary.

Although questions on the application included some regarding the
basics of farming, having such experience made not much of a difference; those chosen, for the most part, were coal miners and mill hands.
Only one-quarter of the original 50 settlers had ever been farmers.[51]

For proponents of the back-to-the-land idea having a bevy of farming experts on call would shorten the learning curve for those chosen to manageable levels, experienced or no. It was quickly apparent to many that each homesteader's "race, ethnic background, and political affiliations"[52] held the preponderant weight in determining eligibility.

Every colony had to have an admissions committee, and Arthurdale's first consisted of Bushrod Grimes and Alice Davis, although the final lineup was Grimes, Eleanor Roosevelt, and Silliman Evans (the fourth assistant postmaster general). Eleanor Roosevelt, disappointed and troubled by the exclusion of blacks and foreigners, stayed away from the whole process, sending a couple of friends in her stead.[53] It was Grimes who went on record with this policy and who therefore unfairly gets singled out as the villain for this piece of Arthurdale's history.

Although maybe unfair, that can happen when you write "[W]e isolated all the colored people we had registered and all the foreigners"[54] and follow it up with a helpful explanation why, as "while the colored people were easy to work with and pliable, they did not make much of an effort on their own count, the foreigners were even worse in this respect."[55]

Such admissions would likely get Grimes arrested today, but he was only part of the general mind-set of his era. People of the time may not have been more racist than people today, but they were certainly more open about it. The people of Reedsville, which lay just to the north of Arthurdale, held protest meetings whose agenda was distress at black Americans being moved into their neighborhood.[56] Eleanor Roosevelt asked the homesteaders themselves to vote on the matter, perplexed that those who had lived in racially mixed Scotts Run in the past would mind doing so now. By a narrow margin, the Homesteaders Club voted to remain all white.[57]

Three reasons were given. The people of Arthurdale, new to the area, did not wish to antagonize their neighbors in Reedsville by pushing the matter. Also, West Virginia laws at the time forbade non-whites to attend the same schools or churches; money would have to be found to build two of each. Last, "real" black people would not wish to live with whites anyway.[58]

Yet, when all was said and done, it was not Bushrod Grimes and it certainly was not the votes of the Homesteaders Club that mattered.

As Grimes noted later, "I have gotten in wrong with Mrs. Roosevelt and Colonel Howe for expressing too many opinions in the past," and although in this matter he was certainly no hero, he was certainly no villain, either.[59] Grimes and the homesteaders were not allowed any say at all in anything, and especially not in such an important matter as settler selection. The homesteaders' vote and the Grimes memos accomplished only one thing: It put them on the dock, too, for condoning a racist policy.

In fact, the policy of racial exclusion was set in Washington, DC For the entire life of the New Deal resettlement colonies, "the program rigidly segregated blacks from whites and class from class."[60] Before 1933 had even come to a close, black organizations were protesting the blatant segregation of the subsistence homesteads program.[61] For all the protests, the men who ran the program shrugged and issued a Kafkaesque response: "[N]o discrimination was made on the basis of race or creed, but consideration was given to homogeneity within the group."[62]

By June 1934, all homesteader selections were being made in Washington, DC, and the bureaucracy had rapidly centralized and hardened. Those responsible for choosing the settlers were instructed to favor people who "seem likely to welcome supervision and guidance from project administrators."[63] But in the beginning, in the haste and confusion that defined the town's birth, for the first wave of settlers the easiest route into Arthurdale, besides being a native-born white, seemed to lie through Bushrod Grimes. Of those who were chosen, it is known that the McNelis family[64] knew Grimes previous to their time at Arthurdale, as did the Houghtons and the Swicks.[65] It is highly likely that they were not the only ones, as the Washington Post took note of Grimes's "long acquaintance with the miners."[66]

Mrs. Houghton years later would remember "he [Bushrod Grimes] saw to it that all the people that had helped him out with the gardening project got homesteads up there."[67] In May 1934, Clarence Pickett, working with the Division of Subsistence Homesteads as a special advisor to Wilson, received a complaining letter that Grimes was only too willing to "slip in people who should not be accepted."[68]

A self-described "West Virginia hick" never to be seen without a bow tie[69] and "somewhat of a perfectionist and a worrier,"[70] Bushrod

Grimes was born the youngest of eight children. Although raised in a world of wealth (growing up in a mansion just outside of Pittsburgh), he never inherited much money and by the early 1930s, he had slipped down the socioeconomic ladder to the "proud but poor" category.

He was born without a name. What his family believes to be his birth certificate has blank space where that information should be, but the date of birth is filled in nicely: February 12, 1885, to be exact. Some old family papers in the possession of his grandchildren refer to him as "Paul Bushrod Grimes," but those close to him called him "Jack." His grandchildren, to simplify matters, called him "Bush."[71]

It had been his question to Eleanor Roosevelt about securing federal funds for his garden program that sparked the events that led to Arthurdale, and when the Division of Subsistence Homesteads was birthed, he put in an application at the suggestion of new West Virginia congressman Jennings Randolph who "assured [him] that the appointment would come through."[72] It did, and on November 10, 1933, Grimes received notice that he was now Arthurdale's project manager at $4,000 per annum salary[73]—about $67,000 in 2010 U.S. dollars. Even after he no longer had any official connection with the town, he continued to try and help any way he could.

As a young man he attended both Penn State and the University of Wisconsin in pursuit of a degree in agriculture, and his greatest desire was to farm the acreage around his father's summer estate in Deer Park, Maryland, a business proposal his father refused. While in Maryland, he fell in love with and wooed his future wife, Sada, by standing outside her window and accompanying her piano playing with his banjo.[74] They were married in 1910, and she gave birth to three daughters, Ellen Jane, Frances, and Joanna.

As with many men, his father, James F. Grimes, formed much of who Bushrod Grimes was to become. Born in 1846 and hailing from Preston County, West Virginia, after serving as a colonel in the Union Army during the War Between the States,[75] Grimes embarked on a very successful career in real estate development; Knoxville Borough, an area now known as Pittsburgh, Pennsylvania's 30th Ward, was his greatest accomplishment.[76] He would move his own family there.

The mansion he raised his family in was the center of community life, and he opened the grounds for all Knoxville residents, allowing them free use of his bowling alley, ice rink, and tennis courts.[77] It was with this emphasis on town pride and what people generally refer to as "neighborliness" that young Bushrod Grimes was raised.

With the one exception of Eleanor Roosevelt, no one had more of an influence on what Arthurdale is today than Bushrod Grimes. Many families were lifted out of crushing poverty—and hence their descendants live in the town today—only because of his willingness to "slip in people who should not be accepted."

Chapter 5

"Spending Money . . . Like Drunken Sailors"

We have greater advantages than any other homestead project in the country.

—Bushrod Grimes, project manager, Arthurdale (1933)[1]

Arthurdale was built in three stages, and from its groundbreaking in the winter of 1933 to the final completion of the 165 homes in 1937, it was a fiasco of epic proportions, giving critics of the FDR administration endless fodder. The most famous of the homes were the first 50—the so-called Hodgson houses, named after the manufacturer from whom Louis Howe had impulsively purchased them. The last 115 homes, called "Wagner" homes after the architect responsible for their design, were started in the winter of 1934.[2] Of the two types, the Wagner homes, being larger and of far more attractive design, were much preferred by the homesteaders.[3] Since the Hodgson houses were too small for some of the child-heavy families, some of those chosen voluntarily delayed leaving the coal camps for Arthurdale until a Wagner was available.[4]

The Hodgson houses were not useless. Properly deployed, they were a popular choice for people who wished for an inexpensive, easy-to-assemble summer vacation home. According to the sales brochure, it took a two-man crew six or seven hours to put one together.[5] Louis Howe, after his foolish boast to FDR that he could have settlers living in Arthurdale by Thanksgiving 1933, likely noticed only the words "inexpensive" and "fast assembly." The homes, although good for a summer stay, were completely useless in West Virginia's harsh winters.[6] One federal official sent up to Boston to examine the homes before shipment "called the houses 'terrible' and 'lousy' even before they left," yet they were purchased and sent on their way regardless.[7]

Six of these prefabs arrived at Arthurdale on December 7, 1933, to the derision of the settlers tasked with assembling them. Depending on the whim of the work crew, they could be put together in an H, L, I, or T shape pattern.[8] The exterior consisted of a thin layer of cedar, with walls insulated by fiber paper. The roof, also cedar, was dipped in linseed oil.[9] As if to highlight the utter incompetence of those in charge of building the town, the Hodgson prefabs did not even fit the foundations that lay waiting for them.

Even when it was *known* that the prefabs were of the wrong size and of flimsy material, the houses, "right up to the last of the group of fifty, were erected according to the original plan, and then were torn down and modified." Some were even painted before their demolition; others were put up, torn down, then rebuilt two or three times over.[10] It was written in August 1934 that "who ordered the houses to be drastically altered, instead of scrapping them, is not of record,"[11] but with the benefit of hindsight, it was likely Eleanor Roosevelt herself, as she is the one who hired an old friend, New York architect Eric Gugler, to go down to Arthurdale and redesign and rebuild the prefabs.[12]

Having previously worked for Mrs. Roosevelt—he had designed her cottage in Val-Kill, New York[13]—Gugler arrived with a gaggle of 10 others and installed them in the Bethlehem Mine Corporation's old commissary building, which lay a short distance from the town.[14]

Taking the prefabs, he "cut them into sections, rearranged parts, built additions, dug cellars, built porches, landscaped"[15] and watched stoically as costs skyrocketed.

A personal favorite of both FDR and his wife, Gugler would leave Arthurdale after the prefabs were finally completed in order to design the White House Executive Office Building.[16] He made the most of his time in West Virginia, though, the journal *American Mercury* noting that some of the prefabs were "rebuilt eight times before they were occupied."[17] By many accounts Gugler was hotheaded, foul-mouthed, and blunt, yet he was a very well connected hothead, politically speaking. Bushrod Grimes complained to M. L. Wilson that Gugler had a habit of directing foul-mouthed abuse at the locals and ignoring any advice Grimes or others at the West Virginia University offered.[18]

For all the resources put at his disposal, Gugler displayed a singular inability to design and build a one-family home; even the simple seemed to perplex him. Following a series of rainstorms in the summer of 1934, "40 of the 50 homes" then completed and occupied experienced serious water damage, as he never bothered to determine whether any downspouts were attached. (Even drainage on the roads left something to be desired.[19])

Despite the opinions of some (such as Bernarr Macfadden) who wished to build simple shacks for the homesteaders, Eleanor Roosevelt wanted something entirely different. As the idea of back to the land was to make country homes as desirable as city ones, it was a battle Mrs. Roosevelt easily won. "The houses were built to her specifications—with every modern convenience and decent amenity."[20] Simply put the houses were, for their time and place, lavish. There will never be another federal housing project of Arthurdale's opulence. You would have to imagine one being built today equipped with hot tubs in every bathroom, flat-screen televisions in every room, and eat-in kitchens with granite countertops to grasp how it looked to 1934 America.

Immersing herself in the town, Mrs. Roosevelt and her close friend Nancy Cook personally oversaw the home furnishing and interior design. Cook had been placed on the payroll at a cool $5,000 per annum[21] (about $80,000 in 2010 U.S. dollars). Wesley Stout, in an August 1934 exposé in the *Saturday Evening Post*, meticulously listed the furnishings provided by the American Friends Service Committee's

furniture-making shops, which, along with a Civil Works Administration
(CWA) project,[22] supplied each homestead with "one double and four
single beds, mattresses and mattress covers, two chests of drawers,
three tables, twelve chairs, crib with mattresses (if needed), blankets,
sheets, pillow cases, curtains, rugs, all free to the homesteader."[23] The
homesteaders, upon moving in, "are going to find them [the homes]
completely furnished and equipped by the government."[24]

The homes were well appointed, with a fireplace,[25] "large closets,
built in bookshelves, and a laundry tub in a room with a window."[26]
Each home was fully electrified, with indoor plumbing, a tub, and
a flushing toilet. Each home had its own well to draw water, with
automatic electric pumps encased in concrete.[27] In each kitchen was
a refrigerator,[28] and every home had a furnace—the Hodgson houses
had ones with a capacity to heat 5,300 cubic feet, vastly larger than
their small footprint.[29] The small, one-story homes had under them
concrete foundations "heavy enough to carry a two or three story
home."[30]

Finally, by July 1934, 43 of the first 50 homes were occupied, and
Eric Gugler and his team packed up and headed back home. Having
wrecked and wasted his way into Arthurdale's history, Gugler was
called away to Washington, onward and upward to his justly earned
rewards, proving yet again that it is not war that is the health of the
state; it is failure. C. E. Pynchon, who took over the Division of
Subsistence Homesteads after Wilson's June 1934 departure, hired
architect Stuart Wagner to complete the remaining homes to which he
would lend his name[31] (150 more were planned, but only 115 were
ever built).[32]

Two stories tall with four bedrooms and a bathroom on the second
floor, without a doubt the Wagner homes, especially the last 40 built
from 1936 to 1937, were the belle of the ball, although Wagner laid
the homes' hardwood floors directly on the concrete foundations,
causing the wood floors to bow.[33] All the Wagner homes were each
and every one slightly different from the others in their layout. Equally
well appointed as the Hodgsons but larger, only six of the 115 had
basements.[34] When the DSH was rolled into the newly created
Resettlement Administration in 1935, the latter added 108 root cellars
and 56 storage houses onto the Wagner homes to compensate.[35]

The last 40 homes were faced with native stone and came in two styles: one-and-a-half-story bungalows and an English Tudor style.[36] They would prove to be the most expensive of all three phases.[37] In November 1933, the DSH had hoped costs "could be kept to an average of $2,500 a homestead,"[38] yet this was not to be for Arthurdale. With the lavish nature of the project, endless blundering, and high cost of labor, despite the DSH intent that "with the completion of the project, the total cost [be] pro-rated among the individual homesteads," the final tally would make such an outcome impossible, considering the meager earning power of the homesteaders.

As early as the summer of 1934, the higher-ups were already floating the idea that the homes should be sold to the settlers not at cost but at what they could afford to pay.[39]

The Blind Leading the Blind

Much money was spent, perhaps some of it unwisely.
— Eleanor Roosevelt on Arthurdale (1949), 171

Although the 1934 comedy *Fugitive Lovers* did introduce America to the Three Stooges, Arthurdale's construction provided many a laugh on its own. Holly Cowen wrote years later of the "almost slapstick quality to the beginning"[40] of Arthurdale, and she was exactly right. The entire building of the town provides posterity with a step-by-step guide on how not to or, to be more accurate, on *whom* not to let build a town. From top to bottom, no one had the slightest idea what they were doing. M. L. Wilson pontificated to his fellow learned in the January 1934 *Journal of Farm Economics* on what was happening in West Virginia, where "low cost, comfortable, and attractive houses" were being thrown up, heralding a new way of life.

He claimed the homes to be constructed at Arthurdale "will be cheap but beautiful, durable and convenient, and adapted to mass production and still utilize unskilled labor in their construction."[41] As with every government venture into private business activity both before and since, supporters assured everyone that "construction will impose no burden on the federal treasury but will result in great gain in national wealth."[42] While Rexford Tugwell added to the din, pointing out that "many mistakes have been made in earlier land settlement projects, and we should prefer to profit by them,"[43] those responsible would instead repeat those very same mistakes, resulting in massive losses to the taxpayer.

Their incompetence was exacerbated by the politicized nature of the entire project, as Arthurdale was to be a shining example of what an activist government could do for the "little" man. Therefore, speed was of the utmost importance.[44] Work was begun before plans had even been finalized, before any decision made as to exactly what was to be done.[45] The first group of men from the chosen families arrived in the winter of 1933 and immediately pitched in to the frantic construction.[46] Bushrod Grimes was wise enough, knowing how impoverished the men were, to arrange for credit at a Morgantown department store so they could purchase work clothes.

During the week the men boarded at either the Arthur mansion or the Red Onion, a small hotel in nearby Reedsville.[47] Echoing the wishes of early back-to-the-land advocates,[48] the men were placed under quasi-military discipline, with a set of Ten Commandments of behavior listed for them to obey. Every man was required, for instance, to shave and bathe at least once a week, make his bed each morning, and turn lights out promptly at 10:30.[49]

The winter of 1933 was typical for the region, with three straight weeks of below-zero weather. In one instance the thermometer hit negative 32 degrees.[50] Nonetheless, construction plowed ahead, foundations were dug in anticipation of the prefabs, and concrete was poured. It was a heady time for Grimes, who reported excitedly to Wilson of "terrific storms and lots of snow," but "we cannot let weather conditions interfere with the progress."[51] Mortar for the home foundations needed to be kept heated over a fire to prevent it from freezing before it was poured, and foundations were covered with straw and tarps at day's end to protect them from the winter storms.[52]

The architectural historian E. Lynn Miller called the $25 million made available by Congress a "blank check,"[53] and the project's immense size lent itself beautifully to padding of both the work force size and the amount billed to the Division of Subsistence Homesteads (DSH). The post office provided trucks to haul the homesteaders around the project and home again,[54] while even the locals piled on to rip some flesh off the taxpayer, with Preston County contributing (and demanding payment for) over $54,000 worth of CWA and Federal Emergency Relief Administration workers to Arthurdale."[55] Marginal players sprinted to snatch at the carcass, and a small local manufacturer parlayed an $872 contract into a final bill of over $2,000.[56]

No one seemed to be watching the funds very carefully, and the decisions made were scattershot at best. A myriad of small, indefensible decisions added to the chaos and cost, as when plans to dig up tree stumps were abandoned, and the stumps were simply chopped off, "which made removal at a later time more difficult and more expensive."[57] As for the larger blunders, a fine example must be Louis Howe's purchase of the land without bothering to first determine the quality of its drinking water. When it was discovered that "a stratum of porous rock lay underneath the land," making it unsafe to drink the water, rather than being fired Howe was given $48,000 more to rectify matters.[58]

Howe's foolish boast that Arthurdale would be occupied by Thanksgiving 1933 had him in a bind, but trouble, like water, flows downhill. Project manager Bushrod Grimes was constantly under the gun to compensate for Howe's stupidity. He seemed to be a favorite lightning rod for the man's edicts. Grimes labored under calls by Howe "not to sacrifice time for money,"[59] and should he dare to venture any suggestions to the contrary, he was brusquely informed, "[Y]ou do it my way or get the hell out of the road and I'll get someone who will."[60] He gamely soldiered on, buried under threats and paperwork, later writing "I continued to sign vouchers up until the time [he was replaced] on the job . . . I knew very little about what I was signing."[61]

For all his problems with Louis Howe, it would be the arrival of Eric Gugler, sent down by the First Lady to deal with Howe's prefabs, that would put Grimes under the greatest strain.

Money Pit

We've had some criticism and you probably heard that over and over again, but that wasn't our fault . . . it was the people that were really in charge."

—Andy Wolfe, Arthurdale homesteader (1991)[62]

In March 1934, Harold Ickes received a letter on his desk from George M. Flynn, Arthurdale's general publishing agent, calling for the firing of W. H. Eubank, the project's construction agent. He offered as reason that "Mr. Eubank is very incompetent and does not appear to have either the experience or ability necessary to carry out the work at a reasonable cost."[63] Fortunately for Eubank, Ickes wisely let him be. By the spring of 1934, it was obvious that he could have closed his eyes and pointed to anyone involved with Arthurdale and much the same charges could have been justly leveled.

Ickes did take his concerns to FDR, although the president casually replied that they "could justify the cost, which will run in excess of $10,000 per family, by the fact that it is a model." Ickes replied that whatever it was a model of, "it wasn't a model of low cost housing."[64] The concept of Arthurdale itself may have been experimental but, as a columnist from the time pointed out, "the houses were not experimental in design or intention."[65]

In July 1934, government officials reported that the average unit cost of the Hodgson homes and outbuildings came to $4,880 each, but likely this figure was excluding the costs that both the CWA and Public Works Administration incurred at Arthurdale.[66] Although the DSH declared that "the structures and other facilities must necessarily be moderate in cost," it at the same time decreed that the homesteaders themselves must be utilized in their construction.[67] Not only did this raise costs due to the miners' inexperience in home building, but when the Department of the Interior declared in October 1934 that "the wage rate and working hour provisions of the NIRA [National Industrial Recovery Act]" applied to the homesteaders, too, "it resulted in raising building costs by one-third."[68]

The homesteaders themselves, although tasked to help with the building of the town, are completely blameless for the fiasco that was its birth. Throughout the history of the project, the homesteaders were told what and how; they were never asked. "The families didn't have anything to do with the planning," recalled homesteader Annabelle Mayor. "[Y]ou know how government projects are. They say this is what you get and that's what you get."[69]

They were not professional home builders; they were for the most part miners with no experience in the trade. Unfortunately, Eleanor

Roosevelt, Eric Gugler, Louis Howe, and all the other politically muscled activists who were calling the shots shared their ignorance regarding how to properly site and build a town.

During the initial stages of construction, no one was more enthusiastic about the dramatic waste than project architect Eric Gugler, who was truly a one-man wrecking crew. The owners of the Hodgson company sent down an employee to assist in the erection of the homes; "he left in disgust" after observing dozens of men gamely taking each house and building, tearing it down, and doing it all over again, often multiple times to the very same home.[70] Gugler assigned up to seven architects to make plans for the remodeling of each house, informing the higher-ups that "when you change plans, it's going to cost a lot of money."[71] Yes, it did.

Especially in regard to the salaries Gugler demanded and obtained for his crew. The large salaries granted sparked the first clash between Grimes and Gugler, the latter taking umbrage when Grimes asked why the staff "draftsman" was being paid $200 per week (roughly $3,250 per week in 2010 U.S. dollars) to draw sketches of prefabricated homes.[72] By the time 1934 rolled in, Grimes was writing to Wilson that he had "arrived at the end of the road" as Gugler "flies off the handle, becomes abusive."[73]

Bushrod Grimes would recall, years later, that Gugler's constant mantra was "I was not sent down here to save money, I was sent to spend money."[74] That he did in a carefree manner, in one instance laying out a barn foundation then ordering it abandoned and covered with dirt because he suddenly decided "it was too near the house."[75]

Had Gugler been a private contractor, he would have been sued into bankruptcy and his professional reputation destroyed, at the very least. The constant delays to the move-in date forced arriving families to take up residence in the Arthur mansion[76] or in nearby coal-mining camps while Gugler built, tore down, and rebuilt some houses up to half a dozen times each.[77] He was intensely busy, just not very productive, and the move-in date kept moving further into the future.

The waste and blunders made such an easy target for the press that even the bureaucracy was forced to admit, sort of, in an August 1934 press release that "mistakes" were discovered and corrected, but all was excused as the unfortunate result of an "emergency problem" that needed swift government action.

How much was all this to cost? Government accounting being what it is, that figure will never be exactly known, but the best guesses point to over $16,000 per homestead.[78] At the time in the very same area one could purchase "an eight room and bath, two story and basement brick house on thirty-five acres" for $5,000.[79]

The politically connected involved in it all were, at least in public, seemingly oblivious to what it all cost. As late as June 1934, Eleanor Roosevelt was assuring a friend that each homestead would come in at $2,600.[80] Less than a week later, O. B. Smart, who had replaced Bushrod Grimes as project manager in April, put the figure at $4,250. Whatever the exact amount, it was an eye opener. Harold Ickes confided to his diary that "we have been spending money down there like drunken sailors."[81] By January 1935, the DSH "allotted an added $900,000 to Arthurdale . . . it also admitted a loss of $500,000."[82]

Later that year Grimes lamented the fact that his father was no longer living, as the elder Grimes had successfully and profitably built a town very similar in many respects to Arthurdale. "I wished . . . I could have fallen back on him for advice,"[83] he wrote, but it likely would have made no difference as politically run ventures are entirely different creatures from private ones. Yet, for all the waste and folly in its construction, there is one consolation to take away from the colossal waste of Arthurdale's building: Even today, almost 80 years on, many of the homes are in excellent condition still and of the 165 built, 162 survive intact.

"Living in a Fish Bowl"

From the earliest days, the community operated under constant scrutiny and criticism.
                              —Stephen Haid, historian (1995)[84]

Whether they were ready for it or not, every settler chosen to participate in the Arthurdale project became in many ways instant celebrities, with all the attendant benefits and drawbacks. Most especially in its first

Pictured here circa 1920, Mother Jones was at the forefront of some of the most violent labor disputes in U.S. history. Sitting to her left (holding a pipe) is Sid Hatfield, pro-union sheriff and instigator of the famous Matewan Massacre of 1920.

Photo courtesy of West Virginia and Regional History Collection, West Virginia University Libraries.

Heavily influenced by the German historical school, proponents of a regulated and planned society, Professor Richard Ely was the leading light of America's back-to-the-land movement. His prodigious work ethic produced the stream of writings that provided the ideological underpinning for Arthurdale. One biographer remarked of him, "He frequently saw himself as a martyr and compared himself to the Hebrew prophets."

Photo from *The Comrade*, 1903.

PROFESSOR R. T. ELY.

Professor Elwood Mead built resettlement colonies for governments in both Australia and California that would provide the operational benchmark that shaped Arthurdale day to day.

Photo courtesy of Library of Congress, 1923.

Most of the families resettled into Arthurdale came from the squalor of Scotts Run. Pictured is part of the Pursglove Mine. Coal company houses, all with bare rooms and no amenities to speak of, rise up in the background.

Photo courtesy of Library of Congress, Office of War Information, 1938.

The men resettled into Arthurdale building the community center complex, June 1934. The profligate waste that resulted from inept federal management of the project shocked the nation.

Photo courtesy of Library of Congress, Office of War Information, 1934.

FDR, waiting to give the graduation address to the Arthurdale High School students, 1938. It was through his personal efforts and decrees that the entire New Deal resettlement program was legislated into existence and funded.

Photo courtesy of West Virginia and Regional History Collection.

Educated by Richard Ely at the University of Wisconsin, Professor M. L. Wilson was a rarity in the back to the land movement—he at one time was an actual farmer. From Arthurdale's birth in October 1933 to his resignation in June 1934, he would oversee the Division of Subsistence Homesteads that built Arthurdale. He warned that "our great industrial cities . . . have been and are failures."
Photo courtesy of Library of Congress, Department of Agriculture, 1924.

The intellectual of FDR's Brain Trust, Professor Rexford Tugwell rejected the idea of subsistence homesteads as practiced at Arthurdale and similar New Deal colonies. A staunch and unabashed socialist, he believed that "the individual good [is] not necessarily the general good." He would run the Resettlement Administration, which was responsible for Arthurdale, from May 1935 to December 1936.
Photo courtesy of Library of Congress, Resettlement Administration, 1935.

One of the few federal officials involved in the town's building who displayed any competence, Bushrod Grimes was the first project manager at Arthurdale, and his involvement in and influence on the town were rivaled only by the contributions of Eleanor Roosevelt. He is seen here in 1949, walking with his granddaughter Ann.

Photo courtesy of the Shannon family.

For the first wave of settlers, FDR's right-hand man, Louis Howe, ordered 50 prefabricated homes from Boston's Hodgson Company. At a time when comparable homes in the area could be had for $5,000, the final tally for each home at Arthurdale averaged over $16,600.

Photo courtesy of Library of Congress, Office of War Information, 1934.

Built for the second and third waves of the resettled, the Wagner-style homes were the most sought after by the miners, some of whom chose to wait longer in a coal mining camp for one to become available rather than move into a much smaller Hodgson-style home.

Photo courtesy of Library of Congress, Office of War Information, 1937.

For the first few years of its existence, Arthurdale was one of the most famous towns in the United States. Tourists flocked from every corner of the country to see for themselves the New Deal's most visible experiment. Pictured is a group of sightseers, circa 1935.

Photo courtesy of West Virginia and Regional History Collection.

Resettled with the second wave during 1935, Joseph and Nellie McLaughlin would raise 10 children at Arthurdale. To this day, a McLaughlin (their grandson, Bob Jr.) still occupies the same homestead they were originally moved into.

Photo courtesy of the McLaughlin family.

The Angel of Arthurdale, Eleanor Roosevelt. While she paid an occasional visit to the other Resettlement projects created during the height of the New Deal, it was Arthurdale into which she poured her heart, time, and much of her fortune. Even once the federal government pulled out of the town, she kept her promise and never forgot the townspeople. Here she is pictured dancing with a resident of the town, May 1938.

Photo courtesy of West Virginia and Regional History Collection.

The Arthurdale school system was unique, and initially used the progressive system championed by John Dewey. The first director, Miss Elsie Clapp, opined, "It's much like surgery. We remove mental and physical impediments and graft on the things that help." Pictured is the high school.

Photo courtesy of Library of Congress, Office of War Information, 1936.

In one area only, of the lives of those resettled, did the federal authorities adopt a hands-off approach—religion. This church was completed and dedicated in 1960. For its opening ceremony, Eleanor Roosevelt, slowed with advanced age, made one last visit to the town and the people she had come to love.

Photograph by author.

few years of existence, the town, its residents, and its supporters were the focus of intense national curiosity. Newspapers both large and small, from the *New York Times* to the local *Preston Republican,* informed their readers (in either positive or negative light) of every detail—and blunder—of the town's birth. Popular magazines from the *Saturday Evening Post* to *Harper's* would combine with them to spill oceans of ink on Arthurdale. Tourists arrived in droves, taking the winding dirt roads far up the mountains, their license plates bearing the mark of every state from sea to shining sea.

For the humble people now living there, it was all a whirlwind of change, one resident later complaining it "got so a man couldn't sit down to his sow belly and turnip greens without some stranger peeking in at the window or walking in to ask some fool questions."[85] Glenna Williams described the initial years as "living in a fish bowl."[86] No group of Americans had ever been so dissected, measured, and pondered upon as the settlers at Arthurdale. It was not all kind; the press could be (and often was) vicious, and the blundering of the people in charge allowed "the struggling community to become the focus of attack for those opposed to New Deal policies."[87]

The most hard-hitting and famous of the negative press reports on Arthurdale undoubtedly was Wesley Stout's piece from the August 1934 *Saturday Evening Post*. In meticulous detail, he tore apart Gugler's folly, and historian Paul Conkin notes that it caused the DSH "acute embarrassment . . . since the article, although very slanted, was factually irrefutable on most points."[88]

It did not take the settlers long to realize, as Dorothy said to Toto after arriving in Oz, that they weren't in Kansas anymore. Between the visitors treating their homes as if they were museums and the settlers themselves as mere props—reputedly so ignorant that they would use their new bathtubs to store coal in[89]—the settlers became a bit taken aback. One of them, William McNelis, asked at a Homesteaders Club meeting "when strangers come in and question us about our homesteads . . . should we tell them?"[90]

Jim McNelis (William's son) recalls the "flood" of tourists during those years, and "it was not unusual, especially on Saturdays and Sundays, to have visitors ask my parents' permission to walk through our house." The visits were so frequent that eventually one homestead was specifically set aside, completely furnished, for tourists to walk through.[91] Some homesteaders took advantage of this odd facet of their new lives and did what people have done since the dawn of history—they began a lively trade with the strangers. Joseph Roscoe would set up a stand on the side of the road and sell buckwheat flour to the visitors.[92]

And it was not only hordes of curious private citizens roaming about the town; government employees and dignitaries were ubiquitous as well. The Farm Security Administration sent photographers to document the project extensively.[93] Eleanor Roosevelt herself gave many a guided tour, one time stopping at a homestead unannounced with a party of eight to walk about the house, the woman who answered the door accepting it with "smiling calm."[94] This lack of privacy was part of the price each homestead family had to pay for the chance at a better life, and all considered it a small one.

Even more important in the minds of the settlers was the reaction of the citizens in the surrounding towns to their arrival, and at first there was suspicion. For some time rumors had been swirling that someone had been looking to buy the Arthur farm. When it broke in the press that the land was in fact to be used for a subsistence homestead, the people in Reedsville were sorely disappointed as they were hoping for a coal-mining operation to move in. They became "very much disgruntled because they hadn't figured on a lot of coal miners from Scotts Run coming into their county and around this section they have a notorious reputation."[95]

From Morgantown to Preston County, the reputation of the Scotts Run miner was not a good one. Those in Morgantown claimed "these people never worked and they never will, they expect the government to support them."[96] One Preston County farmer told a reporter from the *Washington Post* that he intended to welcome the new homesteaders by purchasing "a dog and a shotgun."[97]

It was here, in the decision to build Arthurdale with its own school system, that a chance to assimilate the people into the surrounding area was lost. Robert McLaughlin Sr. recalls, "The only way we had anything to do with other towns was through sports."[98] The point of Arthurdale, though, was not to assimilate into the surrounding area—it was to provide an example of a new way of life so superior to America's traditional individualism that the surrounding area would assimilate with *it*, not the other way around.

Many homesteaders recalled a sense of jealousy and resentment on the part of the locals. Andy Wolfe believed it to be "because we were supported and did receive a lot when we came to the new community."[99] McLaughlin Sr. agreed, believing "I think a lot of the people did sort of hold it against us."[100]

This was inevitable. Along with the decision to accept the lack of privacy, the homesteaders had no choice but to bear the stigma that always resides with those who accept public money. The decision on their part was completely understandable, considering from where they had been resettled.

A Potemkin Village, American Style

[Arthurdale was] a propagandistic showpiece replete with state-sponsored jobs.
—Wolfgang Schivelbusch, *Three New Deals* (2006)[101]

After having been pushed backed repeatedly from Thanksgiving 1933 all the way to June 1934,[102] once the move-in date finally arrived, the homesteaders found their homes completely furnished and built as "the planners had preempted many decisions."[103] Arthurdale was not built with their individual wants and desires in mind; it was built to be, in the words of Eleanor Roosevelt, "a national demonstration which can be seen, photographed, and used as a concrete example of industrial decentralization with subsistence homestead living."[104]

The Russians have a long history of impressing foreign dignitaries by spiriting them through model, synthetic villages full of contented happy peasants, and Arthurdale was, to be blunt, an American version of the same. Arthurdale was so much more to its supporters than a mere village; the charitable component of the project was but a thin veneer over its true purpose, which was to be a showpiece pointing the way to a new way of life led by a New American. Consequentially, from the get-go "the desire to make a showing . . . was very evident."[105]

Besides its deeply held ideological component, the publicity intensified the pressure to present only a good face to the world, and, for its political effect, the fact that those placed into the town were plucked from crushing poverty did much to foster "the rapidly developing image of Franklin Roosevelt as a hero to the downtrodden."[106] Accordingly, everything had to be just so, the grounds throughout shipshape.

The homesteaders were forbidden from modifying their grounds or homes in any manner; to do so first required the consent of the DSH bureaucracy, a long, frustrating process.[107] At a Homesteaders Club meeting in July 1934, it was announced to the assembled that "it is the duty of every homesteader to observe the strictest cleanliness in his own home . . . attention should be called to the necessity of keeping the houses and surroundings clean." A warning was issued that "some of the homesteads are looking pretty ratty."[108] To combat this, the government had the power to enter and inspect any home at will—and "the right of inspection was no empty threat."[109]

The locals in the surrounding area noted all this and took to referring to the town as "Hollywood."[110] In one of the more egregious examples that combined incompetence, waste, and the desire to put on a good show, the *Washington Post* reported that for a publicity photo op, rhododendron, a flower native to Arthurdale, was trucked in from 60 miles away, set about a few homes, then left to rot.[111] (Bushrod Grimes "flatly denied" that the story was true.[112])

The *New York Times* ran a photo spread in its Sunday, June 17, 1934, edition, purporting to show a happy family resettled in their new Arthurdale home. The entire photo shoot was a fake. The family used did not live in the home—in fact, at the time of the story, no families at all had been moved into any of the houses but one, and that was occupied by Daniel Houghton, an unmarried federal employee.[113] The family in the picture was actually that of the project cook, B. B. Luzier, and they lived on the top floor of the Arthur mansion until 1935, when they were selected for one of the homesteads.

The settlers themselves were fully aware of what was going on, one of them (Leslie Bucklew) telling a reporter "four or five times as many people could be helped for what's being spent here than have or will be."[114] Yet Arthurdale was, for all the lack of privacy and waste, a far better venue to live than where they had come from. Just the fact that "everything was neat and clean"[115] was a huge improvement in their living conditions, not to mention how the availability of basics such as regular food and medical care produced a dramatic, marked improvement in the physical condition of both adults and children.[116] Little wonder that Bucklew followed up his complaints to the reporter with "[i]t's better than the mines, anything would be."[117]

And it most certainly *was* a far better place, as Norma McLaughlin recalls with a simple "what a wonderful place to grow up."[118] The people did as people everywhere do quite naturally—they began to form a community among themselves, to feel "like one big family, willing to help someone with their troubles."[119] And standing protectively over them all, fighting off negative press attacks, red tape, and "mean spirited trimming" with one hand while exhorting them onward with the other was Eleanor Roosevelt—the one person who became and remains synonymous with Arthurdale and its people.

The Angel of Arthurdale

The part that Mrs. Roosevelt played in the founding and developing of Arthurdale is a story by itself.
—The Reverend Felix G. Robinson, *Tableland Tales* (1953)[120]

The first baby born in Arthurdale was to the Lyons family on August 21, 1934, a boy they named Darrell.[121] Soon after the Hovatter family also had a boy and named him Franklin, in honor of the president whose efforts made sure he did not arrive into a world of poverty and violence. Three days later the president's wife, Eleanor, was at their homestead to celebrate the event.[122] No other person involved in Arthurdale's colorful history is remembered by the homesteaders or their descendants with such devotion and warm feeling as is Eleanor Roosevelt, and by every account it was a feeling she reciprocated in full. It was a devotion that she would maintain for the rest of her life.

Although she did visit other homestead projects on occasion, "she treated Arthurdale as if it were the only one,"[123] and the press denigrated the town as "Eleanor's pet project."[124] Its blunders became her blunders, the waste her waste, but she broadened her shoulders and took every blow, deflecting it all from the homesteaders as best she could. Despite advice from her well-heeled friends to wash her hands of the whole thing,[125] she continued to defend the homestead with unflagging, if irrational, arguments; she never once backed off her total, absolute commitment to the homesteaders of Arthurdale.

Born in New York during 1884 into a wealthy but severely dysfunctional family, she had for an uncle and godfather none other than President Teddy Roosevelt. Her mother, Anna Hall, was a great beauty and horrendous toward little Eleanor, either ignoring her completely or, when she deigned to give her daughter any attention at all, mocking the girl's awkward appearance by referring to her derisively as "Granny."

Her father, Elliott, showered her with love when he was home and sober, but that was not very often. He adored her, though, and she him, but he adored drinking and drugs more, and when he died in 1894 (two years after her mother had died of diphtheria), she was sent to live in the dark and gloomy New York City townhouse of her maternal grandmother. To the end of her days, her father was the one man she missed most of all.

Early in her life she showed a bent toward social work. Not content merely to throw fundraising parties for the poor, she would actually mingle with them, volunteering in New York City's Rivington Street Settlement House. It was after she returned from an English boarding school that she was courted by, and then married to, her fifth cousin, Franklin Roosevelt, he from a distant, upstate branch of the same family.

Married on St. Patrick's Day in 1905, the next 10 years gave them six children, five of whom survived childhood. FDR, she discovered, was the perfect specimen of "momma's boy," allowing his battle-ax of a mother not only to dictate where they lived and to furnish the homes for them but to treat his wife like a pariah, even saying nothing when she told his children, "I was your real mother; Eleanor merely bore you." The formative years with her own mother doubtless trained Eleanor to accept this stoically, when a more well-adjusted person would have hit her mother-in-law over the head with a blunt object.

Despite it all, Eleanor had found domestic bliss, or at least as much as she would ever be allowed, until her 1918 discovery that FDR was having an affair. Living with her heartbreak, she stayed with him, but their marriage never recovered. Henceforth they would be more business partners than husband and wife, each gathering about them their own circle of friends.[126]

After FDR was stricken with polio in 1921, it was Louis Howe, unique in that he was a friend with both FDR and Eleanor, who would bring her out of her shell, insisting that she learn to give speeches.[127] Under his tutelage the once-awkward, shy woman (who had once walked out of the 1912 Democratic convention in disgust at politics) became a political player in her own right, successfully leading her husband's campaign for the New York governor's nomination in 1924.[128] She was a natural, Without Eleanor, FDR likely never would have reached the presidency. She deserved a better man.[129]

Despite the heavy schedule of her White House duties, Eleanor "immersed herself in all the details of establishing and maintaining Arthurdale."[130] Regardless of what any organizational chart might have claimed, two people—Eleanor Roosevelt and Louis Howe—were the decision makers when it came to the project,[131] and anyone involved in the operation trod very carefully when dealing with the president's wife. She and Howe were the ultimate bulls to burst through any red tape, and "she often reported problems directly to the president."[132]

In addition to all her time, care, and influence, she also added a hefty part of her own income toward Arthurdale. She not only interviewed and hired the personnel for the town's health clinic, but she paid for its initial cost out of her own pocket.[133] She funded all this not only from her own personal fortune but with the earnings from her frequent radio broadcasts and newspaper writings;[134] in 1934 alone, she donated $36,000.[135] When it came time to build the school complex, there was a shortfall of over $63,000, and Mrs. Roosevelt and her friend the financier Bernard Baruch donated money to get the project under way.[136]

She "regarded the settlers with maternal affection," and this would manifest itself in one of the most vivid, warm memories of the town's beginnings—Christmas 1934.[137] She personally donated the funds necessary so all the settlers' children could have something for the holiday, and where once the parents had to "pretend we didn't want any meat so the children could have all there was,"[138] now there was plenty for all.

The previous years had seen the adults bedding down Christmas night on bare floors with newspapers for blankets, shivering along with their malnourished children in decrepit mining shacks. What did they think of as they stared into the darkness, listening to their hungry children cry their way to sleep? What did they dream of when they finally slipped under?

Now, as if by a miracle, the children slept in warm beds with sheets, their bellies full, the furnace stoked and keeping the harsh winter outside and at bay. Everything they could possibly have wished and prayed for surrounded them. The most frequent adjective used by the homesteaders to describe what it felt like to move from the cold, dirt, and hunger of Scotts Run into Arthurdale was "heaven."

That first Christmas was the high point of the Arthurdale experiment.

Chapter 6

The Darkening
of the Light

*For about two years Arthurdale was a model community. After that,
sweetness and light faded.*

—*New York Times* (1946)[1]

B y June 1936, 114 families called Arthurdale home, with a population hovering around 660 souls. It was a young town with
swarms of children running about, 411 strong and the vast
majority under the age of 15. By 1938, by which time the last homes
were completed and occupied, 165 homesteads housed about 1,000
people.[2] In the beginning, during October 1934, then–project manager
O. B. Smart was of the opinion that the homesteaders were "well
pleased and thankful for an opportunity to become independent."[3]

Arthurdale was once referred to as "the nicest ghetto in our nation's history,"[4] and while the words may sound a bit cruel they are not too off the mark. Like all government housing, there are a number of parallels between Arthurdale and such projects. Yet in some important ways there is a chasm between what Arthurdale was and what we see in government housing projects today. It was the first and therefore the most experimental and extravagant of any housing project in history; no expense was spared. Now, 75 years on, the urge and ability to be creative are long extinguished from the federal housing bureaucracy.

Besides the luxurious nature of its physical plant, another striking difference (and one the press mostly overlooked) was the prodigious labor required of the homesteaders to keep their end of the bargain.[5] Half a century after the establishment of Arthurdale, when the furor had died away and memory of the town had faded to a whisper, Hilda Hendershot—who was there from the beginning—was asked, "When you moved into Arthurdale what were some of the things you did for recreation"?

Mrs. Hendershot immediately replied, "Work."[6]

There was no lying about, government-supported lifestyle or no. To move into Arthurdale during the initial years was to commit yourself and your family to long, arduous workdays. The intent of the town's founders was to prove the viability of subsistence homesteading, and the physical labor involved in running a small farm while at the same time working on constructing the town took up much of the homesteaders' days. Ralph Borsodi (at the time running a federal resettlement project up in Dayton, Ohio) had long before "found his subsistence homestead an avenue to freedom and independence, but not to leisure."[7] The homesteaders, too, would discover exactly that.

The confusion and chaos of Arthurdale's building was duplicated by the confusion and chaos displayed in the administration of the town, a direct result of "the many individuals and groups with dogmatic ideas about what subsistence homesteads should be."[8] Nobody was truly in charge; Eleanor and Louis Howe could pop in at any moment and tip everything about, and no single idea held sway. The town, sponsored and protected by the president's wife, would become a hot potato, tossed from one department to the next. Being an orphan in the New

Deal labyrinth exacerbated the problems. Eventually, the constant chaos would wear the homesteaders down to a sullen if grateful submission to their chosen fate.

But for now, during the glory days of the town's youth, with enthusiasm high and the money spigot turned to a full blast, those lucky enough to be chosen felt Arthurdale to be "something close to heaven."[9]

At One with the Land

I dug potatoes nearly all morning. This afternoon I scrubbed and limed the henhouse. There is lots of hard work here. We have to keep at it all the time.

—Homesteader's diary (1935)[10]

In 1939, a team of sociologists and educators from West Virginia University spent a year studying the Arthurdale school system and, by extension, the town itself. Released in May 1940, their report stated, "Subsistence agriculture is the keystone arch of Arthurdale's economy" and followed with a recommendation to expand classes for those who wished to become subsistence homesteaders.[11] Heavily influenced by Eleanor Roosevelt and Clarence Pickett (who provided much of the funds for the study), the report was still singing the old song of back to the land. By 1940, though, most families in Arthurdale—along with all the others placed in subsistence homesteads throughout the nation—had largely abandoned any attempt at such a life. It was simply not economically viable.

At Arthurdale's birth, the decision of whether to farm was not left to the homesteaders; it was a requirement mandated by the town planners. (Arthurdale was not unique in this regard.)[12] Since the Division of Subsistence Homesteads had conducted studies that declared "a family of five should have from 1,200 to 1,500 quarts of milk and from 90 to 150 pounds of butter a year,"[13] cows dotted the landscape and a small barn was built behind each homestead to house them. Pigs and hens were provided; expert advice, seed, and prepared land as well. The homesteaders arrived to find not only a fully furnished home but a fully functional farm as well.

The planners could not have chosen a more knowledgeable and enthusiastic man to lead the Arthurdale subsistence program than Bushrod Grimes. Having ample experience and success running West Virginia University's garden program in Scotts Run, he took to his new role of project manager and agricultural advisor with relish and "launched a detailed plan for the planting of gardens even before the Hodgson houses were occupied."[14] Despite the failure of Richard Arthur to make a successful farm of the same land, Grimes was convinced that after draining and liming it would yield a bounty, and he set off and hired every plow team in the area for $5 a day.[15]

The farm operations were begun in the spring of 1933 and, having to plant and water in the midst of frenzied construction, Grimes had the temerity to ask Howe if building the homes might be halted until the crops were all safely harvested. Howe, in his typical brusque manner, barked at him that "it doesn't make any difference."[16] So Bushrod pushed ahead, and the results equaled his success in previous seasons. His leadership provided "a bounty the homesteaders could not have fathomed in Scotts Run." By the end of 1934, literally tons of crops had been harvested, and using the canning works provided, the residents stored "over 5,000 gallons of canned vegetables and over 1,000 gallons of fruit" for the coming winter.[17]

This was particularly impressive considering that the residents of Arthurdale were for the most part coal miners with little or no farming experience. One resident interviewed years later put it best: "[Y]ou can't become a farmer cause somebody says 'well, you're a farmer now.'"[18] Grimes was a whirlwind, throwing out reams of memos, pamphlets, and advice, all urging the homesteaders on, pleading with them to form study groups and reading circles, constantly reminding everyone that "farm bulletins, farm books, farm meetings, farm specialists, are all available."[19] He was in his element.

Years earlier, Bolton Hall had written that "the overworked and struggling farmer finds little chance to study."[20] The people of Arthurdale found themselves in the same situation, so Grimes's plea to form reading circles went to naught. Nonetheless, by the end of 1934, a rundown of each homesteader's crop yield was proudly produced for the higher-ups, the rows and columns all adding up "food products stored" and "farm crops stored" to their hoped-for market price. In timeless bureaucratic fashion, no mention is made of cost.[21]

It was in the disposal of the settlers' "surplus" crops where the ideology of the back-to-the-land movement (which dovetailed nicely with that of the New Deal as a whole) came into direct conflict with the natural human desire to dispose of their property as they saw fit. As early as March 1934, before any family had even moved into Arthurdale, Secretary of Agriculture Henry Wallace wrote to Harry Hopkins that "they [the homesteaders] should be settled with the understanding that they would grow crops only for home consumption or consumption of their neighbors in the community."[22] There was a fear that if the subsistence homesteads proved to be *too* bountiful they would come into competition with commercial farmers, and such a result would be unacceptable to bureaucrats at the Agricultural Adjustment Administration (AAA). A primary focus of the New Deal throughout the Depression was a desperate attempt to keep food prices higher than they would have been under a free market.[23]

Therefore, any crops above and beyond what was necessary to feed their families were declared "property of the Interior Department,"[24] and a memo directed to all project managers bluntly stated that "the bartering of produce or surplus government property is prohibited."[25] This policy confused and angered the homesteaders, and the minutes to a July 1934 homesteaders' meeting have Grimes trying to mollify them, saying "they cannot prevent us from selling things but in the early stages you must be tactful. In the future things may be sold but not right at present."[26]

In one instance during late 1934, the sale of 8,000 cans of foodstuffs produced at Arthurdale to a store in Pittsburgh created a little firestorm in DC, with the higher-ups repeating "you were to do nothing towards the disposition of these canned foodstuffs or any other products without authority or instructions from Washington."[27]

Grimes was correct, though. As time went on and the belief in subsistence homesteads' feasibility slipped to nothing, the homesteaders began to do what they pleased with their crops. Much of it was donated to the school lunch program,[28] some "divided up amongst the ones that was needy,"[29] and some sold for a "neat sum of money."[30] As it was considered necessary to have at least five or more acres to make a subsistence homestead viable,[31] the declining emphasis on farming can be seen in the lot sizes provided to the homesteads for each construction phase. The first group (the Hodgsons) all had plots of about seven acres;

the second phase of Wagner homes, four; and the last group of homes, a little under three.

The homesteaders did not share the planners' enthusiasm for subsistence farming. Back in 1907, Hall had estimated that a farmer with a 20-acre plot walked over 650 miles per year; while tilling plots far smaller in size, the homesteaders at Arthurdale were doing a good annual walk themselves. Too small for mechanized plowing but large enough to be a burden, the farms provided much-needed food but it would have been far cheaper for taxpayers (and easier for homesteaders) to have had them simply purchase groceries in nearby towns.[32]

Be that as it may, the planners were not out to save money but to prove an idea. So out into the fields they went, all the women and children of Arthurdale working "side by side with their men"[33] weeding, hoeing, and picking throughout the growing season, which lasts about 130 days in that area. The memories of those who recall those times are practically unanimous—they were not big fans. No one recalls digging their hands into the dirt and feeling a cosmic oneness with the soil.

Instead, they felt the heat of the sun on the backs of their necks, the sweat that made dirt cling to their skin, and saw how the long hours spent weeding the carrot bed devoured their days. Norma (Turner) McLaughlin remembered, "[I]t was a lot of work, I hated that kind of thing"[34] while Glenn Luzier agreed: "I always hated things like that . . . as a kid you always hated to have to work in the garden."[35]

As time went on, the Division of Subsistence Homesteads (DSH) was replaced by other organizations less enthusiastic about subsistence farming, and the people simply stopped doing it. Luzier does not recall any extensive farming of the homesteads in Arthurdale after 1940,[36] and a study conducted by the Department of Agriculture in 1942 backs up his memory, pointing to "the minor role of subsistence production in most projects where homesteaders had paid work."[37] As 1940 rolled into 1941, that paid work was provided by the production needs of the war machine. It was this outside income, combined with the dislike of farming, that destroyed any future attempt to make homesteaders play out the yeoman farmer fantasy so cherished by slightly insane academic dreamers.[38]

The Other Half of the Equation: Wage Employment

Of all the mistakes, the most ruinous . . . was the erroneous belief that industry would move to the remote locations of the stranded homesteads.

—Stephen Haid, historian (1975)[39]

Many practical explanations are given for the failure of Arthurdale as a subsistence homestead; the lack of private employment to provide cash wages is the one most frequently cited. The years leading up until the war saw an endless litany of financial disasters, a stream of desperate attempts to get the homesteaders jobs, all futile. The frenzy to get industry to move into the town would "produce mostly frustration and waste."[40] During the first years, construction jobs were provided: As if part of an amphibious assault, the first wave of homesteaders were put to work preparing for the second wave, waiting just over the horizon.[41] What happened, though, when the town had reached its maximum size, the last homestead was occupied, and the last nail was beaten flat? It was enough to keep you up at night.

In a 1942 government study of the program, one finding bluntly declared that "a man living on a subsistence homestead needs a job just as badly as the man in a city tenement."[42] Despite the official-sounding, learned delivery of the report, this was a mere rehash of what had been known all along. A November 1933 circular put out by the DSH stated: "[W]ithout adequate opportunity for wage employment failure will result,"[43] and around the same time Roy Hendrickson, the newspaperman brought by M. L. Wilson onto the DSH staff, wrote a helpful list of pitfalls any successful project must avoid. Prominent among them was "mistaken assumptions about employment opportunities."[44]

Eleanor Roosevelt and everyone else involved were guilty of counting chickens before they hatched, for in this case they believed it certain a factory would be built at Arthurdale, tasked to produce equipment for the U.S. Post Office. With the federal government as its main customer (as close to an eternally assured client as life can provide),[45] the industrial wage half of the subsistence homestead equation would thus be assured and a New World would be theirs. Howe estimated a start-up cost of around $500,000—all of it to be borne entirely by the budget of the Public Works Administration (PWA), not the DSH.[46]

Naturally, this plan struck those in Congress who represented districts already home to such factories as a threat, and even after public assurances that it would "not make any one item needed in post offices" (so as not to threaten the market share of any one preexisting factory),[47] members of Congress sprang to the defense of their privilege. Louis Ludlow of Indiana (where the Keyless Lock Company was employed in making post office equipment) wrote FDR to remind him that "by the nature of its product, [Keyless] has but one patron, and that is the government of the United States."[48]

A reduction for one was a reduction for all, and FDR chose not to push the issue. Ludlow was not the only member of Congress he would anger in establishing a post office factory at Arthurdale, and the president was nothing if not a master politician. There was an ideological element, too, in congressional opposition, with some standing fast against establishing the post office for reasons more lofty than patronage and privilege. A Senator Josiah Bailey of North Carolina felt such an act would "destroy the American Republic."[49]

On March 24, 1934, the House declined to fund the establishment of the proposed factory by a vote of 274 to 111. It was a stunning defeat for the proponents of Arthurdale.[50] The scramble to find industrial employment for the homesteaders would now commence, endless and ultimately fruitless.

The reaction of some in government to the failure to obtain a post office factory was to propose the age-old route of direct taxpayer subsidy, and one Treasury official suggested "loans and payroll subsidies for industries willing to move from urban centers to industrially 'stranded' rural communities."[51] There was no shortage of businessmen eager to hop on that bandwagon, and they "frequently turned to Mrs. Roosevelt and government officials, hoping to take advantage of government financing."[52] The business plans presented ranged from the merely impractical (packaged fuel) to the utterly bizarre (air-conditioned clothes).

With no tenant yet in sight, the DSH began to construct a 10,000-square-foot factory under the economic policy of "build it and they will come, we hope." Work commenced in April 1935, with a set budget of $25,000; "by June 30, the cost had climbed to $31,802.66."[53] (Needless to say, no one was fired.) Despite its completion in the fall of 1935, nothing could be done with the factory; the Comptroller General had ruled that "federal law precluded the use of federal funds for private industry."[54] Months passed, and those who ran Arthurdale, in order to circumnavigate that law, formed the homesteaders into the Arthurdale Association (a cooperative, which *was* allowed taxpayer funds), and the latter purchased the factory for $12,804.[55]

Finally, in April 1936, approval was granted to lease the factory. Howe had approached General Electric about setting up operations in Arthurdale, and the company fobbed off what was an obvious politically motivated loss center to The Electric Vacuum Company of Cleveland, a distant subsidiary.[56] Although Howe wanted the company to sign a 15-year lease, the owner of the subsidiary, Julius Tuteur, was not enamored of the entire idea and insisted on a five-year lease with a six-month termination clause.[57]

In June 1936, the vacuum cleaner factory was finally operational, and at its peak, 29 homesteaders were employed.[58] The owner's son, John Tuteur, spent time trying to line up government contracts for the factory, all to no avail. In 1937, the company closed the factory "for model changes," as the one made at Arthurdale was not in high demand, and promised to reopen shortly.[59] As the downturn of 1937 arose, the company could no longer sustain the losses and suspended operations in August. The factory was idled.

With the Depression deepening yet again and the first factory an empty shell (never again to make a vacuum cleaner), government officials dramatically expanded operations. Two more factories were built, 60,000 square feet in total, to add to the 10,000 already existing. All three were located on the northern rim of the town, along a spur of the Baltimore and Ohio Railroad.[60] The Mountaineer Craftsmen's Cooperative Association, moved up from Morgantown for the purpose of providing jobs, occupied one of the new factories; a tractor cooperative took the other.

In late 1937, the Phillips-Jones Shirt Company (maker of the Van Heusen shirt) leased about 40 percent of the smaller factory, employing at its peak 34 women.[61] The first dozen shirts produced at the factory were ordered by and delivered to FDR, but things quickly went sour. By October, the shirt company had shut down operations for the same reason so many business ventures collapsed at Arthurdale: wage rates all out of proportion to economic reality. The only solution was for wages to be reduced, which was forbidden by law under the National Industrial Recovery Act, so Atlas shrugged (so to speak) rather than continue to lose money. After a White House conference in early 1938, the company agreed to restart operations, and from March to August 1938, it did so, but thereafter the factory again sat empty.[62]

The post office factory, stillborn, and the vacuum cleaner maker and the shirt maker (those last two privately run businesses) all attempted to provide jobs for the people at Arthurdale; all quickly collapsed. For the entire phase of federal control, attempts to lure private business to the town would never let up; even as late as June 1939, Bushrod Grimes was writing to an Arthurdale official concerning "the proposed glass factory."[63] It would all be in vain.

In 1938, three-quarters of the homesteaders were still employed by the federal government, either working on the town itself or in one of the numerous cooperatives.[64] Lack of employment opportunities would drive some away; homesteaders Julia and Joseph Perry would set out for Detroit in 1943. "It was hard for us to leave," she recalled, "but there was no work."[65] The high unemployment rate in the town would never be solved by peaceable means—it would take a world war to do the trick.

The sales pitch for any business to move out to Arthurdale was a weak one. Besides the general economic depression, the sparse population of the area did not lend itself to anything other than local production since a transportation network large enough for an industrial concern of the necessary scale to grant industrial wages was simply not available; that all lay 20 miles north in Morgantown. The community model of subsistence homesteading certainly would not have played well to prospective business owners anyway, as Grimes wanted the operations of any factory to be so managed as to free up settlers for the harvest and planting seasons."[66] Years before, West Virginia coal operators had complained of that very same thing, about their workforce marching off into the hills for farm work and leaving them with disrupted operations.[67]

It would prove impossible to get any industrial employment for the homesteaders, and the planners at Arthurdale simply improvised as best they could. From handicrafts, to cooperative ventures, to taxpayer-funded "jobs" in an alphabet soup of various New Deal agencies, it was a patchwork quilt of make do where they had wished for one, nice, neatly packaged factory, happily churning out post office equipment and jobs for all. With the refusal of Congress to provide that factory, all the hopes and dreams of Arthurdale's supporters would be subsumed much more quickly under the inevitable wave of economic reality.

To defer the day of reckoning, when the last nail was hammered flat and construction was complete, the Resettlement Administration (RA) adopted a policy of deliberately slowing down the pace of building by limiting the maximum number of workers to 402 in any given month.[68] With the reorganization that sent the DSH under the umbrella of the RA, its head Rexford Tugwell saw in Arthurdale's problems the perfect opportunity to introduce *his* surefire solution: worker-owned cooperatives. He was certain they would not only solve what ailed Arthurdale but what, to him, ailed the entire nation: its misplaced emphasis on "rugged individualism."

Cooperation, Debt, and Losses

Enthusiasm for cooperatives seems to have been far stronger among government employees than among settlers.
          —Dianne Y. Ghirardo, historian (1989)[69]

With the chances of getting a private business to move operations out to Arthurdale without heavy taxpayer subsidies looking dim (and with such subsidies being forbidden by law),[70] the planners turned to forming the settlers into cooperative associations. From 1935 to 1939, the town was home to a small galaxy of them, the most prominent being the woodworking shops of the Mountaineer Craftsmen's Cooperative Association, makers of the famous Godlove chair.[71]

Arthurdale was not unique in this regard; all the subsistence homesteads were "frankly communitarian in nature, with industries and services often held cooperatively."[72] The homesteaders didn't have much choice in the matter, anyhow. Yet with few other options, they determined to make the best of it, one of them declaring in a town meeting: "[L]et's try it out and get away from any selfishness or as much individualism as we can and try out some cooperative systems and see if they won't help us."[73] They wouldn't.

Although Rexford Tugwell was the main force behind the cooperative idea, as "the decision to develop the disastrous cooperatives . . . can be traced to his collectivist impulses,"[74] he was far from alone in having such impulses. Wilson must be held responsible, too, as he promoted the idea (along with many other back-to-the-land disciples) and felt "cooperation would effect a beneficial transformation of character" for all who participated.[75] The urge to form the co-ops made sense to them on both economic and social grounds.

It was not just to help move along beneficial transformations of character or to prove co-ops economically viable that such enterprises made their prolific appearance in the town; there was the baser element of politics. The Roosevelt administration suffered acute embarrassment over the dreadful unemployment rate of the homesteaders and wished for anything to keep them off the dole. Although the cooperatives were all funded with taxpayer money, too, they gave the *appearance* of employment, and that was what counted.

This sordid coupling with the political does not lessen the ideological fervor for collective activities held among those who controlled the town. Like Wilson, Tugwell believed that the "cooperative enterprises would reveal the fallacy of individualism and competition," and he made the establishment of such enterprises a major policy objective of his administration.[76] Whether employed by the DSH or the RA, everyone involved had drunk the co-op Kool-Aid.

The funds to start all this were provided under the Federal Emergency Relief Act of 1933, which called for taxpayer funds to "aid in assisting cooperative and self-help associations."[77] Being just such an association Arthurdale fit the bill, so in December of 1935 a loan of $9,750 was provided to open a general store. That same month, a further $12,804 was granted to purchase land for a factory. The following month, $305,200 was made available "for general purposes," creating a grab bag for whatever idea came to mind.[78] Recalling Elwood Mead's taxpayer-supported projects of this kind, easy credit fell like manna from heaven; the homesteader co-ops needed to simply reach out their hand to be buried under a mountain of debt.

In time, Arthurdale formed a medical clinic, an inn, a woodworking shop, forge, general store, gristmill, cemetery, barbershop, dairy farm, poultry farm, general farm, and a gas station. All these cooperatives were wrapped up under the umbrella of "The Arthurdale Association," chartered under West Virginia law in October 1935, and they combined to create a prodigious financial loss. Excepting the woodworking shop, none of the co-ops employed more than six homesteaders, although the inn provided employment to a number of the town's children as waitstaff.[79]

One of the cooperatives used by a wide cross-section of the homesteaders was the general store, opened with much hope on January 2, 1936. Managed at first by Harry Robinson, the secretary of the Arthurdale Association, sales for a time were cash only but with the inability of the federal government to send out checks on schedule, soon a policy of granting credit was offered. Selling various household goods and foodstuffs, after the first month's operations a profit of $36.79 was tallied. That would prove to be the high point, financially speaking.[80]

Although the store was centrally located, sitting on the south side of the town square, a large minority of homesteaders who had a means of transportation shopped instead in nearby Masontown, as the prices there were lower. The general store's higher prices relative to those in the surrounding area were an ironic replication of the higher prices in the coal-mining operator's hated company stores.

The general store was never able to repay the loans used to begin operations, and the fact that health inspectors found it to be "verminridden" certainly didn't help sales. The best that could be said for it, in the words of Stephen Haid, was that it "proved less of a failure than other cooperative enterprises" and even managed to survive for the entire life of the federal project.[81]

Across the street from the general store and built on the site of the old Arthur mansion (torn down at the behest of Tugwell)[82] was the Arthurdale Inn. Described by the same Haid as "disastrous," it proved to be yet another wealth-destroying failure, seeing an average vacancy rate of 60 percent during its lifetime.[83]

Never opened to the public, it was built more as a rest station for visiting government dignitaries and as a place for Eleanor Roosevelt to sleep during her frequent visits.[84] It wouldn't have mattered anyway. The horde of tourists who had once crowded the town had long moved on to other distractions; the inn opened its doors half a decade too late. Even with a dining room supplied from the general store with no markup,[85] it never turned a profit from the time it opened in May 1938. In just a two-year span (1940 to 1941), it burned through almost $7,500 in capital. The Farm Security Administration (FSA), which ran Arthurdale by that time, desperately tried to find someone to lease the inn but failed due to its "disadvantage in location."[86]

By far the best-known cooperative was the MCCA craft shop, maker of handcrafted furniture and the Godlove chair. It was moved to Arthurdale from its home in Morgantown during 1937 in order to provide the colony jobs. Despite a product line that deservedly earned an outstanding reputation for beauty and quality, the prices asked were far too high, a result of excessive wages and a mind-boggling lack of division of labor. A report submitted by an employee of the Department of Commerce expressed shock to find "each workman started on a piece and carried on each operation himself to final completion,"[87] as if Adam Smith had never been born.

By the end of 1937, a loss of about $25,000 was all the cooperative of 40 employees had to show for its efforts,[88] but, this being a government-run operation, as a reward, a new home was built for it with "an expensive dry kiln and other improved equipment" at a total additional cost of $40,000,[89] and a sales office devoted to its output was opened in the community center building.[90] The dry kiln was no panacea, and during 1939 and 1940, the shop lost just shy of $45,000.[91] By 1941, the FSA had seen enough and refused any further loans to prop up the MCCA. Soon after, the factory was leased out to a manufacturer of radios and record players. Come the end of 1942, that company, too, had shut down operations.[92]

The fetish for tilling the land died hard, and Tugwell, having come to admire Stalin's work in Russia with that great man's emphasis on the industrial sized, ordered his RA to ramp things up on the agricultural side. The RA "vastly increased the acreage" on the colonies it had inherited from the DSH.[93] Arthurdale was no exception, and three additional tracts of land totaling 458 acres[94] were purchased for $19,000 to accommodate the desired diary, poultry, and general farm cooperatives.

The idea for dairy and poultry co-ops had been shot down earlier by a panel of government experts who declared it to be "not an economically sound proposal,"[95] but with $305,200 burning a hole in their pockets and pressure to provide jobs, the concept was revised and put into action. From the very beginning the co-ops bled money. Once again the homesteaders were used to build all the facilities, resulting in the same waste, low productivity, and inefficiency as when they had built the houses. "The cost of the barn, feed rooms, and dairy house amounted to approximately $9,600, whereas two private contractors had bid the same specifications for $3,730 and $3,470, respectively,"[96] and here $6,000 disappeared in a flash.

The poultry farm was constructed in like manner. The facilities built (which included two barns converted into laying houses, one three-story, and 40 small laying houses) showed labor costs that a government inspector regarded as "exceptionally high."[97] At its highest peak of operations, approximately 3,000 laying hens and "a very fine pure-bred herd of Jersey dairy cows" were put to the task of paying back all the money sunk into the operation, but it was a hopeless endeavor.[98] Both the dairy and poultry cooperatives would fail to turn a profit.

The dairy opened for business in February 1938,[99] and by October of the same year it had already produced losses of almost $3,000; these were chalked up to high feed costs and wage rates that averaged twice that of local, privately run dairies. In addition, the handful of homesteaders chosen to work on the farm had little idea how to run a dairy or properly maintain the herd, and neither did their federal overseers. Between 1938 and 1941, actual production fell by 35 percent.[100] This, coupled with the foolish attempt to "pay industrial wages" for a job that could not support it,[101] led the FSA to shut down operations during the war and sell the dairy farm to West Virginia University, which got the whole shebang for a single dollar.[102]

The result of the poultry cooperative was decidedly the same; high feed costs and wage rates exceeding those of local private poultry farms by almost three and a half times over saw to that, so the six men employed equaled 21, far too large for the task. A government inspection declared the operation to be poorly managed, with employees in need of more training and better supervision. After operating at half capacity for its first few years, it was decided to lease out the farm, as had been done with the dairy. It seems there weren't any takers, as in April 1942 a "detailed audit report of the project indicated that the poultry facilities appeared to have been abandoned."[103]

The general farm also experienced the same problem of high wage rates and low productivity, and "became a general dumping ground for residents who had nothing to do."[104] It was leased out in April 1939. One further attempt to create a viable co-op within Arthurdale was a tractor factory, an extremely capital-intensive undertaking funded with $325,000 in tax money funneled through the FSA. Of that, $125,000 was used to prepare the factory and get things up and running, leaving $200,000 for operating capital.

Coming to an agreement with the American Cooperatives, Inc. (a multistate organization of six Midwest farming cooperatives) to supply new tractors, the operations commenced in the spring of 1939. An Iowa businessman protested the entire idea and wrote "if you take a Virginia coal miner and put him in a tractor factory and pay him with government money . . . you make a mighty rotten tractor."[105]

He was not the only businessman protesting. The Battle Creek, Michigan–based tractor manufacturer Duplex Machinery Company sued the federal government, for until the Arthurdale factory had come along, it had supplied tractors to the very same American Cooperatives. "It cited unfair advantage" as it was forced to compete against a business backed by taxpayer funds and claimed that the loss of business had resulted in the termination of 200 men. The case was decided in Duplex's favor and $41,000 was given as compensation.[106]

Mostly, it seems, the American Cooperatives agreement simply siphoned the factory's capital base dry, leaving the Arthurdale Association with a monumental loss of over $106,000 after only one year's operation. Never able to generate sufficient revenue to cover costs, by April 1940, the tractor factory was closed.

The net result of the cooperative fetish of Tugwell, Wilson, and their fellows was a massive waste of taxpayer money and a swath of abandoned and underutilized buildings. Designed with the political motive to keep as many homesteaders "off the dole" as possible, the

economic goal of proving the superiority of co-ops over private ventures, and the ideological goal of creating a "better man," this entire
episode (in the words of historian Haid) "cannot be waved aside as
being of little consequence."[107] The wage rates paid were vastly out of
line with the revenue generated from the products offered and proved
yet again that it is not the business owner who sets wages but the consumer. Every government auditor and observer from the time invariably
indicated that the high wage rates was the fatal disease. Yet there was
something more than that in their failure.

As the Salvation Army report had warned back in 1903,[108] the
co-ops encouraged idleness. This is why the homesteaders themselves
were not too enamored of the cooperative idea.[109] The comments on
the operations of the co-ops echoed those passed down throughout
history whenever such attempts had been made. In May 1939, one
official blamed the losses on the high wage scale and "the inability to
secure the maximum productive labor from homesteaders employed."[110]
The homesteaders themselves put it more bluntly, complaining to a
New York Times reporter in 1946 that "their cooperative efforts were
supporting 'a bunch of loafers.'"[111]

At no time, though, was failure an option; it would have
been far too politically embarrassing to the Roosevelt administration.
Consequently, despite all the unemployment among its residents, one
homesteader recalled, "[T]here was more employment in Arthurdale
than in [nearby] Reedsville and Masontown put together."[112] Despite
the record of dismal failure, all the waste and destruction of the co-ops
did account for one thing: It kept the town on the map, floating on a
turbulent sea of taxpayer money.

Pleasantville

*Arthurdale's failure to support itself by bringing in local industry is
offset by the rich community life it brought the homesteaders.*
                    —Nancy Hoffman, author of *Eleanor Roosevelt
                        and the Arthurdale Experiment* (2001)[113]

Even in Utopia there is sadness. One Arthurdale woman born into an
abusive home summed up her life on the project with a heartbreaking

"there are plenty of things that stand out, but they are all bad things, I prefer not even to think about them."[114] For all the lavish surroundings, and for all the attempts to make them into a New American, the people of Arthurdale were and remained people, flawed like the rest of us. Every town has its secrets, and in Arthurdale some drank too much[115] and some parents, if the record is to be believed, beat their children into a hardened shell. It was no hell, and it was no heaven. Arthurdale lay somewhere on the scale of life more toward one end for some, more toward the other for the rest; for most, though, it was decidedly toward the heaven end.

Almost all of the children were not beaten and almost all of the families gathered sober in church each Sunday, but for all the look of normalcy, life for the homesteaders was different from what would be considered in their time as "American." The level of political control over their lives was of a degree that no American of the time could even fathom. But for the children of Arthurdale, those born in the town and those young when they were brought there, that life struck them as entirely normal; it was all they knew. They had a definitive sense, however, that living in Arthurdale was somehow different from the life of the children in the surrounding towns. This is not to say it wasn't a happy life.

Joseph and Nellie Jane McLaughlin moved into SR-7, a two-story Wagner built for the second wave of homesteaders, arriving after a stay in the nearby coal-mining camp of Burke. They had been waiting there a year for the new home's completion. Mr. and Mrs. McLaughlin and their children, eventually to number 10, would be moved into the neighborhood that lay just south of the community center, along Route 92, which bisects the town.

The family, never rich to begin with, had a well-developed sense of the "make do." Joseph McLaughlin was a woodworker and hand-made some of the furniture that outfitted his new home. Though the McLaughlins themselves were moved from the town of Harmony Grove, just outside of Morgantown, Nellie Jane had a skill common to many women of Scotts Run. She could make a comfortable dress out of "feed and flour sacks,"[116] so her daughters would have something to wear the next day. She was kept busy raising her children, all of whom remember the smell of freshly baked bread waking them every

Monday, as that was when making eight or nine loaves was listed on her hectic schedule.[117]

Despite a home well appointed with every modern convenience, the family was far from well off. The "make do" in their parents' DNA was noticeable in the children. After two of the boys (Robert and Joe) had partnered with another to deliver newspapers, they saved enough to purchase a bicycle that "was on the goin' all the time,"[118] passed from child to child, as it was the only one they had.

Baseballs were made of tightly wound "old clothes" that you couldn't bounce, but "you could shoot." The children found ways to improvise as the need arose and did what children do the world over: played.[119] The McLaughlin household was the gathering place for the area children.

Larry, the youngest boy, was delivered March 22, 1937, in the Arthurdale clinic, but while undoubtedly the most coddled and spoiled (as all youngest boys are), it was his younger sisters, Linda and Glenda, born January 21, 1941, who displayed the foresight to be born twins, the first recorded at Arthurdale. Eleanor Roosevelt gave a pair of baby blankets to congratulate the parents and commemorate the occasion.[120]

The family possessed that indispensable accoutrement of the genteel family: a piano. One daughter, Norma, played and provided the voice[121] and when out of the home sang in the church choir run by Pastor Felix Robinson.[122] Dances were frequent on the weekends and were held in the community center and then, after the completion of the school, in the new gymnasium.[123] They were well attended, and whenever she was in town, Eleanor Roosevelt would happily participate. Of all the dances, the Virginia Reel was her favorite.

The activities of the town were funneled through a buffet table of clubs, all formed to promote a sense of community. First formed was a Homesteaders Club with six officers led by the first president Andy Goldstrom, and from this would arise a "recreation committee" to help things along. The emphasis was on guided, collective activities, and Andrew Wolfe, one of the six officers, recalled the focus as "community this, community that, everybody worked together."[124]

Besides the Homesteaders Club (which was for the men only), the women formed the Eleanor Roosevelt Farm Women's Association, which was to last well into the 1990s.[125] Crafts, a band, acting, and reading circles were organized and encouraged by town planners who wished to manage the settlers' free time as well as their workdays. Glenna Williams fondly remembered the club activities, feeling the clubs were necessary. "We had to, the community didn't grow like other communities. We were transplanted down here, there had to be something to bring us together as a group."[126]

In one area only did the government stay studiously aloof from meddling into the private sphere—the matter of religious worship was left entirely up to the homesteaders, and they responded on their own by holding prayer meetings and church services in their homes and eventually (in a move that would have sent an American Civil Liberties Union lawyer into screaming fits) in the newly built school complex.[127]

For the homesteaders, Arthurdale was an oasis of security from a depression that stretched around them, vast like the Sahara. Despite the lack of employment on or off the project, "the homesteaders at Arthurdale were well cared for."[128] As winters set in, the smallest children would each find a snowsuit purchased for them by Mrs. Roosevelt, her thoughtfulness made bright by the kaleidoscope of colors she chose.[129]

Dr. John Fullmer, the son of the ingenious James "Lon" Fullmer,* looked back on Arthurdale as "an outstanding place to grow up . . . you knew everybody."[130] As the town was completed in the late 1930s, observers reported, "There is an abundance of natural facilities for play and recreation."[131] The memories of the children of Arthurdale, in particular, are happy ones.

It was a far cry from the hopelessness of Scotts Run, and the days of dodging the stray bullets flying about were forever put aside for these lucky few. Edna Day reveled in the happiness of being able to "walk anyplace in Arthurdale and you wouldn't be afraid."[132] For the most part, especially during the first years, it seems the homesteaders confined most of their walking about to the project grounds.

A survey of the town conducted in 1939 referred to it as "an island of social and economic isolation,"[133] and this confirmed the fear that

---

*Lon Fullmer was a man of many talents, one being an extraordinary ability to replicate antiques. A copy he made of a sixteenth-century astronomy instrument called a Tycho Brahe armillary sphere is now part of the Smithsonian's collection.

subsistence homesteads "would become federal islands on the order of Indian reservations."[134] There were a number of reasons for this outcome, from the intent of the planners to the resentment and jealousy of those in surrounding towns. Some who grew up in Arthurdale recall the tension, and doubtless this played a part in keeping the homesteaders to themselves. "We just were in our own little town and did our own thing"[135] was a common refrain.

The fact that the homesteaders arrived with the fearful reputation of Scotts Run coal miners did not help matters.[136] As time passed, though, the town was slowly integrated into the fabric of Preston County and the artificial barriers crumbled, helped along by the closest towns becoming "trading centers for the people of Arthurdale."[137] George Washington once spoke approvingly of the "civilizing effects of commerce" between peoples, and Glenn Luzier and Dr. John Fullmer can attest to that. With the passage of time and easing of tensions, both would marry Preston County girls.[138]

For now, though, the locals used the term "homesteader" in a derogatory fashion,[139] and "jealous" was the most oft-repeated term used by the settlers to describe the attitude of those in local towns, all the resentment directed at Arthurdale because "we had something they didn't have, that the government was giving us something that they didn't give them."[140] Besides the taxpayer money, the highly visible trips by the First Lady and her continued generosity to the homesteaders must have rankled the locals.

Medical care was one such "something" that was provided to the people of Arthurdale as "the First Lady saw the homestead communities as a 'unusual' opportunity for experiment in socialized medicine."[141] The 1936 establishment of the well-equipped infirmary was unique throughout Preston County; the surrounding area suffered from such a shortage of doctors that one night a desperate, armed group of outsiders literally kidnapped Dr. Lehman (Arthurdale's town physician) in order to secure medical help.[142] Despite federal regulations that strictly forbade him to practice outside the project, the gun was a far more persuasive argument.

Dr. William E. Zeuch of the DSH was, like Mrs. Roosevelt, an enthusiastic booster for setting up medical infirmaries on each project, seeing it "as the first step towards socialized medicine."[143] At first

Arthurdale's infirmary was supported by Eleanor Roosevelt herself, the money routed through the American Friends Service Committee,[144] but once the project was put under the umbrella of the RA and was reorganized as a cooperative, taxpayer money was made available as a subsidy. This marked a watershed, as it was "the first time the government has supported group medicine."[145]

At first, any family who paid a $1 monthly fee was able to use the clinic, but as time went by and the losses and delinquent accounts piled up, the fee was raised time and again until it reached $9 by 1939.[146] As 1946 arrived and the government was exiting the project, the infirmary was shuttered. Without taxpayer subsidies, it would have been closed far earlier, as the lack of wage-paying employment never ceased to plague pre-World War II Arthurdale.

In a 1936 study, the average income per family was estimated to be $687 annually (roughly $10,800 in 2010 U.S. dollars), and "many families came to Arthurdale carrying a financial indebtedness" to boot.[147] Things did not improve with time, as a 1940 study estimated $467 as the average annual earnings,[148] although others placed it around $840 to $960 (roughly $13,000 to $15,000 in 2010 U.S. dollars).[149] Whatever the level, it was not enough, and in early 1939, the FSA lowered rents for all homesteaders to an average of $9.99 per month.[150] (This was less than the $10.54 a 1933 DSH report cited as minimum for a $2,500 homestead.)[151]

The lack of work was ameliorated by placing homesteaders into the various New Deal agencies designed to "make jobs," and the National Youth Association (NYA) opened a branch in town, using the community center's basement as a mess hall.[152] Years later Joseph Roscoe, a homesteader who participated in the program, was asked what work they performed in Arthurdale. He laughed and admitted: "You got me there. . . . I can't remember what they really did."[153] One use that the NYA could be put to was shown by future president Lyndon Johnson, who used his time as a member to build the political machine that would one day take him to the White House.[154]

The homesteaders were used as much as possible in the continued building and maintenance of the town, but there were not nearly enough positions available.[155] Any remaining building projects were deliberately slowed down to extend employment, and the New Deal policy of favoring "more primitive, labor-intensive techniques" over the efficient was evident throughout the life of the project.[156] The dramatic rise in costs and the deliberate delays engendered coupled with the use of unskilled homesteaders to build the facilities led one official to assert "that there was actually a movement underfoot to sabotage the whole project."[157]

The people made do as best they could, improvising jobs as they could think of them. Joseph and Julia Perry, the youngest couple moved into the project, took some of the vegetables from their garden plot and sold them for cash, allowing them to buy a compressor that Joseph used to paint cars for extra money. Although such behavior would have struck the bureaucrats deep in the AAA as a treasonable act as the "excess" food belonged to them, the cash gave the Perrys the ability to buy a 1933 Ford Coupe. They kept the car in the small barn behind their home, the one the planners were bent on their using to house a cow.[158]

The opening of a large strip-mining operation right outside of Arthurdale also highlighted the different worldviews of the settlers and the federal bureaucracy overseeing them. When the *Morgantown Post* reported in February 1938 what the Fairfax Mining Company intended, Bushrod Grimes wrote to Eleanor Roosevelt that "this operation should not be permitted,"[159] as, in his mind, large-scale mining operations and farming didn't mix, yet by such time it's a wonder why he was bothering over subsistence farming at all. The strip mining went ahead all the same.

The end result, when all was said and done and the mining operation moved on, would give to Arthurdale's children the gift of a freely provided swimming hole, perfect for the summer heat, 75 yards wide, a mile long, 10 to 15 feet deep, and with "lots of diving points." Both Glenn Luzier and Dr. John Fullmer recall the swimming hole left behind with far more fondness than their recollections of working in the subsistence gardens.[160] Granted the benefit of the swimming hole was in hindsight, but considering the chronic lack of employment available to the homesteaders, it is a wonder that anyone, at all, would suggest any business project be halted.

Then came World War II, and the needs of the war machine were so insatiable they reached all the way up the mountain roads into

Arthurdale. Suddenly there were more jobs available than homesteaders. When the last federal project manager it would ever know—
Milford Mott—arrived on the scene in December 1941, "the
unemployment problem had been solved."[161] Even before Pearl Harbor,
the president sent directions to the War Department to set up a plant
in the town, and by April 1940, Silman Manufacturing Company was
occupying part of the moribund tractor factory, churning out walkie-
talkies and flares for the Army and Marine Corps while employing
nearly 100 people.[162]

By 1943, the Hoover Aircraft Corporation had arrived and set up
operations extensive enough to occupy all or part of three factories and
the inn,[163] and among them, Silman, and the huge DuPont defense
plant established at Morgantown, the homesteaders had their choice of
well-paid industrial work at last.[164] Wages soared,[165] the last vestiges
of subsistence homesteading were happily abandoned, and some old
miners even returned underground, where wages of $10 per day were
common.[166] The endless worry over jobs at last was over; all it took to
solve the problem was carnage unleashed on a global scale.

The homesteaders took it in stride, gratefully. Andy Wolfe, working
in the general store cooperative, remembered the war as a time when
things were "goin' real good . . . business was doin' much better . . .
everybody was working."[167] Surprisingly, despite being in his mid-30s
with three children, he was drafted into the Navy. He found that he
was making more money there than at the store and wanted to stay in,
but after a little over a year and a half, he was honorably discharged
and returned home.

It was a different experience for some, as 121 men were taken from
the town and transferred into the military. A young girl named Ruby
Wolfe looked about the town and felt "lonely, not many boys around
to date."[168] Her part of the story ended on a happy note. A young
Arthurdale resident named Maynard Weaver would return home after
the war and marry her.

In fact, all the town's wartime stories end on a happy note,
for despite seeing so many of its men off to war, not a single one was
killed in action. Not one blow to the town's future was struck from a
foreign direction. The biggest blows to the survival of the Arthurdale
project would come domestically, in the press attacks and the halls of

Congress. While the world at large had already begun to forget it and eventually the press would lose attention, at no time did Arthurdale suffer a shortage of enemies who wished to bring the experiment to an end.

It always remained too visible a target, one too large and tempting to pass up. This was a direct result of its size and purpose, as Eleanor Roosevelt wanted the town to be a living, breathing exhibit of a New America, with up to 100,000 people visiting annually and the nearby West Virginia University opening a research unit devoted to its study.[169] So while after the first few years the flood of civilian visitors slowed to extinction, government employees continued to watch, measure, and record the homesteaders to an extent no other town in America's history had ever encountered. The experiment chugged along, now mostly unobserved by the public.

The historian Paul Conkin once referred to Arthurdale and its kind as "a social show window" that reduced the settler to "a human mannequin in a great exhibit."[170] Each homesteader adjusted to this as they could. Some took it with good humor; others were a bit taken aback. It was the press attacks that affected them most deeply, not too surprising considering a 1934 *New York Herald Tribune* piece that referred to them as "federal sheep in a prophylactic pen, eating federal fodder from a porcelain trough."[171]

When the waves of outside visitors were crashing heaviest against them, the homesteaders' patience certainly was tried time and again with a "typical visitor on a sort of sociological souvenir hunt . . . [that] asks them the most intimate and personal questions as though they were a species apart from himself."[172] Taking it all in stride, Viola "Chris" McNelis actually enjoyed them and asked each one to sign a register she set out in her home. By her simple act of hospitality we have an excellent record of how often an original settler in Arthurdale received sightseers. Within a two-year period, Mrs. McNelis collected over 1,200 signatures, most of them on weekends.[173]

So many rumors were written as fact and so many tall tales passed off as true that the people of Arthurdale began to join in the fun themselves, making up stories and passing them along to gullible reporters.[174] One favorite concerned a fictitious homesteader fresh from the coal camps, utterly ignorant and annoyed that the "indoor spring" he was drinking out of (actually a toilet) had a lid that kept falling down on his head.

It is likely that the homesteaders themselves invented the anecdote of settlers who, having never beheld an indoor bathtub, instead used them as coal bins. This story had enough staying power that even 60 years later, a nephew of Bushrod Grimes would write a letter claiming that "when the natives moved in, they used bathtubs to store coal."[175] (I came across no record that anyone ever did so.)

Yet for all the jokes, negative press, and wide-eyed tourists, it was Washington, DC, that released the thunderbolts that ultimately would bring the project to an end. That was only logical, as the project was maintained purely by its being plugged into the New Deal apparatus. Opponents knew that to kill the project, it had to be unplugged. As early as 1935, the comptroller general was challenging the legality of every dollar spent on the project,[176] egged on by the habitual reference of Senator Thomas Schall of Minnesota to the town as "the communist project" and the "West Virginia commune."[177] These attacks, coupled with the lack of autonomy, red tape, and unemployment, had by the late 1930s sapped all the enthusiasm from the homesteaders.

As the first settlers moved in during June 1934, Eleanor Roosevelt took a group of friends on a tour of Arthurdale. One of them asked a housewife how she felt about the town. "It is paradise for us," the woman replied.[178] By 1940, however, after seven years of federal control and communal living, the rose had lost its bloom, and "the cooperative spirit so evident at the beginning of Arthurdale is fading."[179]

The planners of Arthurdale had run up against the unavoidable error of all utopian schemes: They had populated the brave new world in their heads with angels and the one down on earth with human beings.

Chapter 7

"A Human Experiment Station"

It seems to me the time has arrived . . . a human experiment station is being established. We are doing a laboratory job which will be useful and far-reaching in its ultimate results.
—Eleanor Roosevelt on Arthurdale (1934)[1]

By the end of 1939, FDR's Resettlement Agency (RA) had selected and resettled about 14,000 families.[2] Although the most publicized, Arthurdale was far from an only child; it had three siblings and many cousins. The federal resettlement project birthed a bit fewer than 200 colonies, and they stretched across the continent; one even sailed the cold waters of the northern Pacific into Alaska.[3]

Devolving from the frenzied activity of 1933, in late 1937, Secretary of Agriculture Henry A. Wallace* had declared resettlement activities to be "only a minor part" of his department's functions.[4] While it lasted, the experience of those resettled presented a vast contrast from the pioneers of old. The hardy folk would not arrive to tear a living out of the earth and battle those already upon it; here a working farm awaited, all the natives long ago slaughtered or safely corralled onto distant reservations by the U.S. Army; here a home bearing all the gifts the modern world could offer trumped a crude log cabin. And, for a time, these new pioneers had caught the attention, if not the admiration, of the American press.

More so than material comfort, what set the colonies off from those that came before was the degree of political control over the lives of the resettled. As they were living on a stage set, this was inevitable. The political value of Arthurdale as a real-life, living experiment of what FDR and his fellow travelers' hoped-for new world would look like necessitated that everything be on the up and up, and that accounts for why the lives of the resettled were regulated to such an extreme. It quickly became apparent to them that they weren't living a "normal" American life any longer.

With the lack of work available on the project and the necessity of shelter for the National Youth Association members based there, by October 1940, resettled families occupied only 141 of the 165 subsistence homesteads. The three waves of settlers had crested by then, and those who moved in, out, or were thrown off the project did so in dribs and drabs. The town, now grown to 2,283 acres, had settled into as normal a routine as permitted.[5]

The director of the town school and "community activities," Elsie Clapp, wrote a letter to Eleanor Roosevelt in early 1936 that speaks to the extent of bureaucratic control over the town. Breaking down the people much like an army unit, she presents a detailed inventory of the town residents, listing them by the jobs they had performed prior to their resettlement (the majority had worked in the mines, 60 of them as "hand loaders"), what jobs they currently held on the project (most were listed as "laborers"), and a compilation of all adults, both male and female, by age and fitness for work.[6]

---

*By 1937, the RA fell under the Department of Agriculture.

Diving below the color of their skin, Clapp also broke them down into national background, finding that 70 percent were Scotch-Irish and 25 percent Pennsylvania Dutch, but thankfully "both elements had lived so many generations in America that there is no group consciousness on their part."[7] Instead, the homesteaders' cliques seemed to arise from differences in wages, as the lack of work had worried them for two years now.

It was perplexing for them to discover that the promised material benefits, all to arise from this new life at Arthurdale, were turning out to be unfulfilled. They likely had little idea that material things for the colonists were not the primary focus of those who ran Arthurdale, as when Eleanor Roosevelt stated in a 1935 *Washington Herald* article, "What we are trying to do is to create for those who have endured poverty a more bearable poverty."[8]

It was not a world of plenty that was sought after; the goal was a world where the spark of revolution would be snuffed out forever and a new, improved American would arise. Arthurdale was always, from the first to the last, touted as the laboratory from which that new American would stride forth.

Machine of the Gods

There was so much bureaucracy.
  —Glenna Williams, original settler, Arthurdale[9]

Some gods demand blood, some gold, some a simple prayer—the Division of Subsistence Homesteads, in all its manifestations, demanded paper. In July 1934 C. E. Pynchon of the DSH sent out a memorandum addressed to all section chiefs. Called "Drawing, Issuing, and Registering Forms," it outlined, in three dense pages, the proper procedure to create even more forms for people to fill out.

For example of the paper vines that quickly strangled the town, from the memo's "Section II, e" it is required that "a fifth designation indicating the date of registration" should be used, preferably along the lines of "SH-A 1-a" or "SH-A 1-a/7-14-34," and when submitting a new form (along with a "purchase request (SH-65 2)," it was imperative that both first be signed by the section chief, there to be sent on to "the Methods Section" somewhere in the division's rapidly expanding belly, and, after securing approval, to be sent along to the "supervisor of purchases." One entire building in Arthurdale was given over to administrative matters.[10]

For simply selling produce grown in the town, it was required that the project manager "obtain three bids from three different sources on Form 33 . . . the bid forms, when prepared, shall include Form 36,"[11] and the powers that be weren't kidding, as not one month later that same C. E. Pynchon was reminding everyone that when using Forms 33 and 36, "one copy must be posted conspicuously in a public place."[12]

Clarence Pickett, a veteran of large-scale relief efforts who knew of the logistics (and flexibility) required for their success, was stunned by the "endless rules." Years later he recalled, "I did not know how many things one cannot do under government regulations."[13] The hypergrowth and centralization of political power over the resettlement communities, which quickly subsumed the hoped-for "democracy" of local control, would add up to a bewildering array of forms to be filled, permissions to be denied or delayed, and bureaucratic stairways to nowhere.

Following close on the all-encompassing nature of control propounded by Franklin K. Lane[14] and given life by Elwood Mead at Durham and Delhi, everything came from the political authorities who ran Arthurdale: all the jobs, houses, loans, edicts, and education. Rexford Tugwell foresaw in 1929 how the nature of an Arthurdale would make it "unable to escape the necessity of much government activity if an industry [agriculture] so individual and independent was to be welded into a machine with national purposes."[15]

The machine was kick-started by the $25 million allotted in Section 208, and flush with cash but vague on specifically how it was to implement its desired plans, the DSH declared itself "a continued program of long-term character."[16] What *Harper's Magazine* referred to as "this great scattering of the destitute"[17] was officially begun on August 23, 1933, and M. L. Wilson (chosen to be director) began with a secretary, one full-time assistant, and a part-time staff of four.

A public call had been made for states, towns, cities, and lonely farmers to mail in their vision of Utopia and hope against hope that it would be chosen and made real. Within a short time, an avalanche of resettlement proposals—the best of which, if taken together, would have cost $4 billion to implement—inundated Wilson's small crew. Some were well thought out, others were racist missives asking for the removal of black Americans to rural, out-of-the-way areas. Then there were those simply lunatic, like the ones calling for "the complete decentralization of New York, Philadelphia, and Chicago."[18]

Wilson quickly leaned away from unsolicited, unprofessional offerings and toward the familiar, and soon enough "stipulated that any proposal would have to have . . . the cooperation and planning aid of the state colleges of agriculture."[19] The size and scope of his kingdom had exploded; from a humble beginning that occupied a mere three rooms in the Department of the Interior, within two months it had 22 employees, and by the following summer the administration personnel alone numbered over 300 and took up three floors[20] with another 1,850 persons coming under the division's umbrella.[21]

The intellectual cream of that division were brought over by Wilson from the Bureau of Agricultural Economics, and he put them to work on "research projects on part-time farming in 33 states, marking one of the most extensive research programs" of such a nature ever undertaken.[22] Because Wilson, like many of his fellow dreamers, stubbornly ignored past attempts and insisted that what was being undertaken was an idea fresh and untried, "experimentation" was to be the modus of operation. He liked to sit about with his fellows and "temper bureaucracy with philosophical discussions in the rapidly expanding New Deal."[23]

The most star-powered of these philosophical discussions formed voluntarily and held its first meeting in September 1933. With a roster that included Wilson, Henry Harriman (president of the U.S. Chamber of Commerce), Senator John H. Bankhead, Harold Ickes (secretary of the Interior), Rexford Tugwell, Bernarr Macfadden, John D. Black, and William Green (head of the American Federation of Labor), it took the name "The National Advisory Committee on Subsistence Homesteads,"[24] and its recommendations would provide the skeleton on which the DSH was constructed.

Eleanor Roosevelt was caught up in the excitement of the moment, too, gushing in the *New York Times* that "there is nothing so exciting as creating a new social order."[25] The living room of the Luziers' apartment atop the Arthur mansion was the scene of a number of relaxed meetings of the mind for DSH officials and Eleanor Roosevelt, she pacing the floors with a baby Glenn Luzier in her arms.[26]

The disciples of resettlement had all the resources that anyone could hope for at their disposal; a vast harvest of taxpayer funds lay at their feet. They had everything, in fact, but an idea of how actually to implement that dream which they couldn't quite define. All that was produced for a plan of action was a tepid "the best use of the available appropriation will be made by setting up demonstration projects which will point the way to a program of a permanent character."[27] For all speeches, articles, books, and big brains purchased at the finest colleges, when they finally got their chance to put their dream into reality, they simply winged it.

The proponents of Arthurdale were honest in their dealings and pure of heart—the November 1933 circular printed by the DSH promised resettlement projects would be located only "with reference to the principal 'problem areas' of the United States."[28] The program, though, was infested with politics from its very nature, and the five homestead colonies established within Senator John Bankhead's home base of Jasper and Birmingham, Alabama, certainly raise the eyebrows.[29]

Secretary of the Interior Harold Ickes was frankly appalled at Wilson's loose handling of taxpayer funds, plus he did not think much of the man to begin with.[30] In a quick series of executive orders and decrees, the entire structure of the DSH was rapidly centralized.[31] Wilson held fast to his support for local decision making, and he did, in fact, hold it honestly and ardently. His disgust at the quick centralization of power rendered the DSH inhospitable to him, and on June 30, 1934, he resigned and took along to a new post in the Department of Agriculture many of the original core who had arrived at the DSH with him. Pynchon, who had come on board only a few months prior, became de facto head of the division.[32]

From that time forth, the DSH would become the unwanted stepchild of the New Deal, shunted from one parent organization to another, exacerbating the already chaotic administration of the settlements. Christened in 1933 as the Division of Subsistence Homesteads within the Department of the Interior (the bureaucrats named Arthurdale "SH-WV-2, Region IV"), there it remained until May 1935, when it was folded up into the RA. From then until December 1936 it lay still, but like the orphan it had become was shunted off to the Department of Agriculture, first retaining the RA tag until an internal reorganization in September 1937 kept it in house but under the FSA. It would not find peace until October 1942, when it landed in the Federal Public Housing Authority, curled up within its National Housing Agency until it passed away in 1948.[33]

The division was a hot potato, both politically and career-wise, as it was not only under the harsh glare of a hostile press and growing congressional opposition but within it resided Arthurdale, which bore the close, personal attention of the First Couple and (until his death in 1936) FDR's right-hand man, Louis Howe. Taking the division under your domain meant dealing with all three of them. From Howe, who was a blizzard of memos demanding information on small, decentralized electrical stations he wished to have power the colonies (and on top of that he also had an odd fixation to make everyone grow flax), to Mrs. Roosevelt, who was running "a parallel administration" in tandem to yours,[34] to knowing that FDR's desk was routinely covered with questions, complaints, and documents regarding the most trivial of details concerning the resettlement colonies,[35] administering the DSH was what ulcers are made of.

Some critics panned the ideology that underpinned the entire project, too, *Harper's Magazine* accusing it of being a plan to "diffuse the social risks of revolt,"[36] which it was. Doubtless, the FDR administration used fearmongering about a communist-led revolt to sell the idea to the public, press, and politicos and used the available monies to engage in patronage. Yet for many, Arthurdale was a cherished dream put to motion, their fondest wishes made real. In a 1931 speech, FDR had called on the listeners to "plan a better distribution of our population,"[37] and at long last here it was. Both Howe and Mrs. Roosevelt maintained an in-depth, close eye on Arthurdale. Weekly progress reports were delivered to the White House so they both could watch unfold what Howe called "the economic and social benefits promised by the subsistence homesteads program."[38] Wilson summed up the feelings of its deepest acolytes when he proclaimed they were "laying the basis for a new type of civilization."[39]

Democracy and *cooperation* were the buzzwords of that new civilization, and it was believed the new world they were bringing forth would not sit still within Arthurdale but spread across America in an orgy of voluntary, thankful imitation. The project was created so every-one could see the benefits to "speeding and guiding industrial decen-tralization."[40] A subsistence homestead was officially defined as "a modern but inexpensive house and outbuildings, located on a plot of land upon which a family may produce a considerable portion of the food required for home consumption."[41] But there was a problem, legally speaking.

The powers granted in the frenzy of FDR's First 100 Days that gave life to the program were due to expire on June 16, 1935, unless renewed by Congress, which would decline to even vote on the matter.[42] Foreseeing this outcome, on April 30, 1935, FDR simply issued an executive order legislating the program into permanent exis-tence. His decree not only continued the funding of all the resettlement projects but also raised them to the stature of a cabinet-level entity, creating the Resettlement Administration with Rexford Tugwell as its head.[43] In response to this blatant assault on its powers, Congress gave not so much as a squeak in protest.

Openly collectivist and bejeweled with degrees from the finest universities, of all of FDR's Brain Trust (the gaggle of intellectual advi-sors he'd gathered around him) the most intellectual was Rexford Tugwell. His drive and intellect produced an endless stream of articles, speeches, and books, while his public exhortations to establish a cen-trally planned, collectivist America led to warnings for parents to keep their children from getting a hold of those books or within hearing range of those speeches.[44] He would quickly expand the RA into a behemoth so large it had its own telephone network, with over 13,000 employees spread across 16 divisions. He established headquarters in one of Washington's more storied private mansions.[45]

By 1936, Tugwell had become a political liability to FDR and resigned,[46] but his ardent belief in work collectives—and his disagree-ment with the idea of small, subsistence homesteads—was a primary motive behind Arthurdale throwing away so much wealth on trying to implement the co-ops. He fully realized and accepted the fact that his desires would subvert the restrictions of the Constitution and would be a political imposition into the private sphere of American life to an extent formerly unknown.[47] But he had a new world to build, and thus anything was but a small price to pay. In this acceptance of the incessant meddling into what was formerly private, he was far from alone.

He was a man who left his mark on America's political landscape. Tugwell's resignation from the Brain Trust ended Arthurdale's control by the leading intellectual lights of Ely's teachings. From then on until it was put to sleep, the New Deal resettlement program would be run by career bureaucrats.

Progressive School, Progressive Man

The new homesteaders had to learn to . . . rid themselves of the individualistic tendencies developed in Scotts Run, and begin life anew.

—Amanda Griffith Penix, author of *Arthurdale*[48]

From its very beginning Arthurdale was a young town. The resettled West Virginian coal miners tended to have large families, so upon the opening of the school, 36 preschool and 246 older students were in need of an education.[49] With the school complex still on the drawing board, the Arthur mansion (among a few other buildings) was put to the task, and now a crowd of almost 300 students waited outside the mansion, together on its great lawn. The administrators took care of the preschoolers first; the older children had to wait their turn. It was a beautiful day and the children, in their timeless manner, immediately started forming friendships. "What grade are you in?" was the popular icebreaker.[50] Being that Arthurdale was a "progressive" school, the answer was "none," as for them grades would no longer exist.

Among those who embraced the idea put to the test at Arthurdale, all their desires and hopes for the success of their creation of a New American were embodied within the town's school. Education was to be the pottery wheel upon which God's children would be remolded and improved, and the school system would for a short time become to them the most interesting and important component erected in the laboratory of Arthurdale. For the first dozen years of its life, the high school at Arthurdale was distinguished by having either Eleanor

Roosevelt or (in 1938) FDR deliver a commencement speech to the graduating class.[51]

Clarence Pickett, at whose suggestion Mrs. Roosevelt hired Arthurdale's first principal, Elsie Clapp, stated afterward that "one of the most important things that we undertook was the establishing of a special school . . . a school which would train the young people of the community to fit into the kind of environment which we are attempting to create."[52] Like the rest of the town, the children were to be improved upon in preparation for that environment, but with a much greater chance for success as they were younger and needed to "unlearn" that much less than their parents.

For a time the school was considered the epicenter of progressive education and a tangible experiment that would prove worthy of its promise. The school would also draw a stream of visitors; the nursery had two-way mirrors through which visiting experts could observe the children, and for its first few years Arthurdale's school system was "a hotbed of study for outside researchers."[53]

The idea behind it was quite a leap from the days of teachers instructing on reading, writing, and arithmetic. Something else was now desired, the task expanded from teaching the basics to an active pursuit of molding the child. A 1940 report on Arthurdale's school conducted by teaching experts openly expressed that "public education has an opportunity as well as the responsibility for the development of the whole child."[54] During its initial years, most especially under its first two principals, Elsie Clapp and E. Grant Nine, Arthurdale's school system pitched into the task.

No expense was spared, and a huge complex was erected on the north side of the town. It boasted 50,000 square feet of floor space, 1.14 million square inches of glass windows to provide light, and seven independent buildings (a nursery school, primary school, intermediate school, administration building/cafeteria, secondary school, gymnasium, and pottery building). The school employed five janitors and a night watchman to maintain things and watch over "several separate heating plants" that kept out the cold.[55]

It may have been extravagant, but it had a grand purpose. In the words of Clapp, "there are no bounds, as far as I can see, to what it could accomplish in social reconstruction."[56] It was assumed, explicitly, that the grinding poverty so many of the resettled had endured had so beaten them down that it was necessary they be "taught how to live" again. This assumption was not unique to Arthurdale but woven into the back-to-the-landers' tenets for decades.[57]

The people of Arthurdale would be rebuilt using the techniques and ideas of the Progressive movement's foremost educational expert, John Dewey, who gave to America "the most important intellectual supports for interventionism and a degree of collectivism."[58] Clapp was one of Dewey's foremost disciples, having first read (and been captivated by) his works while she was still in college. For her, school was an all-encompassing thing: "[T]he community is the school and the school in all its activities and interests is Arthurdale. . . . [it] supplies the ideas and ideals, the interests and news, the life of the community."[59]

Clapp's desire was for the school to "revive the cooperative, demo-cratic spirit," which she believed to have been stripped from American life by the industrial revolution.[60] The assumption of control over the town by the RA was no threat to this worldview, as Tugwell, too, believed school to be one of the "instruments available for social reor-ganization."[61] The ideal of progressive education elevated "the idea of a managed society" high upon its banner.[61] Education was to be the primary agent used to transform America into that society.

Those who ran Arthurdale's school system also held onto the notion that free markets were a social evil. At the 1932 Progressive Education Association, it was argued in one panel that "educators needed to help reform the structures and institutions of American capitalism."[63] Clapp worried about the miners resettled from Scotts Run; "being in the shadow of urban Morgantown, they had been disturbed by . . . bour-geois cultural standards."[64] One route used in the school to fix any such disturbance was its newspaper, the *Arthurdale Builder* (We're Building for a Living Democracy!), which would replace "gossip, rumor, and hearsay [with] . . . accurate information."[65]

The *Saturday Evening Post* in a 1937 column gives a rundown of one example of this technique, when the school newspaper ran a student-penned tale entitled "Shut Up!," those being the words the capitalist at the center of the story implores the inquisitive student with, lest his workers overhear their conversation and realize how they were being "exploited."[66]

Like Tugwell's insistence that the distinction between public and private was meaningless, Clapp's view of the school asked "Where does school end and life outside begin?" and answered "There is no distinction between them."[67] The school was "concerned equally with the development of individuals of all ages,"[68] and a panel of experts seconded that idea in 1940, calling for the town to "use the nursery school, the homes, and community enterprises even more extensively as laboratories for experience in dealing with family problems."[69]

Such pervasive imposition into the life of the community was not possible without a high degree of paternalism, and for all the love poems written to sweet democracy the progressive educators poured out of their hearts, "Clapp and government officials were constantly concerned about the homesteaders' ability to make judgments and at times overruled the wishes of the homesteaders."[70] Being overruled would last for the townsfolk until such time as they themselves demanded an end to the progressive education methods practiced at the school, and while the names of Elsie Clapp and John Dewey may have faded from memory, to this day their idea of what education should be retains its force.

A Little Village in Itself

She considered all of us; everybody in the community was her pupils.
—Jettie (Boggs) Eble, Arthurdale homesteader[71]

Elsie Clapp dubbed it "a little village within itself" and that the Arthurdale school system certainly was.[72] Officially hired on July 7, 1934, Clapp joined Eleanor Roosevelt, Clarence Pickett, and John Dewey on the school's advisory committee,[73] and always her ideas were strongly supported by the First Lady,[74] who lavished the school with her own funds. Clapp was born in 1879 into wealth and raised in Brooklyn, New York. Like Elwood Mead and Richard Ely, she made good use of her family's well-stocked library, earning herself a prodigious education.[75] Being of superior intelligence, she found Vassar College none too challenging and complained that "classes may be dull, but at least I have this library."[76] She transferred to Barnard, eventually earning a master's in philosophy in 1909 from Columbia University. It was at Columbia where she began with Professor John Dewey what would become a lifelong, mutual admiration.[77]

From her younger days she ran with a reactionary crowd, moving within circles that contained Bill Haywood of the Industrial Workers of the World and John Reed. (His 1917 dispatches from Russia's October Revolution earned him enshrinement in the Kremlin Wall.) As with Eleanor Roosevelt, Clapp was motivated to social work by her exposure to poverty, in this case from her time with the Patterson Silk Workers' Strike Organization during 1922. It opened to her the tenements of New York's Lower East Side.[78] Similar to M. L. Wilson, Clapp was bitten by the bug of democracy, once marching in a Woodrow Wilson Inauguration Day parade with 20,000 other woman suffragists, all demanding to be allowed in on the fun.

At the time she was hired to run Arthurdale's school, she was one of the progressive education movement's most prominent names and principal of the Ballard Memorial School near Louisville, Kentucky. The system was compromised of 212 students scattered about one- and two-room schoolhouses in the area, all of them run on the principles of John Dewey. In tandem to her teaching duties, Clapp also chaired the National Committee on Rural Education for the Progressive Education Association.[79] For the planned progressive school at Arthurdale no better candidate could have been chosen.

Clapp took her pledge to make the school the center of community life to heart, and clashed with the project managers as to just who was in charge at Arthurdale.[80] She considered herself de facto town mayor and behaved in a manner appropriate to the title. Empowered by her close affiliation with Eleanor Roosevelt, she added to the organizational chaos and "acted as an intermediary between homesteaders and Washington"[81] on a wide array of issues. She even fought Andy Wolfe (a homesteader on the project) as to whether he was allowed to cut trees on his property.[82] When she departed after the 1935–1936 school year, "few missed the paternalism of her ideas and methods."[83]

Clapp was once quoted as insisting that "the school should not be established at excessive costs,"[84] but she didn't really mean it. She worked closely with both Eric Gugler and Stuart Wagner in the design of the school complex,[85] and like the rest of the town, it was luxurious and overlarge. Even she "did not pretend that all these buildings are necessary."[86] Although nine one-room school houses—ill-equipped and sporting outdoor privies—lay within a four-mile radius,[87] the children of Arthurdale enjoyed a well-appointed complex that "resembles those found on the grounds of some of the more favored country day and boarding schools."*[88] Ironically, the complex she put so much of her time and energy into would not open to the children until after Clapp's departure.

One student remembered years after, "[W]e had a lot of unique things in our high school," and for that time and place he wasn't kidding.[89] The gymnasium alone boasted a large stage with dressing rooms, lockers for both home and visiting teams, showers, rooms for orchestra practice and prop storage, and "the best basketball floor in West Virginia."[90]

A complex of such size was tough to maintain to begin with, and it was built of "a relatively impermanent type of construction" that made it expensive to keep up. It did not help that the heating system was improperly installed, turning one room into midsummer while leaving its neighbor freezing in deep winter. "Obviously," pointed out a study, "this means inordinate fuel consumption."[91] At first most construction and maintenance costs were paid for not by the federal government (which at the time still mostly respected the constitutional constraint on such expenditures) but by a confluence of private contributions and different organizations. The teachers' salaries were higher than those prevailing elsewhere in the county (Clapp's alone came in at $6,000 per annum, or $98,000 in 2010 dollars)[92] all of them paid for out of the pockets of Mrs. Roosevelt, Bernard Baruch, and other private individuals.[93]

Soon enough tax money began to slosh in from the federal level, and by the 1938–1939 school year, 44 percent of operating funds came from the Preston County Board of Education;[94] 41 percent from the FSA, Works Progress Administration, and Public Works Administration; and 15 percent from private donors.[95] Although such an arrangement

---

*The 1940 *Report of the Survey of Arthurdale School* was of the opinion that the school was big enough to support 250 more children and that the nearby Masontown School was "rather crowded."

kept the lights on, it threw the school into an organizational chaos that matched the town's. Having so many interested parties caused the chain of command to "become somewhat tangled, with authority and responsibility in many instances so scattered as to lose any semblance of system."[96] Expenditures per student averaged from 19 to 180 percent higher than for other county schools,[97] but no long-term plan was ever created for continued funding of what Preston County on its own clearly never could afford.[98]

The local *Preston Republican* worried aloud about this problem, commenting in late 1936 over the "Roosevelt monstrosity" being thrown onto the backs of the county taxpayer.[99] It was clear even to its adherents that "were the support now provided by private funds and the several federal agencies to cease," Arthurdale's student body would notice a serious change in the program.[100] Although the material support lavished on the school made it stand out from the crowd, it was the educational experiment conducted there that made it truly unique.

Clapp's methods to instill a progressive education felt that "'learning' in this connection is to be understood as acquisition of moral and spiritual values rather than those usually associated with . . . bookish and academic implications."[101] The progressive methods used at Arthurdale were so outside the loop of standard procedure that the state refused to grant the system accreditation until 1938. Instead of the traditional, structured classroom setting, the children (who were divided into classes not by age but by the interests they expressed a partiality for[102]) were sent into the surrounding fields to "learn by doing," boys were sent to home economic courses and the girls to shop class.[103]

The progressive education movement believed that "the curriculum . . . should not be hampered by traditional and formal courses of study, nor by standardized grading and grouping of students."[104] At the time such teaching methods were beyond comprehension, with even the friendly 1940 West Virginia University (WVU) Teachers survey noting "that teachers measured the outcomes of teaching by any other means than observation was not clear in the early days."[105] Yet it was a clear purpose not to have any grading at all. According to the next principal, E. Grant Nine, "the school shall provide for the maximum amount of creative expression on the part of the child. It should hold at a minimum all repressive measures that tend toward teacher domination."[106]

Fitting in perfectly with the back-to-the-landers' desire for a fixed rural population, the school (again according to Nine) worked to prepare students "for work available in this resettlement community."[107] The very mention of the word "coal" was dropped down the rabbit hole as "little systematic effort was made by teachers to make mining and related work part of the curriculum."[108] Mining coal was part of a dark past; the future belonged to the cooperative life of subsistence farms.

Adults were strongly encouraged to show "community spirit" and take advantage of the myriad activities that Clapp put together. Believing them necessary to revitalize a local culture that industrial life had crushed out of them, she pushed the homesteaders to express themselves through folk singing, fiddle playing, handicrafts, and performance of mountain ballads, as these were "essential features of American rural life."[109] (Clapp, though, made sure to expunge all ballads whose lyrics extolled labor violence.)[110] Some responded enthusiastically. homesteader Elizabeth Fullmer, for example, took the weaving classes to help with the stress of raising 10 children and "that there settled my nerves better than anything else."[111]

To be a teacher in such a system was summed up perfectly by Clapp: "There is no ease, little leisure, much work, great happiness."[112] The hours required were prodigious; one teacher who worked at Arthurdale from 1936 to 1938 can "only remember having two free evenings."[113] Besides endless reports to be written, community activities that they were required to be a part of, and their work during actual class time, all were expected to study John Dewey's writings and discuss them at meetings held in Clapp's home on weekends and after hours.[114]

Despite the higher pay granted, the turnover among Arthurdale's teaching staff was a problem, especially at the high school level.[115] During the 1940 school year, of 17 teachers on staff, seven were brand new, and only two had more than five years' experience within the system. In the high school, six of the nine teachers were in their first year.[116] There were a number of reasons cited for this, the most prominent being the uncertainty of long-term employment at a school touted as "experimental" and the long work hours expected of those employed.[117]

For all the thought that went into the progressive educational approach, by 1940, even so sympathetic a group as that which conducted the survey for WVU (funded in part by the American Friends Service Committee) was flatly declaring that "the better half of the pupils . . . are not in reality what may be called 'superior' pupils"[118] and strongly recommending that the school move more toward "definite planning and more sequential execution of plans" in the basics.[119] More than anything, it was the reaction of the parents of Arthurdale that sealed the fate of the progressive school.

In January 1936, the homesteaders voted to seek accreditation from West Virginia so that their children could attend college at WVU, if they so chose.[120] Clapp's progressive methods did not jibe well with the requirements to attain that goal, and seeing the writing on the wall she left Arthurdale in the summer of 1936, turning her post over to Grant. While he was undoubtedly sympathetic to Clapp's philosophy and methods, a decided turn toward book learning replaced lesson plans that were determined off the cuff and on the spot.[121]

Clapp's reaction to the lack of accreditation was to note: "None of the three students to be graduated . . . was planning to go to the university."[122] Although some hold this up as "snobbishness" on her part, the goal of the school system was, like that of the town at large, not to broaden horizons and set the goalposts high but to keep people content and in one place. A college education would broaden the mental horizons of, and wanderlust in, the affected student. Subsistence homesteads were designed for multigenerational use; hence the school's emphasis on preparing students "for work available in this resettlement community."[123]

The homesteaders were bound to figure out the limitations that were being assumed on their behalf, and soon enough, as Mrs. Roosevelt recalled, "we finally realized that the kind of experimental school which Miss Clapp established was really not satisfactory to the people."[124] At a February 26, 1936, meeting, the people of the town passed a resolution "demanding that the Arthurdale School come under the school system of West Virginia."[125] The homesteaders simply had higher expectations for their children than the progressive educators, and time proved their concerns valid.

One homesteader recalls "as I look back on it we didn't get a very good education at Arthurdale. I even had to go to school extra to get enough credits to even get into the university,"[126] and he is far from alone among former students who felt that way.[127] Glenna Williams remembers her worry over whether the course work offered at the school would force her to go live with her sister back in Scotts Run "and go back to University High to get my diploma."[128] Robert McLaughlin Sr. was never taught cursive penmanship and to this day still prints.[129] A young student Joseph Roscoe wrote an essay about "boys and girls complaining they couldn't tell" what grade they were even in.[130] Such concerns and experiences of the students were bound to get back to and worry their parents.

Not everyone felt negatively about the school. Dr. John Fullmer remembers his math teacher (Robert Calvert) as outstanding and feels his time at Arthurdale left him well prepared for college. He did not stay at the school through graduation, though, being pulled away to Masontown High for his senior year by the charms of a young student named Marlene Kay Morgan, whom he would one day make his wife.[131] Despite how he felt about the progressive education he was receiving, "she was much prettier than Arthurdale school"[132] and after 56 years of married life, five children, and five grandchildren none could argue with him.

With the homesteaders expressing displeasure at her educational methods, by August of 1936 Elsie Clapp could write to Mrs. Roosevelt that "we have all finally withdrawn from Arthurdale."[133] Sad but accepting of the homesteaders' will, Mrs. Roosevelt would reply: "[W]hile of course it isn't as good a school, the people do seem able to go along on their own initiative."[134] The progressive methods used at Arthurdale would soon begin to slowly wither away, and by the time World War II arrived, the school was, to all intents, almost indistinguishable from the rest of Preston County.[135]

"This Highly Restricted Mode of Life"

The homesteaders . . . were left with little latitude for decision-making. Even the most trivial of matters had to pass through the hands of Washington officialdom before action could be taken.
                                        —Stephen Haid, historian (1975)[136]

When the National Advisory Committee on Subsistence Homesteads drew up its 15-point platform, one of its central tenets was a paean to democracy suggesting "a maximum of local initiative and responsibility with adequate federal supervision."[137] Its members may as well have asked a hungry lion to nibble. From FDR, to Tugwell, to Wilson, to Pickett, all involved with Arthurdale were firm believers in planning, and what is the point of being a planner if you cannot order people about?

In October 1933, Secretary of the Interior Ickes announced the opening of Arthurdale and stated, "It will undertake to return to usefulness . . . men who are victims of the period of planlessness which I hope we are leaving behind."[138] Being planned, Arthurdale by its very nature was controlled; its residents lived under what a 1940 report dubbed "this highly restricted mode of life."[139]

A study by the Bureau of Agricultural Economics in 1942 claimed that "it was sometimes difficult to discern the extent to which they advocated what prospective homesteaders wanted, or . . . what they thought the prospective homesteaders ought to want, or deserved."[140] From the very beginning, the DSH openly declared that besides merely providing homes, "important social objectives will be served as well."[141]

Wilson outlined those social objectives as the "attitudes and lives of the families who occupy these communities must be integrated so as to provide a new and different view of life and a new and different set of family values."[142] And in Arthurdale, being a laboratory tasked to bring forth this desired change, "the government was determined to exercise control over both physical and social aspects" of the homestead.[143]

It is ironic that idealists in far-off Washington, planning other people's lives over leisurely dinner parties, praised democracy while setting down in great detail the lives of others. Clarence Pickett wrote a few decades later that "it is true that there was a period when these communities were . . . in a dependent relation to government,"[144] and in Arthurdale, as throughout all the other resettlement colonies, that dependent relationship was the most important, overwhelming fact of life.

From merely being nagged to clean up their yard to the extreme of eviction, the town's residents were closely supervised by the federal authorities. (Clapp, in a 1936 letter to Eleanor Roosevelt, includes on

it a helpful list of "men who are most indignant about conditions.")[145]
"The fear of being kicked out of Arthurdale if they didn't live up to
the government's expectations was real for many homesteaders,"[146] and
a May 1939 letter from J. O. Walker (the director of the RA) to Eleanor
Roosevelt stated that "we have . . . gone over each family with the
result that five have been eliminated."[147] Within one week, all five
families were gone from Arthurdale.[148]

A detailed report was submitted for the file of each family removed.
One of them, that of a James Lawrence, gives a glimpse at how deeply
into the private lives of the resettled the disciples were willing to go.
It was noted that he "has not been buying at the co-op store" and,
despite a policy of its being, at minimum, strongly frowned on had
been renting out half his acreage to another farmer. He had an "unusu-
ally ruddy complexion" and the writer suggested, "It would be well to
investigate his temperance."[149] Lawrence and his family were thrown
off the project in May 1939. The other families removed were done
so for a variety of reasons, such as failure to pay rent, drinking, infidel-
ity, and "lack of community spirit."

This deep diving into the lives of those resettled was born of necessity, as any laboratory experiment must be controlled else it isn't much
of an experiment. In a January 1936 "Case History of Dallas Earl
Riley," the man and his family were subject to investigation of their
past, all family members, credit with local businesses, wages, physical
appearance, state of home and yard, and their "attitude and personali-
ties." It was noted that Mr. Riley enjoyed reading Western stories and
was deemed acceptable to remain on the project despite being "mule
headed over what he thought to be his rights."[150]

The contract that was required to be signed by those resettled into
Arthurdale spelled out rather clearly that the political authorities held
all the cards. They reserved all mineral rights, could inspect the property
at will, forbade "intoxicating liquor of any kind" on the project,*
forbade any change in layout or ownership, specifically tasked the family
to adhere to "a general plan for . . . a subsistence homestead," and granted
themselves the right to cancel the agreement "without any reason or

---

*Like Prohibition everywhere else in America, by many accounts this clause was
completely ignored.

cause therefore."[151] It is no surprise that the homesteaders, without exception, referred to their "mortgage" payments as "rent."

For each and every task, from the layout of their homes to how they would run their businesses, "the perimeters for community decision-making existed only within the narrowest of limits."[152] In what must have been one of the more insulting moments for the men, the Homesteaders Club wished to hold a beer and oyster party to celebrate its first anniversary and Elsie Clapp, the school principal, refused to allow it.*[153] A letter from 1937 has Bushrod Grimes complaining about the "use of army tactics with the homesteaders."[154]

Grimes himself was not immune to the effects of power and wrote in September 1934 of his plan to prevent the homesteaders from growing whatever crops they wished; instead "we should plan to have the homesteaders raise grain and forage for an expected cooperative dairy herd. If you agree with me the homesteaders should then be rounded up."[155] Already a plan had been decided for a "cooperative dairy instead of allowing individual homesteaders to keep their cows," but then everyone was allowed to keep cows if they pleased.[156] It was but one example of how the plans constantly changed on a whim as Arthurdale was "in the experimental and testing stage."[157]

Much of the everyday was planned on behalf of the resettled, all of whom, according to Eleanor Roosevelt, "must be taught to live."[158] Those who ran the Arthurdale project believed themselves to be just the people for the task, as they glittered with all the college learning that money could buy and had in their hands political power, a tool in which they had boundless faith. Rexford Tugwell considered government the means through which "neighborliness had to be expressed."[159] They had a profound distrust of individual action, excepting their own.

Any action on the part of the homesteaders (such as complaining) that did not conform to the plan was frowned upon, and Elsie Clapp for one thought "it would be well for them (the homesteaders) to concern themselves with such questions [on school matters] rather than their restricted matters of personal gain or rights."[160] The Homesteader Club had no power whatsoever and was more of a sounding board

---

* They retired instead to a bar in nearby Reedsville.

for requests to be passed up the chain of command, and the various meetings to which the homesteaders were called to by the authorities were "pep talks," not negotiations.[161]

The homesteaders adjusted as best they could, and Clapp felt they were "slowly adjusting to the situation. A good many things are still not clear to them. They understand very slowly."[162] It was difficult to get anything done when the authorities in Washington were paralyzed with indecision, afraid to make any move concerning Arthurdale on their own, lest they anger Eleanor Roosevelt or Louis Howe.[163]

No one at any level felt it prudent to allow the homesteaders any autonomy. The prevailing attitude toward the homesteaders' abilities was summed up by Bernard Baruch in 1936: "[W]e must set them on their feet and on sound feet or they never can stand."[164] The introduction of the collectives only increased the intrusions into the homestead, and a 1937 report finds that "no steps have been taken to release the control which government maintains over every detail of co-op activities. Indeed, there is more control than there was a year ago."[165]

Tentative plans were floated regarding the time when the homesteaders, declared ready to stand on their feet again, would be released from political control. It was widely felt that any emancipation should take place gradually. In 1939, RA director Walker declared that "my feeling is entirely one to retain some control in order to protect the homesteaders as much as possible in the next step—that of learning to operate their places and maintain themselves. With this thought in mind, I have figured on 20 years."[166]

The back-to-the-land activist and publisher Bernarr Macfadden wrote long before that the resettled would care for little and "will be satisfied with enough to eat."[167] Doubtless that played a part in the beginning, but once their bellies stopped growling, like all men throughout history they began to desire more, such as the power to make their own decisions. Yet bureaucrats are always reluctant to detach from the host, so as late as 1940, contemporaries reported that "the future is not in the hands of the homesteaders but of the federal government."[168]

Although it is impossible to calculate the exact effect years of outside control had on the people of Arthurdale, that it had an effect is impossible to deny.

The Jamestown Effect

These men and women are expected to abide in peace, this arbitrary disposition of their future.
　　　—Letter, E. G. Swift to M. L. Wilson (1933)[169]

During the early life of the DSH, at the time its mailbag was stuffed to bursting with proposals, plans, and pleas from across America, a letter made its way from Los Angeles into the hands of M. L. Wilson. Written on October 24, 1933, by a man named E. G. Swift, it is a 13-page dissection of the entire subsistence program on both practical and moral grounds. While one of Wilson's concerns was whether "this new pattern of life can develop without a great deal of social control,"[170] Swift was already certain that the answer was no, that nothing would develop from the back-to-the-landers' "quick-sand of a theory" and, more important, the people subjected to such heavy social control would react in ways the planners likely never thought of.[171]

For all the ink spilled over the idea and the multitude of historical examples they could have brought to bear on it, the question of how people would react to the level of control required to create the New American was given little thought. Among the Smart Set who held fast to the theory, the assumption was that the people resettled, once the educational benefits of the school took hold of their minds and the abundant (but not *too* abundant) flow of goods from the collective workshops poured out before their eyes, would themselves become acolytes of subsistence homesteads and collective living. When all was said and done, Wilson and all "envisioned a new improved man, with new attitudes and new values."[172]

As early as 1934, the organizational chart of the DSH was beginning to resemble a computer motherboard, and with all the overlapping federal and state agencies involved, along with Eleanor Roosevelt, Louis Howe, and Elsie Clapp thrown in for good measure, "decisions by government agencies were often arbitrary and resulted in inconsistent policies."[173] It was not easy to live under such a regime.

Years later Annabelle Mayor said of all the visitors and the lack of privacy: "[W]e didn't resent it as much as we probably should have."[174] The main resentment among the resettled seemed to center on each other's lives, specifically on the subject of wages and the differentials among them.[175] In 1936, Clapp remarked, "The men reminisce always about their first day on the project when they were all paid an equal sum for whatever work they did and deplore the fact . . . they are now paid different amounts."[176] Besides wages, any jobs on the project given over to outsiders were also a source of consternation.

Because everything was provided through political channels (and the homesteaders were not privy to the account books) and all work was done in common, people became distrusting of each other, wondering who had the better angle. The Homesteaders Club became the stage of "petty rivalries and suspicion,"[177] Bushrod Grimes recorded in late 1934 of one meeting where the men fell to arguing with each other over how and when to divide the communally raised produce.

"A good many accusations were flung back and forth," he recorded, but it was not the first time. The meeting was but one of a series of "continued bickering which has been going on among some of them for the past two months."[178] Three years later, he was still writing about Arthurdale's "jarring cliques, jealousies, intolerance, and here and there domestic problems."[179] A *New York Times* article from 1946 surmised that "the bickering of its residents doomed it to failure,"[180] but that was untrue—the bickering was but an effect, not the cause, of Arthurdale's collapse as a subsistence homestead.

The uncertainty over the timing and terms of how the resettled would be granted title to their homes was one of the biggest sources of friction. The *Washington Post* reported in early 1934 that "the method by which the homesteaders are going to buy their homes and land has not been finally settled."[181] The settlers were well aware of what a disaster, from a financial standpoint, the building of the town had been, and the impossibility of ever earning enough to pay for their homes even should they be able to obtain a full-time job (jobs that were, for the most part, unavailable) weighed on them. For this problem, like every other on the project, the only means of relief were political.

Politics being such a large part of the settlers' lives, that was the natural and proper angle to take to obtain employment. Homesteader Andy Wolfe felt he was supplanted in his job at the co-op farm because others "was a little bit better connected with Bushrod Grimes," and he should have known what he was saying, as he was first hired in like manner.[182] Full-time, secure employment was scarce, and the homesteaders watched for openings and resented any "outsiders" being brought on. Leslie Bucklew complained to the *Pittsburgh Sun Telegraph* in 1935 that "they've loaded up the administrative offices with a lot of political hacks and not one of our girls can get jobs even as stenographers."[183]

The Homesteaders Club came to have one very important function—it was a way to collectively organize for purposes of political agitation, "to bring pressure to bear for something."[184] Andy Wolfe recalled in 1987 how it worked. "[We'd] go in there and if there was anything difficult, we'd go in and discuss and 'course a committee was formed to approach the officials of the government."[185] The settlers from the first took this route. In October 1933, a group of homesteaders' wives wrote to Eleanor Roosevelt saying "we do not want to ask anything," then added a litany of requests for how they would like their future homes to be furnished, for indoor plumbing, living rooms, and "a large kitchen."[186]

The efforts at agitation seemed to have been concentrated above all on jobs and wages. In March 1936, the homesteaders voted to ask West Virginia Senator Rush Holt to launch an investigation of Arthurdale concerning "wage discrepancies," and they hoped "to let the proper government official know that we are not receiving sufficient money to live up to the standard of living that has been set for us."[187] As late as October 1940, the Homesteaders' Club wrote to J. O. Walker that "we, the homesteaders, feel that the cut in wages we received a year ago should be restored."[188]

Wages, though, came from jobs, and their scarcity had the homesteaders scrounging for them where they could, even writing to Eleanor Roosevelt that "many jobs in the construction department on this project return a bigger monthly wage, jobs homesteaders could be doing, but which they are not permitted to do."[189] A constant need to agitate for both the petty and the important defined much of the interaction of the homesteaders with the federal bureaucracy, and as the settlers had so little freedom to make their own decisions, it was inevitable that Clapp, as early as January 1936, was making note of "habits of idleness and desultory work patterns" among the project's young adults.[190]

This was seconded in the worries of a mother who wrote in her diary in 1937 that "some people say they are done with hard work forever—the government can keep them," and she made efforts to see that her children did not "get in with that crowd that drinks and boasts about not working."[191]

By 1939, with the collective experiments obvious money pits, work still scarce, and distant bureaucrats still in charge, "a study of the reactions of the young people tells something of the philosophy of their elders." The authors of the report claimed the "present background of uncertainty and unrest"[192] had filtered down into the children, and "A casual observer in the Arthurdale High School is aware of an absence of physical vitality and mental aggressiveness . . . there is no great amount of initiative on the part of the students, and there is a general air of indifference."[193]

Being on the receiving end of the public till had an effect on the recipients. In 1930s America, there was a definite stigma attached to those getting public money. One homesteader remembered: "I recall that I felt a little inferior to other people . . . I guess maybe you thought that you were kind of on welfare or something."[194] But far more insidious than the feeling of shame was welfare's long-term effect—the longer any man remained on it, the stronger the dependency it will breed within him. Doubtless there were instances of this in the town; homesteader Luther Zinn recalled, "Some wanted everything given to them."[195] One historian even claims "when their school bus broke down, the homesteaders actually sent it to the White House garage for repairs."[196]

As the focal point of many a request for help, Eleanor Roosevelt was subjected to a stream of pleas.[197] Although the homesteaders may have done this out of habit, she was an easy means to cut through the endless red tape. While she was blessed with patience, even she was moved to consternation as "they seemed to feel the solution to all their problems was to turn to government"[198]; the First Lady did not understand that during Arthurdale's time under federal control, turning to government *was* the solution, and the only one at that, to all the homesteaders' problems.

Wilson believed "in communities where substantial numbers of citizens look elsewhere for salvation, self-government ceases."[199] There was no self-government in Arthurdale. In March 1940, *Harper's Magazine* sent a reporter to check up on the town and he noted, "[L]ife under paternalism like that has its effect, and it is not altogether salutary. It is perhaps an understatement to say that it saps initiative."[200] Everything had devolved, in the writer's opinion, into "an attitude of grateful resignation."[201]

A report from 1940 recorded "few outsiders can realize the cumulative effect" of living under the control of others, with plans "completely imposed from above, and repeatedly altered."[202] The New American who emerged from Arthurdale was the same one who had always emerged from such collectivist ventures. He can been seen in Jamestown, Plymouth Rock, and Durham and Delhi and moves about in a group, but one of a number of bickering cliques, each and all resentful and suspicious of themselves and others.

Rather than a vastly improved human being striding forth, all the experiment of the back-to-the-landers had delivered were jealous cliques, passive dependency, and a broken-down school bus.

Chapter 8

At Long Last, Arcadia

I believe Arthurdale has a future. It depends on us people here.
—William McNelis, Arthurdale homesteader (1942)[1]

If you approach Arthurdale from the north, coming down from the I-68 Interstate along Route 7, you will twist up the mountains around curves and through a number of hard-looking towns. As always, a Dairy Queen appears around one corner, a reminder that even in Appalachia you are still in America.

Just north of Arthurdale, you drive through Reedsville and turn south on Route 92, crest a hill, and now you see it laid out in front of you; it is a decided change from all you have just driven through. Say what you will about government incompetence—the town is nicely laid out; my wife immediately crowned it "pretty." Unlike the tired miners' shacks that squat beside the mountain roads behind you, the homes here are painted white and pleasing to look at, separated from each other by well-manicured lawns and small fields.

As you enter the town, you pass the site of the old factory buildings, unseen from the road and off to the right. A bit farther on and to your left appears Elsie Clapp's school complex, its original buildings all long abandoned but one—the school gymnasium where FDR and Eleanor Roosevelt once gave a decade plus of high school commencement addresses. The floor of its basketball court still gleams.

Drive a bit deeper into Arthurdale and you see a stone Presbyterian church to your left, followed by the inn. Across the street on your right lies the town center. For decades after the federal withdrawal, the complex sat abandoned to the elements, slowly rotting. Now the community center stands well maintained, as do the surviving auxiliary buildings erected around it. The town center is now the heart of the Arthurdale museum.

The Forge and Administration building appear as they did during the New Deal, likewise the old co-op gas station. Other sections of the original center, such as the general store where Andy Wolfe once clerked, are long gone, lost to fire or neglect. The town today has about it an air of not wealth but contentment. But that is now. In 1942, if a news reporter is to be believed, the town presented a different picture. "The houses look dingy and are in need of paint . . . the dirt roads are quagmires."[2] It was wartime.

Since the late 1930s, the initial energy of the New Deal had been dissipating[3] into a hardened bureaucratic shell. With the fires of true belief dimmed and the nation needing to fund a war, the more obvious policy blunders were coming under an increasingly critical eye—and Arthurdale was at the top of the list. By 1943, even Calvin B. Baldwin (head of the Farm Security Administration [FSA]) was telling Congress that the resettlement colonies should be released into the wild, so to speak.[4] The process of selling off the homesteads was put into high gear.

After all the embarrassment, and the fact that the loss to taxpayers was almost total, those responsible for Arthurdale had one concern above all in mind that they communicated to Milford Mott, the town's last community manager, in very clear terms: "For heaven's sake, please keep us out of the press." They need not have worried, though; except for a brief flurry of snide obituaries in a few newspapers, the American public had moved on.

The liquidation process was already under way by early 1942.[5] The settlers were informed they were to sign a purchase contract or give up their homestead.[6] It should have come as no surprise; the administrators had been telegraphing their intentions to liquidate the project for some time. Homesteader Alice Whittaker believed that "it was sort of a gradual thing that I think they (the other homesteaders) knew it was coming."[7]

By the time of their sale, the average appraised value of a home in Arthurdale was $6,000.[8] Dividing the total cost of the entire town among the homesteads equally, it was estimated that each had cost an average of around $16,600 to build.[9] They were sold to the homesteaders at prices ranging from $750 to $1,249.[10] The inn and the three factory buildings were sold to a Baltimore furniture manufacturer. Four of the school buildings were deeded over to the Preston County Board of Education for $1 (the nursery and elementary schools, made over for war production, were sold to a Philadelphia manufacturer after the conflict ended), the dairy and general farms were sold to West Virginia University for $1, and all undeveloped land was turned over to the Department of Agriculture.[11] Come April 1947, everything had been sold off, and all federal employees withdrawn from Arthurdale.[12] It was over.

The actual cost of the project is impossible to determine; the tally of destruction is never to be known with certainty. The FSA listed the total cost for Arthurdale at $2,775,276, and that was on October 31, 1937.[13] Five years later, they had the accumulated costs of Arthurdale at $2,744,724.[14]

The FSA estimated an 87 percent loss.[15] In 1942, the *Chicago Daily Tribune* cited $2,646,000 as the total cost of the town's construction,[16] and if we consider the value of a 1937 U.S. dollar versus that of a 1947 U.S. dollar, each house at Arthurdale cost about $25,706,[17] so the actual loss to taxpayers was likely higher than any calculation extant. No one will ever know the true cost, in dollars and cents, of the Arthurdale experiment. It is best to just take the word of historian Dr. Paul Conkin that Arthurdale "resulted in a tremendous loss"[18] and leave it at that. There is no way, either, to measure the unseen: the economic costs of the redistributions to Arthurdale not directly before our eyes. In those we must include, for example, in the unseen cost of Arthurdale's co-op tractor factory the 200 Duplex Machinery Company men thrown onto the bread line by it. Doubtless, there were others.

Even with the sale of the homesteads to the settlers, the bureaucrats did not wish to let go; they still wished for the resettled to conduct subsistence farming and, above all, not sell "their" homes for a profit.[19] The "sales" contracts to the homesteaders, as first offered in 1942, were funded for 40 years at 3 percent[20] and called quitclaim deeds. The contracts took a page from the coal company sharpies of older days (who had snapped up land from the farmers of Scotts Run) and reserved all mineral rights to the federal authorities. Settlers were not permitted to sell or lease the property without the authorities' consent, and combined with other conditions the contracts "left the client completely under FSA supervision."[21] In 1944, Congress struck down all restrictions in the sales contracts, granting homesteaders unfettered ownership of their property.[22]

Looking back, if there is one incident at Arthurdale about which those resettled agree almost without exception, it was that the price at which they were offered their homes was extremely generous, to say the least. It was determined by a number of factors, the overriding one being each homesteader's ability to afford it. Any rent the people had paid in the years leading up to the liquidation was deducted from the final sales price,[23] pushing an already affordable price into fire-sale territory. Bertie Swick, who along with her husband, Jacob, and their two children were one of the first to move onto the project, declared that the sale was effected at "what I'd say a very low price."[24] Andy Wolfe, also one of the very first resettled, flat-out opined, "I do know one thing that I didn't buy it, they gave it to me. I'll say it that way."[25]

It was the final culmination of years of struggle. Even as late as 1941—a full eight years after ground was broken on the project— federal authorities were still trying to determine the price and conditions under which they would allow the homesteaders to be granted ownership.[26] After all was said and done, when cooler heads in Congress prevailed, the remnants of the back-to-the-landers had to drop all restrictions on ownership, throw overboard all their dreams to retain control of the settlers' lives, and simply walk away. Alice Whittaker remembered, "My parents were really elated . . . you know they really owned their property now."[27] Finally, at last, the homesteaders had what they had always desired above all: a place to call home.

The worries of government officials that the resettled, once given title to the homes, would turn into dreaded speculators sell out, and pocket the money were, in the case of Arthurdale, largely unfounded.[28] Doubtless a few did, and Andy Wolfe excoriated them: "Those people didn't appreciate what the government did for them—to my notion."[29] Seventy-five years on, all the original adult homesteaders but two had died, but go to Arthurdale and you will have no trouble locating their children and grandchildren. Where once the neighborhood rang with the shouts of Joseph and Nellie McLaughlin's children, you will now find the family of Robert McLaughlin Jr., their grandson, occupying the very same home.

Elwood Mead, who had striven mightily for just that outcome, would have been pleased as punch.

The Sleep of the Just

You can't tell anybody that grew up in Arthurdale that it was a failure. No, it was our savior.
                        —Glenna Williams, Arthurdale homesteader[30]

Dr. John Fullmer, whose parents were resettled in the town during 1935, argues, "I feel good about what Arthurdale did for the people of Arthurdale."[31] Every government program has, by its very nature, winners and losers. Some could point to the low sales price offered to the resettled and the lavish subsidization of their lives while under federal control to make the claim that they were undoubted winners from the New Deal's redistribution of wealth. On the face of it, that claim is indisputable. Yet in a 1942 news article, one homesteader, O. C. Brown, when asked about the offered price of his home, responded, "Dirt cheap? Not at all, when you look into it."[32] There is something to be said for his take on the matter.

Looked at more broadly, beyond the simple matter of dollars and cents, I would agree with Brown. The homesteaders paid a steep price for their homes; in fact, we all did. Although they were undoubtedly better off than in the coal camps in material terms, life on the resettlement projects was worse in terms of the lack of independence from outside control. With the intimate meddling into their very personal lives, in the matter of personal independence those resettled into Arthurdale took a decided step down. The reaction of many to the federal withdrawal from Arthurdale was relief—they finally could begin to get on with their own lives, in their own way. Homesteader Robert Day was of the opinion that "[i]t's always good to see rules and regulations are being eliminated where you can go ahead and do things on your own and enjoy your freedom."[33]

Numerous reports, not only from hostile pressmen but also contained in federal reports and internal memos, pointed again and again to widespread disillusionment and bitterness among the homesteaders while under federal control. Partly this was due to a simple clash of desires. While the intellectuals, in their tweeds and bow ties, wished for the people at Arthurdale to embrace their ideals and become what they considered new, improved human beings, the resettled were looking for nothing more than a safe port from the Depression's storm where they could raise their children, own a home on a bit of land, and otherwise be left alone. The planners laid out a detailed course of action for people they had nothing in common with; whom they also just simply did not understand.

The resettled deeply appreciated the bounty turned over to them but they were men, and like all men were possessed of pride. A 1936 report commissioned by the federal government concluded of those at Arthurdale: "[H]owever grateful they may be for what has been done for them, they would prefer the opportunity to make their own way."[34] Instead of a simple helping hand up, the settlers found that they were considered—and treated like—helpless children in need of supervision and control. It is unnecessary to ask how the members of the Homesteaders Club, men with children of their own, felt when they had to go to Elsie Clapp, the school principal, and ask permission to hold a beer and oyster party, or ask how they must have felt when she said no.

Arthurdale is a story with no hero. Although the policy prescriptions of the subsistence homestead boosters ran roughshod over the rule of law, Clapp remarked of the homesteaders, hungry and desperate not two years prior, that "the Constitution, the Supreme Court, fascism, are outside their concern at all."[35] The former were hungry for power, the latter were simply hungry. The behavior of the former is unforgivable; the behavior of the latter, while sad, is completely understandable.

Those resettled at Arthurdale cannot be blamed for jumping at the chance to improve their families' circumstances, to go from the harrowing existence of a coal-mining camp to a world of plenty—at least to do so would require a harder heart than I possess. One resident was exuberant to escape, claiming "we can have a cow if we make money enough and they say we can have a Ford, too."[36] Years later Bertie Swick remembered that "we came because we wanted a better place for our family to grow up,"[37] and who can hold that against any of them?

Glenda (Stump) McLaughlin stated the matter simply: "Those who were able to move there, why wouldn't they have wanted to?"[38] Julia Perry recalled, "[T]hose were some of the best years of our lives during very difficult times for so many people in our country."[39] Florence (Groves) Hovatter remarked on how her mother used to say, "[T]his must be what it's like to move into heaven,"[40] a common sentiment among the resettled. To blame any family for making the decision to accept what was offered—and the federal grandees had no legal power to offer it in the first place—is to ask a man to play the hero. Most men are not heroes, and any parent, listening to their hungry children crying themselves to sleep at night will grasp at any chance to ameliorate their plight. Who can cast a stone at all the parents who accepted the chance to move into Arthurdale?

Eleanor Roosevelt remarked of them, "The people who moved into Arthurdale had many new things to learn; many new experiences to encounter; many things to forget, before life could become normal to them." Once the experiment was terminated and they were left alone, life went on for the people at Arthurdale. No longer the care and concern of those in faraway Washington, the seasons still changed, and the children of the resettled began to scatter across the nation. Those who remained behind developed an extreme aversion to any outside control—the postwar attempts to incorporate the town were voted down[41] out of fear of taxes and restrictions on the use of their property.[42] The age-old desire of Americans for "land and little control over how they settled it"[43] was, despite all the wealth and effort spent on the homesteaders, still deeply ingrained within them.

During the time when the project was being shut down, the boys began to return home from the war and, in an amazing feat of pure luck, every single soldier from Arthurdale came back alive. Yet death has a firm ally in time. The swimming hole left behind by the nearby strip-mining operation, so beloved of the town children, would claim one of them. When the war stoked a renewed demand for coal, the men began to flow back to the mines and the danger of the job. Edson McClain, who played clarinet in the Arthurdale band, would die in a 1942 mine explosion that claimed over 50 others. Seven months later, his wife would bear a daughter who would never meet the man whose name she bears.[44]

Now on their own, the people of the town did what they had to in order to hold onto their homes. Human nature being what it is, there were some who had grown used to being taken care of[45]—that kind quickly left. In the end, the settlers in Arthurdale were lucky in escaping the debilitating effects of public welfare before it could become too deeply ingrained within them or their children. One homesteader reminisced years after about it: "[T]he older people remembered and their children came up under the memories of the former years."[46] Those older people who remembered what it was like to live on your own terms, without any outside direction, were critical in pulling the town out of the sullen apathy it had been cast into.

The mines were a well-paid option for some of the men, and the irony of commuting from Arthurdale back to the Scotts Run mines was not lost on them.[47] James Fullmer would go one better and open up his own mine,[48] while Ellen Estep's husband commuted to the Pittsburgh steel mills, coming home on weekends.[49] Until he was able to find a job in Morgantown Joseph McLaughlin would commute to Virginia, also coming home on weekends.[50] Following the death of FDR in 1944, much of the New Deal was dismantled, and the economy, vastly more free, finally began to recover. In the end, those who stayed did so because they wished to; they had developed a bond with the area and their neighbors.

The decision as to whom to people the town with, while doubtless racist toward nonwhites and elitist toward all, succeeded admirably in collecting the cream off the top of the coal camp population. The records strongly hint that Bushrod Grimes, completely outside the approved channels of a bureaucracy that was still too new and porous to prevent it, did much to get the families he knew and respected from his days working in the camps into a home at Arthurdale. His knowledge of the camp populations were an invaluable contribution to the makeup of the town; like a veteran beat cop, he knew all the ne'er-do-wells to avoid choosing.[51]

In their time, the overwhelming majority of the people who populated the project may have been poor whites, but I would bet money that they were never poor white trash. They were overwhelmingly decent, churchgoing, and—most important—family oriented.

Those virtues were their saving grace.

The End and the Beginning

I think Mrs. Roosevelt—President Roosevelt, too—would have been really proud if they could come back now . . . to know that we are still here.

—Alice Whittaker, Arthurdale homesteader (1991)[52]

It had taken the townspeople years of stillborn efforts, pinching pennies, and ardent prayer, but finally the church had been completed. Sitting just south of Elsie Clapp's old school complex, the stone exterior was cut and erected by the people themselves. They had built the church with their own hands, like all of the original buildings in Arthurdale, and this time with their own time and money.[53] Standing before a backdrop of woods, the church exudes the care and effort that went into it. Even more so than the finest stone Wagner house, it is the most beautiful structure in the town. Its dedication ceremony would mark the last time Eleanor Roosevelt would visit Arthurdale.

The passage of time had taken a toll on her health, and while she visited Arthurdale with less frequency than in the past, she always managed to return.[54] Advanced age now prevented her from traveling

much, a distinct change to her accustomed lifestyle of constant movement. From the time that her husband had reached the pinnacle of
power, Eleanor Roosevelt became an international political player
in her own right. Yet for all her worldliness and the rarefied air that
was her natural milieu, she never forgot the people of Arthurdale.

She had always gone the extra mile for them, always turned in
whatever effort was required to help see them through. With her
unblemished record of care for them and her having been their guardian
angel in the struggles against an imposing bureaucracy, it was only
natural for the townspeople to ask her to give the dedication address
for their newly built Presbyterian church, and it was only natural for
her to accept. It was September 1960.

Jennings Randolph, now a member of the Senate, introduced Mrs.
Roosevelt to the assembled worshipers.[55] A local businessman named
J. W. Ruby owned the inn and invited her to stay in the exact same
room as she had done so many times in years past.[56] It was to be one
final visit to say good-bye to old friends and look about at the result
of all she and her fellows had worked for. She returned to her New
York estate (Val-Kill) the next day and would never again set eyes on
Arthurdale. Eleanor Roosevelt died in New York City on November
7, 1962.

To this day, the memory of her burns bright in Arthurdale, and
every year the townsfolk hold a New Deal Festival that, despite its
name, is more a celebration of her than anything else. Although never
a homesteader herself, Eleanor Roosevelt is, in their hearts, as much a
native of Arthurdale as any original settler.

When the project was terminated and the property returned to
private ownership, she had made a vow that she would not forget
them—it was a promise she kept. Until her death, a stream of young
men and women from Arthurdale would obtain jobs in Washington,
all with her help. Henry DeGolyer, whose sister Eleanor was named in
the First Lady's honor, rose within the ranks of NASA to become the
chief accountant for the entire agency. He first entered its halls with
the help of the first couple.[57]

Mrs. Roosevelt kept a personal list of all the Arthurdale people she
had placed into the Washington orbit and had them to the White House
for dinners and other occasions. James McNelis recalls being invited to

a reception for the Queen of England.[58] Where once he had been an awkward boy dressed in dirty overalls who danced the Virginia Reel with the First Lady, he now dined confidently on presidential china.[59] Another child of Arthurdale, James Davis, ate at the White House "about three times" during his tenure in DC.[60] They were not alone. Every year, Mrs. Roosevelt would have the entire graduating class from Arthurdale, along with the teachers, over for a White House luncheon.[61]

The look of the town itself has changed over time as more people have moved in, plots were subdivided, and homes were expanded. Arthurdale is now, for the most part, a bedroom community for nearby Morgantown and West Virginia University. In the early 1990s, the last of its roads were finally paved. The number of homes within the original area has about doubled, and many of the Hodgson and Wagners are customized to such an extent as to be barely recognizable. This last was intentional, as a 1933 Division of Subsistence Homesteads memo promised that "[h]ouses are planned so that they may be conveniently expanded without destroying the design of the original unit."[62]

At the core of Arthurdale, as in any town, is a group of civic-minded citizens. Not political hucksters with the easy promises and hearty handshakes, but ones who volunteer their own time and money for the common good, ones you find manning the tables at the bake sales and staffing the local museum on weekends. Due to its unique history, Arthurdale has a notably large and active core. In 1985, under the leadership of Glenna Williams (whose father used to hold Sunday school on his front lawn), they formed Arthurdale Heritage[63] and tasked themselves with repairing and maintaining all the long-dormant, rotted community buildings. Using nothing but volunteer labor and what little money they could scrounge up, they had done such a remarkable job within five years that the town was entered into the National Register of Historic Places.[64]

Even more important than the preservation of the dilapidated community buildings, the Arthurdale Heritage Foundation sought to preserve the memory of the town and conducted a series of interviews with some of Arthurdale's original settlers (those first 50 moved into the Hodgsons in June of 1934) along with others from the following two waves. Almost all the interviewed are now deceased, but the audiotapes show that despite all the ideas and money burned in the effort, the resettled do not come across as superhuman New Americans, just as merely human. To a stranger listening to these homesteaders, what is notable is the humility in their words and tone; they were light-years away from the arrogance of those political grandees who wished to remake them into something they never were and never wanted to be.

Arthurdale means so much to the people who live there not because of any historic place it holds in the annals of American history but because of the memories it holds in the annals of their own personal histories. Those interviewed, just like everyone else, order their memories around life-changing events, most of them social—births, deaths, marriages, the times shared with neighbors, the banding together of the people from a group of homesteaders into neighbors, friends, and in some cases spouses. Although Elwood Mead and others believed it possible for proper cooperation and town pride to come about only under expert direction through collectively organized clubs, human beings are by nature social creatures, and the people of Arthurdale did very well without them. In the end, Arthurdale did not make these people; these people made Arthurdale.

The people who live there today have a sense of pride in Arthurdale that stems in part from all that took place there in the context of history, but mostly for the fact that it is home, the place where their families were raised and, in many cases, blossomed.* Although they are grateful for the chance Arthurdale afforded them, in the end they made it, and continue to make it, under their own steam.

Years after the frenzy had calmed, a homesteader named Elma Martin was asked her thoughts on whether Arthurdale was a success. She gave the only accurate reply to the question that is possible: "Part of it was and part of it wasn't."[65] The history of Arthurdale falls into two distinct parts—its time under federal control and its time under the peoples', pre- and post-1947.

Those resettled into the town were not alone in how they responded to communal life—the archives are full of observations on how other

---

*In the case of original settlers Clarence and Elnora DeGolyer, they *really* blossomed. Their 11 children multiplied into 120 descendants.

homesteaders in other resettlement projects responded to the political control. There is a sameness about those observations that speaks not only to the mind-set of the average rural dweller in 1930s America but also to the timeless, donkey-like stubbornness of human nature. How many of the powerful throughout time have tried to bend it to their hopes and dreams, all for naught?

In late 1935, Mary Meek Atkeson, a native of Preston County, wrote for the magazine *Country Gentleman* about Arthurdale and the chaos it was experiencing. Over a decade prior to the federals' decision to withdraw, she provided what would turn out to be the perfect solution for the town: "It's success in the coming years is likely to be brought about, not by importing more and more experts to study its problems, but by turning its management back to the mountaineers."[66]

Although Arthurdale is a story with no hero, it is not a story devoid of hope, for it was the very people resettled into the town—looked down on as helpless, dirt poor, and ignorant by the politically powerful who put them there—who made a successful go of it. Where Eleanor Roosevelt, M. L. Wilson, FDR, and Rexford Tugwell, despite the boundless wealth at their disposal and all the academic credentials on their walls, proved to be utter, bumbling failures, the people themselves succeeded. Despite the high-sounding speeches, can't-miss ideas, and well-funded programs that the federal boosters could provide, what was needed to make a success of the town, to make it a sustainable, desirable place to live, was for the elite simply to go away.

So while the people of Arthurdale may host a New Deal festival each year in memory of Eleanor Roosevelt, and although they may honor her above all, it is more fitting that they should look about at each other and honor themselves.

The success of Arthurdale is their story, and no one else's.

Epilogue:
To the Victor, the Spoils

It is not possible to experiment with a society and just drop the experiment whenever we choose. The experiment enters the life of the society and can never be got out again.
—Professor William Graham Sumner (1840–1910)[1]

World War II had fallen upon the American people, and by then Arthurdale had slipped into the quiet anonymity from which it has never escaped. The little mountain town was pushed to the bottom of America's mental toy chest; the nation now worried over the great struggle, not "Eleanor's pet project." Treated for the most part as an embarrassment, it rested deep within the National Housing Agency, a subsection of the Federal Public Housing

193

Authority—its final home.[2] The fires of first love faded and the initial enthusiasm now long gone, Arthurdale was already forgotten. No longer did hordes of tourists drive up the mountain roads to see the dawning of a new way of life, or strangers peek in at windows to ask some fool question.

War grants to some its illusion of beneficence, and as during World War I, the hyperdemand to feed World War II had West Virginia manic busy; jobs were easy to find for the homesteaders, even more so as the induction of 121 of its young men into the military further exacerbated the sudden labor shortage. With congressional opposition growing against continued funding of the resettlement communities and a steady paycheck at long last delivered to the homesteaders, after nine years it was finally time for the American government to begin its withdrawal from Arthurdale.

In April 1942, the magazine *Nation's Business* ran a hastily timed obituary for the town, "Passing of a Great Blunder," reporting that the Farm Security Administration (FSA)* had announced all the property was to be sold off to private interests and the experiment terminated.[3] It had become official—the acolytes of the back-to-the-land movement had again fallen short; the promised New American had failed to appear. Those resettled into Arthurdale had remained stubbornly human.

The historian Paul Conkin once asked if the entire idea behind the federal subsistence program was up to the task in 1933. "Arthurdale and other homesteads provide no clear answer," he decided, and here I respectfully disagree. Arthurdale and its siblings, and the massive losses they caused for taxpayers, clearly tell that subsistence homesteads were not the answer to alleviate the harsh effects of the Great Depression. In *A Place on Earth*, the 1942 federal study of the subsistence homestead program, the authors concluded that the entire concept "constitutes a flight from the heart of the problem."[4]

Arthurdale is not to be held up for any especial ridicule; all the problems, failures, and bickering among the settlers recorded during its time under federal control were also recorded, to a greater or lesser degree, across all the New Deal resettlement projects,[5] as they have

---

* Arthurdale remained under Farm Security Administration control until October 1942, when it was transferred to the National Housing Agency.

been recorded across all collectivist land settlements throughout our nation's history. This was to be expected, as they each suffered from the same fatal flaw, the one Ebenezer Howard highlighted in 1902 when he observed in his *Garden Cities of Tomorrow*, "Probably the chief cause of failure in former social experiments has been the misconception of the principal element in the problem—human nature itself."[6] This was to have consequences, both immediate and long term. For the immediate, Arthurdale as a subsistence homestead was a failure.

Other warnings, from both historical and contemporary sources, had argued against once more digging up the back-to-the-land idea but they, too, went unheeded by those who created Arthurdale. One, a 1933 speech by Dr. R. W. Murchie, a professor of rural economics, gave a learned rundown of past resettlement colonies and delivered what he felt to be their lesson for policy makers: "Any scheme of extensive land settlement has very slight chance of success; even with expert direction, careful selection, and an elaborate 'after care,' the results obtained are hardly commensurate with the cost."[7]

During 1932, Dr. John D. Black, a noted agricultural economist and friend of M. L. Wilson, testified before a congressional committee in regard to the proposed McFadden resettlement bill. His testimony, which stood out from the others by its calm, erudite manner, concluded that "any sweeping plans for setting up colonies are impractical at this time."[8] He was ignored, and just shy of a decade later, after the squandering of so much of immeasurable value, the Department of Agriculture study reached the exact same conclusion: that "subsistence homesteads do not justify the confidence that many people have placed in them as a relief measure."[9] According to a writer for *Harper's Magazine* in 1940, the town is "chiefly valuable as showing what not to do."[10]

For the people resettled into Arthurdale, the larger picture of the project's sustainability was far less important than the opportunity to get their families out of Scotts Run, to be granted a chance to move their families away from the lowest circle of the Great Depression. The people chosen for Arthurdale had, and their descendants still have to this day, strong feelings of loyalty toward Eleanor and Franklin Roosevelt. It is an undoubted fact that they were plucked out of crushing poverty and placed into Arthurdale by presidential edict—the idea of subsistence homesteads was, in the words of FDR himself, "one of my own pet children."[11] For that, they feel a gratitude that is completely understandable.

Yet to call Arthurdale "charity" would be incorrect. Although Glenna Williams years after spoke of how "the government provided" everything at Arthurdale,[12] it is important to remember that "the government" did no such thing. The taxpayers provided, and none was *asked* to provide the funds to build the town, any more than Thomas Jefferson would have *asked* his slaves to bring in the crops. Whatever the superficial appearance may be, without the act of voluntary giving it is not charity.

There is no getting past the point that Arthurdale, when you look below the surface, produced results that were, in the prophetic words of Professor Murchie, hardly commensurate with the costs. There is no arguing that the material goods provided to those chosen for Arthurdale lifted them out of dire straits, yet, like everything in life, it came at a cost, one not restricted just to those directly involved but spread across the nation and down through time.

The future seeds of what America has become were first planted at Arthurdale. Although we can take lessons from all that happened, 75 years later, what is done is done, and it is far too late for tears.

Collective Dispossession

We made so many mistakes here.
            —Eleanor Roosevelt on Arthurdale (1960)[13]

The reasons for the failure of Arthurdale and the other colonies were legion, yet they all were birthed from a common source. The colonies' founders had tasked themselves with an impossible mission—to change human nature—and how does one go about such a thing? As for the practical nuts and bolts of the matter, the dollars and cents, the same conclusion reached by the California State Land Settlement Board regarding the collapse of the Elwood Mead's homestead at Delhi can be leveled at those who ran Arthurdale: "The colony was managed by inexperienced men of academic type, to whom the public trough is a free institution, economy and practical judgment were lost sight of."[14]

The people who managed the town's affairs and the blundering circus their efforts presented shocked witnesses and homesteaders alike. They had never before seen Keynesian pump priming in the flesh and had yet to become inculcated with the view of its necessity. "The idea of mixing government and business was not strictly new, but it would still be novel, in 1933,"[15] and the blatant, prodigious waste of public money in a time of economic distress was a new, peculiar thing to American eyes. The press in particular took notice.

For the back-to-the-land disciple, the question as to whether these experiments were self-sustaining was not high at all on the list of important things to consider. Franklin Howe demanded that "we must think more of man and less of wealth,"[16] and the colonies were designed "to change a society in which emphasis is placed upon money into a society in which emphasis would be placed upon ideals."[17] With such a mindset, heavy financial losses were certain.

In response to the articles and broadcasts that exposed their incompetence, those who administered Arthurdale clamped down on the release of information to the press. By 1936, a wall of bureaucratic silence began to be erected against unfriendly news reporters, declared a column in Nation's Business.[18] Three years later, the same reporter was investigating Arthurdale again and revealed to Bushrod Grimes that "they [FSA officials] just don't seem to want anybody to know what is going on—at least when the facts are not flattering to the project."[19] The monthly reports from the FSA to FDR outlining the state of each resettlement project were quickly stamped "confidential."

Some of the reasons for the collapse of Arthurdale as a subsistence homestead are obvious, like the part of an iceberg visible above the ocean's surface. For instance, that the income to be earned from the available jobs could never enable the homesteaders to pay for all that was provided is the part we can see. But there was far more to it than that. Four decades on, it was written by the historian Bruce Beezer, "as the newness wore off and no real changes seemed to happen, the true nature of Arthurdale became clear; it was an artificial community created on a hope to regain the past."[20]

It was the hubris and arrogance of those who pushed things along, their utter disdain for individual rights and the rule of law combined with a belief that they could improve on human nature itself; those were what the iceberg was mostly composed of and hidden beneath the waves. There was the true source of its danger. It produced the perfect mind-set to grow the blinders necessary to keep the fanatic from opening his eyes to the danger his actions introduced into the body politic.

The willful delusions of the back-to-the-landers never dimmed, before, during, or after the entire experiment. From M. L. Wilson insisting in 1933 that "there is little light thus far that can be shed on many of the problems" sure to arise from Arthurdale,[21] despite numerous historical examples (not to mention his own personal experience) that he could have drawn on, to Rexford Tugwell in 1958, claiming that of the millions loaned by the Resettlement Administration, "the government got almost all of it back,"[22] despite the massive, across-the-board losses sustained throughout the life of the homesteads, neither facts nor figures could penetrate their armor, something contemporaries made repeated note of.[23]

Their all-encompassing arrogance was perfectly encapsulated in a speech Wilson delivered in November 1934. He spoke approvingly of a notion held by one school of "social philosophers" (college professors) who believed America to be in such perilous straits "through lack of appreciation of science," as embodied by all those blessed enough to have attended college. To turn America back to the path of sustainable prosperity required "social invention of a high order," and Wilson wondered aloud about the rising "super-governmental economic and social intelligence" they were building to show the way forward.[24] The rare glimpse of such "super-governmental" intelligence would deliver ludicrous spectacles such as the findings of a 1937 committee organized by FDR and tasked to study Arthurdale; its report declared that 58.79 percent of each homestead's income must be derived from industrial employment, their guesswork gussied up to the one hundredth decimal.[25]

The economic platform of the back-to-the landers consisted of a self-righteous, moralistic disdain for laissez-faire combined with a desire to restrict production and raise prices. The entire idea of encouraging handicrafts on the subsistence homesteads was to turn the resettled away from the factory system of mass production and become islands of economic autarky.[26] All the back-to-the-landers were possessed by a false memory of a golden era that America had once enjoyed "before the period of the great industrial city," the rise of which they declared had removed economic security and leisure time from the common man's life.[27]

When the men of Arthurdale's Mountaineer Craftsmen's Cooperative Association gratefully abandoned the manual production of furniture for higher-paying factory jobs elsewhere, it made Clarence Pickett "ask questions about our civilization."[28] He, like all his fellows, failed to understand that mass production of goods is production for the masses, that its economy of scale makes possible the lower costs of production and hence lower prices for the working masses, that it is the very division of labor they wished to do away with that makes possible a higher standard of living. Pickett's reaction to the homesteaders' desire to improve their lives spoke not only to how ignorant he and his fellows were of basic economic principles but to how disconnected they were from the daily experience and desires of their fellow citizens. In Pickett's case, he was a decent man and his heart was in the right place; his head was not.

At the root of the financial disaster experienced on all the New Deal resettlement projects was the institutional refusal to come to terms with humanity's natural possessiveness, our ingrained attachment toward and love of personal property. The New Americans they were striving to create had no such "selfish" motives and would happily work for the "common good," content with whatever proceeds of their labor they would be given leave to keep. Productivity will collapse in the absence of clearly defined (and protected) property rights, and collapse it did on all the cooperative resettlements.

From the get-go, those resettled bitterly fought to take possession of their homesteads and to be paid for their labor in a manner both fair and easily understood; no amount of prodding, pleading, and "education" could change this.[29] Even as early as 1934, newspaper reports from Arthurdale made note of the "possessive spirit of the homesteaders, already feeling that the land and homesteads are theirs."[30] The Resettlement Administration (RA) expected hardy independent-minded yeomen farmers to emerge from a world where they had been dispossessed of all property—the exact same error that Elwood Mead had blundered into at Durham and Delhi. The RA's refusal to allow unhindered ownership of the homesteads, all the while insisting that the resettled behave as if they owed what they clearly did not, would cause much resentment and disillusionment for all parties concerned.[31]

According to the conclusions of *A Place on Earth*, "a great wariness should be present to prevent the imposition of community houses and cooperative enterprises,"[32] something that should have been known already with the disastrous example given by reports of past collectivist settlements sitting on the library shelves. Yet at Arthurdale, too, "a lot of the work was done in common,"[33] a form of organization that encouraged idleness and led to endless bickering among the homesteaders as to the division of shares.[34]

As in all past collective efforts, "the ambitious settler did not like the manner in which the less ambitious settler worked";[35] as early as July 1935, the idea of communally farmed land was looked down on by homesteaders at Arthurdale, who were glad "to be managing their own land and not getting confused about shares in labor and produce on community land"[36] once the practice was ended. One later explained to a reporter that "they used to try to make us share up around here but there were too many loafers trying to live off the rest of us."[37]

The promoters of Arthurdale themselves had a distain for profit, their laudable disregard for the materialistic buttressed by the fact it wasn't their money they were squandering. It was easy for Elwood Mead to write in a paper published just after World War I: "In land settlement carried on as a public matter, profits from land sales are made secondary to rural progress,"[38] and that attitude on the matter held fast 17 years later, when an RA official assured the First Lady, "[O]bviously the government does not want to or should not make a profit on the homesteaders."[39] With this sort of mind-set and nothing (for them) to lose, the losses piled up.

In a 1958 talk that was more sermon than speech, Rexford Tugwell defended the resettlement colonies' lavish nature from a position of moral superiority versus the businessman. "We provided sewer and water systems, schools, parks, and other utilities. No speculator did any of those things; in his projects the home buyer had to expect that his house would begin to fall apart in a few years."[40] All Tugwell had to do to disabuse himself of such a delusion was speak to Bushrod Grimes concerning his father, the private developer James F. Grimes. There is much to admire about the life of the elder Grimes.

When he died in January 1916, the community newspaper from the area he developed—Knoxville Borough, now Pittsburgh's 30th Ward[41]—eulogized him perfectly: "Infinitely greater than he that taketh a city is he who buildeth one."[42] As his son would decades later, the elder Grimes built homes so "many of whom had lived in the hollows and soot and grime, were enabled to live in healthfulness."[43] A local historian wrote of how he never lost sight of the "cultural and spiritual values in the life of a community."[44] He provided a library out of his own pocket, gave over land for any church his customers (and neighbors) wished to build, and opened his property for public events. The attitude of so many of the back-to-the-land acolytes toward men like him was one of knee-jerk disgust and hostility. Their minds, so deeply prejudiced against the businessman, could not fathom how profit could come about in conjunction with honest endeavor.

It is men like James F. Grimes who built this country and created (rather than destroyed) wealth in the process; he made a profit while making a city. After the end of World War II, it would be private home builders who enabled the urban populations to disperse into the countryside. Businessmen such as William Levitt—the man largely credited with creating America's postwar suburbia—would build homes on a scale that dwarfed the most fevered dreams of any back-to-the-land booster, and they did it profitably, at a fraction of the cost of homes built with public funds.[45] Those responsible for Arthurdale were, in contrast, like a plague of locusts, consuming far more than they gave. For every home built at Arthurdale (at over $16,000 each), how many were prevented from being built elsewhere? When the homesteader Leslie Bucklew told a reporter that "four or five times as many people could be helped for what's being spent here than have or will be,"[46] he knew what he was talking about.

For all their educational pedigrees, the people who put the Arthurdale experiment into operation were spectacularly incompetent, and this, coupled with the fact that their plan, though detailed, was a mishmash of contradictions and wishful thinking only exacerbated the problems. Sadly, because the wealth they were spending with drunken abandon was for the most part not their own, from the very beginning a distinct lack of fiscal discipline resulted in heavy losses for American taxpayers—the tally at Arthurdale alone exceeded $2 million worth of their workdays.[47] At Arthurdale, the return to the taxpayer was pennies on the dollar, at best. What men like James T. Grimes built cost the taxpayer not a dime.

Bushrod Grimes would die on September 1, 1957, and now lies interned in Pittsburgh's South Side Cemetery, about a two-hour drive north of Arthurdale. His grave is unmarked but possible to find. A giant sycamore tree crowns the top of a hill in the graveyard. You walk up until that tree stands above you; now under your feet lies the Grimes family, Bushrod and his wife, Sada, with their daughters Frances and Joanna alongside. What announces their location is that which resides in your head because you know a secret; the tree above you is more than a tree, it's a living gravestone.

From under that tree you can look down from the top of the hill upon Pittsburgh's 30th Ward spread below and see what the Grimes family left behind. Row upon row of two-story homes, each with a front porch for hot summer nights and an attic ready for the mother-in-law; they fall away from you and then rise up again, climbing the far ridge. The Grimes mansion is long gone, but much of what James F. Grimes built is still with us.

You could say that the Grimes family plot is unmarked, but I would argue that notion; their monument is easy to find. Just look for Pittsburgh's 30th Ward, and there you have it.

Flowers for Algernon

The mind is its own place, and in itself
Can make a Heaven of Hell, a Hell of Heaven.
                                        —John Milton, *Paradise Lost*

Judging by their words, actions, and writings, it is proper to say that FDR, Wilson, Tugwell, and all the rest were, at minimum, extreme reactionaries with a deep admiration for Benito Mussolini's fascism and, in the case of Tugwell, Stalin's communism. Although the fact that both Mussolini's Italy and Hitler's Germany also instituted subsistence homesteads during the period of the New Deal does not automatically make FDR and his fellow travelers fascists, it certainly should give one pause.[48] There is no rational argument that the Constitution granted U.S. politicians legal power to create resettlement colonies. The answer as to who was imitating whom is rather obvious.

This is not to say that those who initiated the subsistence homesteads were evil-minded men; the truth is quite the opposite. Yet they had within them a willingness to plant a little evil today in the hopes of growing a better tomorrow. They were practical minded, "scientific" if you will, devoid of principles for guidance, and disdainful of all warnings, as they had been to college. In both their political and economic musings, they did not give more than a passing thought for the long-range consequences of their actions other than to promise their undoubted beneficence. Well-intentioned, noble men (as they fancied themselves) would always run the powerful machinery of state they were erecting.

They had to the man a hatred of individualism, particularly when expressed in the free market, about which they had little good to say. The more honest among them, such as Wilson, took a page from Karl Marx and did not deny that mass production under a free market system had dramatically raised the standard of living for the working masses; they asked instead "whether its fruits have been equitably distributed"[49] and they were certain the answer was no. Through their experiment at Arthurdale, they intended to raise the New American who would adhere to the collectivist values that they so cherished.

Eleanor Roosevelt was open in her admission that Arthurdale was "from the start a laboratory in every way."[50] The back-to-the-landers' answer to the Depression was to show a better way of life, one unconcerned with property past a bare minimum, with people always willing to pitch in to a never-definable "common good." Such Americans would be grown in isolation in West Virginia but soon, with their public release, all society would turn away from the selfishness of individual life.

For years prior they had laid out in somber academic journals this coming new world in loving, if vague, detail. Yet "for all the idealism which went into the creation of Arthurdale, there was very little faith in the people"[51] and even less understanding of human nature. Ebenezer Howard had warned against politically directed land colonies, saying "two chief difficulties appear to present themselves. First, the self-seeking side of man—secondly, his love of independence and of initiative."[52]

Mary Behner, the Scotts Run missionary, lamented the ignorance of local conditions and the arrogance of those outsiders who wished to help. In a 1934 diary entry, she wrote, "What a gulf between class— what little understanding there is. The biggest hindrance to our work is the attitude of people who think they are the very helpers."[53] The *New Republic* was of the opinion that when it came to the resettled miners, "Union Square in New York never understood these people."[54] Arthurdale was an attempt to impose a new way of life and a new set of values onto a people with whom those who drove the experiment had little in common and even less understanding of.[55]

They were convinced that, in the words of Eleanor Roosevelt, whether the people of Scotts Run were aware of it, "they were alive, but they were dead as far as any real living was concerned."[56] It was an elitist attitude that the locals were bound to notice, one of them complaining "they [the government officials] didn't think nobody knowed a thing unless he'd come from a thousand miles away."[57]

In college they earned more than academic credentials—they left with an insufferable arrogance and a deep-seated belief that "science," as embodied by their plans, must be the new guideposts for American society to move forward. In them, America's Age of Planning had arrived. They fancied themselves as all-knowing philosopher kings, failing to realize that any college, being a human institution, is just as stuffed with fools, morons, imbeciles, and the occasional genius as any good corner bar. An overwhelming pride and self-righteousness is the distinguishing mark of their writings and speeches—they exude an unshakable confidence. This, combined with their grasp on political power and the hold that a particularly crackpot scheme had on their minds, would have immense consequences for this country. The future, and our present, belonged to such minds as made Arthurdale.

Since the actual human being encountered at Arthurdale was vastly different from the one they had imagined would be resettled and remolded, the resettlement colonies were subjected to a minute regulation of the day to day in an attempt to get the homesteaders to behave in a manner befitting the New American. One homesteader on Arthurdale complained to the press (anonymously) that "every time you turn around, there's some government regulation staring you in the face,"[58] and toward the end of the experiment, it was recorded that the homesteaders believed that "Arthurdale could have been made a going concern if there had been less meddling and regulation from Washington."[59] Ironically, the end result of Arthurdale was a carbon copy of how Elsie Clapp described life in a coal camp—a place where "no civic responsibility was demanded of them, where they did as they were told and where they bought on credit in company stores."[60]

Although those who promoted Arthurdale sang repeated hosannas to democracy (Clapp insisted a progressive school "grows by concurrence and consent),[61] they specifically attempted to exclude those deemed "extreme or emotional in [their] political or economic beliefs"[62] and to fully convert those resettled to theirs. The progressive school was labeled in *A Place on Earth* as a means "to change the homesteaders' habits of living to conform to what we, not they, think they ought to be."[63]

Wilson claimed that "any plan to be successful must be organized in its local administration so that it works with and not against human nature"[64] but, like most within the movement, he held at the same time a snobbish elitism toward the people resettled. To him, those placed into the town were "helpless in doing anything for themselves . . . when it comes to doing anything besides mining coal."[65] As if they were charged with a town full of children the federal bureaucrats promised to release control over the settlements only "as soon as the ability and responsibility of such groups seemed to be established"[66] as determined by the bureaucrats themselves. J. O. Walker (the director of the RA) and his 20-year-long withdrawal timeline from Arthurdale came from this elitism.

In the beginning, back in 1934, Arthurdale's project manager reported that the people were "thankful for an opportunity to become independent"[67] from the coal company control. Yet within a few years a reporter looked at the political control over the resettled lives and wondered "whether there is great difference between that and the restrictions now placed upon them by life upon the project."[68] In 1934, *Harper's Magazine* decried the position of the homesteaders, isolated and at the mercy of a political entity that provided everything, as "a sheltered peasantry" who, in an ironic twist, now "must accept whatever terms are offered" not from the coal companies but from a new boss: the absentee owners who administered Arthurdale from faraway Washington.[69]

This was but a natural outcome of the ideological mind-set of the back-to-the-landers, with their love of planning. Arthurdale was a planned community, in the 1930s sense of the term,[70] and "those who shrank from the degree of social control necessary to operate the machinery,"[71] such as Wilson and the activist and author Ralph Borsodi were quickly pushed aside. The "arbitrary disposition" of the settlers' lives was a necessary consequence of planning, as "the greater the extension of collective planning, the greater is the likelihood that a larger number of individuals will have to be coerced."[72]

Arthurdale was not unique in this regard, as force was a necessary component of any large-scale resettlement activity, from its very method of funding to its practical application on the ground. Secretary of the Treasury Harold Ickes received a letter from the field in 1934 complaining that certain residents of designated slums, in this case at West Virginia's Montana Mines, did not wish to be resettled, but "with the government on the scene, the independence of those mountaineers was indeed hopeless."[73] Whenever an individual's private property stood in the path of a planned resettlement colony, he would be threatened with eminent domain if he showed any reluctance to sell.[74]

In the 1942 federal study of the subsistence homestead program, it was stated that the wish of the planners for the resettled to engage in subsistence farming (a desire not shared by the resettled themselves) led to "the adoption of restrictions upon the traditional rights of individuals."[75] One later account concluded that "if one were to measure the success of Arthurdale in terms of an experiment to return to people a sense of control over their lives, then it was not a success."[76] The settlers went from cursing the coal operators to cursing the bureaucrats in Washington[77] and the coal operators never meddled in the personal lives of their workers.

Glenna Williams inadvertently touched on this when she said that "they were trying to get a group of people that would make a success of their dream."[78] It was never about those resettled into Arthurdale and their dreams; it was about those with the power to impose their plan and their dreams. In his book on the subsistence homestead program, Dr. Paul Conkin remarked, "Planning itself denotes purposeful endeavor and is, therefore, an activity possible for all men. To plan is to be human."[79] That was an important point to make about Arthurdale. To plan is to be human.

Wilson once asked, "Are we justified in making experiments with . . . family in the same way that we experiment in agriculture with . . . grain, grasses, and the dairy cow?"[80] From the humanist point of view, if Arthurdale was an experiment, what did that make the people placed into it? More to the point from a humanist point of view, what did that make the people who placed them into it? To not allow your fellow human beings to make their own way under their own will is to deny them their humanity, to reduce them to a speck of grain, a blade of grass, or a dairy cow.

In the end, Wilson answered his question in the affirmative, that it was justified to experiment with people. "If and when these planning boards get to the problem of planning our human resources, they will be doing something of tremendous significance to the family"[81] was his opinion. The idea—which lay at the ideological core of men such as Wilson and FDR—that people are a type of raw material to be harnessed by the powerful and directed toward a goal of their choosing was put into action through the subsistence homesteads program, and with the passage of time, that idea has woven itself into the fabric of the American political mind.

That, more than anything, is the tragedy of the Arthurdale experiment.

Back to the Future

At the time of an act, one is not likely to realize its future ramifications.
—Eleanor Roosevelt (1949)[82]

The people who created Arthurdale had a vision, however vague, of what they wanted to create. The town would "provide a prototype for fundamentally re-orientating and reorganizing American life along more humane lines."[83] The First Lady felt the project's value lay "in the suggestions it is making,"[84] and we are what we are today because we followed the suggestions first laid out in Arthurdale.

For all the press and debate sparked by the subsistence program, it was the long-term implications that stood highest in the eyes of those who thought it through, and the welfare state as we know it today arose from Arthurdale and all the other New Deal programs, exactly as its opponents predicted and exactly as its proponents wished.[85] From federal housing projects, federal intrusions into education, and socialized medicine, the seed was first planted at Arthurdale.

Looking at the town, one congressman declared that the "state socialism" taking place "violates the fundamentals of American philosophy and sets a precedent that will hound and plague the country for years to come."[86] The 1930s were a time when many people admired the fascist and communist political models and wished to replicate their methods of "planning" here in America. To a larger extent than they could have hoped, and to a larger extent than the Constitution allows, that wish was granted.[87]

Crises from whatever source are welcome allies to those who wish to grab power. History is replete with such examples, and what happened to the rule of law during the Roosevelt administration is yet one more instance of short-term concerns trumping the long. Secretary of Agriculture Henry A. Wallace observed at the time that "at a certain point of misery and destitution, nations cease to think about liberty and think only about bread."[88] By the time FDR had come to power, America had reached that point. With an economic depression of unprecedented severity and duration laying over their lives, some of our forebears lost any care for such high-sounding principles as the rule of law and the diffusion of power. Security from want was their greatest desire[89] and the political elite of America was only too happy to promise it in exchange for free rein.

Wilson outlined his "three elements" for a strong, stable nation as "security . . . leisure time . . . community."[90] When FDR addressed Congress on January 4, 1935, his declaration "I place the security of men, women, and children of the nation first"[91] was telling. Neither he nor Wilson mentions "freedom" and upholding the rule of law that preserves it. Arthurdale itself was created far outside the bounds of law.

The fact that the imposition of their plans were blocked by the Constitution proved to be of little consequence. Wilson pointed out that "on philosophical grounds [the back-to-the-landers were] willing to pay the price, whatever that may be, for . . . the gradual reorientation and redistribution of the workers."[92] For the supporters of the subsistence homesteads, the rule of law was not a barrier, just a thorn in their side. If it forbade what they wished to do, destroying it was but a small price to pay.

Conkin referred to subsistence homesteads as a "broad program of community building that had no well-defined legal basis,"[93] while *A Place on Earth* states that "established administrative law and procedures had not been devised to serve social enterprises of the sort."[94] During the Great Depression, Congress abdicated its responsibility to keep the executive branch in check—the separation of powers collapsed. The Resettlement Administration was legislated into existence and funded by presidential decree; never at any time did it receive a stamp of approval from Congress.[95] It simply existed, a little army 13,000 strong, a pet project of one man and his close friends.

FDR had asked for "broad executive powers to wage a war against the emergency, as great as the powers that would be given to me if we were in fact invaded by a foreign foe,"[96] and he was granted much of the power he asked for, far more than any president in the country's peacetime history and far more than Congress had any right to grant. Yet at no time did Congress ever grant Roosevelt power to resettle thousands of Americans across the continent, and certainly not to develop "a new way of life." The subsistence homestead amendment was quietly slipped, unread and unknown, onto the enormous National Industrial Recovery Act, which no one read, either, for that matter.

When Congress allowed that amendment to lapse into oblivion, FDR simply went ahead and continued the program, regardless. Even before he ascended into the White House he had already bragged of an incident where a "good friend" of his "aided and abetted me, shall I say, by avoiding and evading the letter, while keeping to the spirit, of the Constitution of the United States."[97] He was not a man with any respect for the Constitution he swore to uphold and defend, and in 1930s America, he was far from alone in this regard.

Clarence Pickett recalled years later, "[T]here was a general realization that we must not let regulations . . . prevent our acting with promptness and reasonable adequacy."[98] West Virginia congressman Andrew Edmiston declared his support for funding the post office factory at Arthurdale not on any constitutional grounds but "if for no other reason than for the courtesy extended to our First Lady of the land, if this be but a whim of hers, we should carry on and make this homestead project."[99] There was a general abdication of responsibility, not only by Congress but by the American citizenry as a whole.

During a 1933 conference on resettlement proposals, an agricultural economist from the University of Minnesota, Professor O. B. Jesness, blithely sidestepped his responsibility as a citizen by declaring "I do not intend to argue the question of the Constitutionality of these proposals. That is a legal question I am not qualified to discuss."[100] Those who should have known better actually encouraged disrespect for the law, as shown by a helpful memo from the Attorney General's office to Louis Howe in 1933, pointing out that Section 208 (the Subsistence Homesteads Amendment) "confers very broad powers upon the president."[101]

It was here that the subsistence homestead program did the greatest damage to the country: its long-term effects on the political structure of the republic. The building of Arthurdale was an action far outside the bounds our Constitution grants to the federal politicians. Sustained by nothing more than the whim of the president, given life by a series of executive orders, it made a mockery of Congress and the rule of law. The Great Depression was a time of economic crisis, and "the period had many of the earmarks of a great wartime effort."[102] War always puts on exhibit the propensity of a frightened people to fall in lockstep behind the schemes of a demagogue; crisis is the premier means to centralize power.

It was under the assault of the Roosevelt administration, using the misery of a great depression as its battering ram, that the political class in America finally breached the walls of the Constitution for good and swept the field; FDR's rule ended the American people's long-standing aversion to the government's nosing around in the private sphere. The introduction of the New Deal programs destroyed forever what little still remained of the constitutional republic and its limits on federal power. Arthurdale was made possible not under the rule of law but simply "through the power and will of our president."[103]

The effect of Arthurdale on our way of life took hold in the American mind, and it was there that the greatest victory for its supporters was attained. Rexford Tugwell spoke years later about the time that saw FDR's rise: "There are crises in human affairs . . . whose demands for action overwhelm all the warnings and cautions it is possible to marshal."[104] As long before as 1922, Elwood Mead had noted that "there is no longer any opposition to state aid nor the methods by which it is given."[105] By the time of the Great Depression, FDR simply bumped his wheelchair into the republic's edifice and it collapsed, rotted to a hollow shell by years of Progressive inroads.

In an appearance before a House investigation committee in 1934, a Dr. Wirt gave warning about what he considered the dangerous, revolutionary change in America's idea of government embodied by Arthurdale. Pointing out that it was not considered as a relief or stimulus project, he asked the gathered congressmen "What, then, is it?"[106]

That is an important question, and the answer should never be let out of our national memory—because therein lies a warning and a rebuke to what we have become. Behind the Potemkin-like attempts to dress it up in perfection, despite the material goods lavished on the homesteaders and the thin veneer of "charity," at base the subsistence homestead of Arthurdale was—in Eleanor Roosevelt's words—"a human experiment station." It was a morally repulsive attempt to "improve" upon human beings who were considered somehow less than ideal in the eyes of the powerful.

It takes an outsize ego to look down upon your fellow citizens and play with them as if they were so many lab rats. Arthurdale represented a completely new view of the purpose of government in America. No longer would the political elite merely protect the sanctity of liberty by upholding the rule of law; a new purpose had arisen—to improve their fellow citizens.

From that first attempt at Arthurdale, the idea that animated it has spread like wildfire over America—every day new laws, new taxes, new regulations are passed, all with one thing in mind: to stop ordinary people from smoking, being poor parents, gaining too much weight, having too much money, or whatever the latest social engineering fad

may be. Such is life in modern America. The idea of improving humanity through political means has moved far overseas, to the very edges
of our empire.

Starting with a 1932 observation that "all workers in the United
States are now inevitably bound together in common interest, that no
great group can slide downhill without tugging dangerously at the
security of all the others,"[107] now, with the expanding footprint of
America's military and the expanding political power of its rulers, it
is today declared by our president, Barack Obama: "[T]he security
and well-being of each and every American depend on the security and
well-being of those who live beyond our borders."[108]

In northwestern Iraq lies the city of Tal Afar, once home to over
200,000 people yet now reduced, postinvasion, to about 80,000. Even
here America's mania to improve upon the raw material of humanity
has set down roots, and it is here, 75 years and 6,000 miles away, that
we repeat what was so wrong with the entire Arthurdale experiment.

In 2006, the mayor of the town, in a simple statement that we
should take to heart, chided the American garrison commander about
all that had been and was being done to make the city inhabitants
embrace "freedom and democracy." "What you are doing is an experiment," the mayor said, "and it isn't right to experiment on people."[109]

Not to mention useless. Human nature is what it is, no matter
how many trinkets you hand out, how many heads you lop off, or how
many prayers you direct on high, any new way of life, "society," is
too big a structure for any human intellect to build from scratch and
bring into life by force; it is something that evolves on its own. The
authors of *A Place on Earth* concluded that "administrators of a project
should leave the development of its social organization strictly to the
homesteaders."[110]

And even if it were possible for the powerful to create entire new
societies by decree, would it be moral? For both the big and the small
things in life, people have a right to find their own way, on their own
terms. The resettled people were dispossessed of their most valuable
piece of property: the right to choose for themselves.

In a 1942 newspaper article on the town, the author observed that
"it is not as if anything had been learned from Arthurdale and similar
follies: the same players remain on the stage and the same lines are being

spoken."[111] For that matter, nothing has changed today, either. We still hold the same idea in our hearts, speak the same lines as before, and build more castles of sand. For Rexford Tugwell, "the important thing, in the long run, is the conscious striving for new national directions."[112] Seventy-five years later, it is safe to report that America's future belonged to Tugwell's kind.

So while we can point out the lessons our forebears should have learned from Arthurdale, highlight their mistakes and folly, we need to keep in mind that even with the benefit of hindsight, we, too, are none the wiser.

Acknowledgments

Writing is a solitary endeavor that requires one to quietly sit for days (sometimes months) on end, typing at a keyboard, taking notes, or reading piles of source material. Publishing a book, though, requires a team effort and a lot of luck. This book would not exist but for the kindness of friends, the willingness on the part of many (former) strangers to open up their lives to me, and a patient understanding on the part of my family who saw me but rarely, if at all, for long stretches of time. I have many people to thank, and even more to apologize to.

It was the prodding of a dear friend, the financial journalist Caroline Baum, that got me to gather all my notes and pitch my obsession to a publishing house, and it was just my good luck to meet Pamela Van Giessen, the editorial director at John Wiley & Sons, who consented to take a flyer on a new author. I cannot thank either of them enough.

My editor at John Wiley, Emilie Herman, was a joy to work with and always kept my thoughts marching in a straight line instead of veering off into tangents. Despite my complete lack of mastery of the English language, she never physically threatened me, not once, though I remain murky on a semicolon's proper usage. Thanks also to Todd Tedesco, my production editor at Wiley.

All the staff at the New York Public Library's research wings were ever helpful and polite, and I am blessed to live so near such a world-renowned collection of historical documents. My thanks also go to Jim Bantin of Southern Illinois University. The staff at the National Archives, both the main center in College Park, Maryland, and FDR's personal library in Hyde Park, New York, were also of great assistance. The staff of the West Virginia and Regional History Collection at West Virginia University in Morgantown has my gratitude, especially Michael Ridderbusch, Christy Venham, Catherine Rakowski, and Harold Forbes for their many efforts on my part.

The board members at Arthurdale Heritage, Inc. were extremely kind and open-minded; they never hesitated to answer a question and even granted access to the town archives to not only a complete stranger but also someone critical of the very New Deal that created Arthurdale. Rick Rodeheaver, Amanda Griffith Penix, and Jeanne Goodman were patient, kind, and understanding regarding all my requests and questions, and have my eternal gratitude.

The people of Arthurdale, both those who still live there and those who have moved away, surprised the New Yorker in me by their kindness and quickly offered hospitality. I spoke with many of them during my visits and would like to particularly thank all those who consented to be interviewed and share their family histories: Dr. John Fullmer, Jim McNelis, Robert McLaughlin Sr., Larry McLaughlin, Glenda (McLaughlin) Stump, Norma (McLaughlin) Turner, Linda (McLaughlin) Honchell, Glenn Luzier, Julia Perry, and Ann Shannon have my heartfelt thanks. Of immeasurable help in opening up many a door to me was Robert McLaughlin Jr., who has not only become a friend but also got me addicted to buckwheat pancakes.

Many thanks for all those who gave of their time and advice or otherwise helped move things along: Bernard Griffin, Keith Friedman, Janet Fiorenza, Robert Arancio, Rick Imperiale, Mark Gilbert, Kate Wood, and Eileen Curtis, wherever she may be. I would like to thank all the people at LewRockwell.com (and Mr. Rockwell himself), Mises.Org, Stephen Cox of *Liberty* magazine, David Beito of the University of Alabama, Dr. Nigel Ashford of the *Institute for Humane Studies*, Alexander McCobin of the *Students for Liberty*, John Tamny of *RealClearMarkets*, Michael Terry of Canada's *Echo Weekly*, the staff at Cape Cod Compositors, and Dr. Robert P. Murphy. A special thank-you to Brooklyn's DJ Jon Porter, who provided the soundtrack to many of my work hours.

All the opinions, mistakes, and shortcomings of this book are mine and mine alone.

This book is a small memorial in memory of John David Fernandez of Columbia University—God rest his soul.

I cannot thank (and apologize) enough to all my friends and family (especially my mother), the ones who watched me fade into nothing for the past few years so I could produce this book. Last, I need to thank above all my wife, Dorothea, and my son, Casey, for their endless understanding—you can both have me back now.

C. J. Maloney
New York City
November 2010

Notes

Introduction

1. Byers, Michael, "Brave New Town: Revisiting Arthurdale, WV," *Preservation* (March/April 2006), 32–37.

2. Niall Ferguson, *The Pity of War* (New York: Basic Books, 1999), xxiii.

3. Malcolm Ross, "When Depression Blights a Great Area," *New York Times*, Jan. 31, 1932, Sec. 5, 6.

4. Lee A. Gladwin, "Arthurdale: Adventure into Utopia," *West Virginia History* 28, no. 4 (1967): 311; and Louis Howe Papers, 1934, FDRL.

5. Paul K. Conkin, *Tomorrow a New World: The New Deal Community Program* (Ithaca, NY: Cornell University Press, 1959), 6.

6. Kathleen Cullinan and Beth Spence, "Arthurdale: The New Deal Comes to Preston County," *Goldenseal* 7, no. 2 (Apr./June 1981): 7–25.

7. Stuart Patterson, "Constructing Ideal Families in Ideal Communities: The Case of Arthurdale, West Virginia." Manuscript, Emory University, April 2002, 4.

8. Bruce Beezer, "Arthurdale: An Experiment in Community Living," *West Virginia History* 36, no. 1 (1974/75): 18.

9. R. W. Murchie, "Land Settlement as a Relief Measure," from *Day and Hour Series #5,* University of Minnesota, 1933, 5.

10. Conkin, *Tomorrow a New World*, 327.

11. H. J. Haskell, *The New Deal in Old Rome* (Auburn, AL: Ludwig von Mises Institute, 2009), 97–103.

12. Albert V. House Jr., "Proposals of Government Aid to Agricultural Settlements: 1873–1879," *Agricultural History* 11 (Jan. 1938): 61.

13. Murchie, "Land Settlement as a Relief Measure," 9; and Conkin, *Tomorrow a New World*, 13.

14. Murchie, "Land Settlement as a Relief Measure."

15. Conkin, *Tomorrow a New World*, 40.

16. House, "Proposals of Government Aid to Agricultural Settlements," 47–49.

17. Ibid., 46–66.

18. Ibid., 59.

19. Conkin, *Tomorrow a New World*, 41.

20. Ibid., 21.

21. William E. Smythe, "New Homestead Policy for America," *Review of Reviews* 65 (Jan.–Jun. 1922): 296. Elwood Mead would actually be the author of a congressional bill calling for $500 million to be set aside for such colonies. See also Conkin, *Tomorrow a New World*, 53.

22. Conkin, *Tomorrow a New World*, 27–28.

23. Michael Byers, "Brave New Town: Revisiting Arthurdale, WV," 32–37.

24. Paul K. Conkin, "Arthurdale Revisited," in Bryan Ward, ed., *A New Deal for America* (Arthurdale, WV: Arthurdale Heritage, Inc., 1995), 23.

25. Andy Wolfe, Interview transcript, June 11, 1987, Arthurdale Heritage, Inc., 4.

26. T. R. Carskadon, "Hull House in the Hills," *The New Republic* 79 (Aug. 1, 1934), 312–314.

27. Rexford Tugwell, *The Battle for Democracy* (New York: Columbia University Press, 1935), 143.

28. Amity Shales, *The Forgotten Man* (New York: HarperCollins, 2007), 54.

29. Patterson, "Constructing Ideal Families in Ideal Communities," 4.

30. Bushrod Grimes, Memorandum. West Virginia University, Arthurdale Project Papers, West Virginia Regional and History Collection, A&M 2178/Folder 3.

31. Nancy Hoffman, *Eleanor Roosevelt and the Arthurdale Experiment* (North Haven, CT: Linnet Books, 2001), xv.

32. "Denies Endangering Sewickley Seam," *Black Diamond* 72 (May 1924): 619.

33. "Will Buy M. & W. Railway," *Washington Post*, June 2, 1923, 5.

34. Ronald L. Lewis, "Scotts Run: America's Symbol of the Great Depression in the Coal Fields," from Ward, *A New Deal for America,* 1; and Amanda Griffith Penix, *Arthurdale* (Arthurdale, WV: Arthurdale Heritage, Inc., 2007), 9.

35. Matthew Yeager, "Scotts Run: A Community in Transition," *West Virginia History* 53 (1994) p.7–20.

36. Sidney D. Lee, *". . . And the Trees Cried"* (Morgantown, WV: self-published, 1991), 22.

37. Ibid., 9.

38. Yeager, "Scotts Run: A Community in Transition."

39. Letter, Floyd B. Cox to Rexford Tugwell, July 10, 1935, *Project Records, 1935–40 West Virginia,* Records Group 96, National Archives, College Park, MD.

40. Hoffman, *Eleanor Roosevelt and the Arthurdale Experiment,* 8.

41. Transcript, "West Virginia," WV History Film Project, www.wvculture .org/history/wvmemory/filmtranscripts/wv.html.

42. Clayton R. Newell, *Lee vs. McClellan: The First Campaign* (Washington, DC: Regenery, 1996), 34.

43. Howard Burton Lee, *Bloodletting in Appalachia: The Story of West Virginia's Four Major Mine Wars* (Morgantown, WV: West Virginia University, 1969), 51.

44. Hoffman, *Eleanor Roosevelt and the Arthurdale Experiment.*

45. Louis Stark, "Fare Worst in Mines of West Virginia," *New York Times,* Nov. 29, 1931, N39.

46. Sandra Barney, "You Get What You Pay For: The Political Economy of Health Care Delivery on Scotts Run, 1920–1935," in Ward, *A New Deal for America,* 28.

47. Lee, *". . . And the Trees Cried,"* 46; "Unionizing in West Virginia," *New Republic* 66 (Apr. 4, 1931): 289; Clarence Pickett, *For More than Bread* (Boston: Little, Brown, 1953), 34; Dr. Ruth Fox, "West Virginia Coal Mines," *The Nation* 133 (Sept. 9, 1931): 257; Transcript, "West Virginia."

48. Lee, *". . . And the Trees Cried,"* 44.

49. Fox, "West Virginia Coal Mines."

50. Charles R. Joy, "In a West Virginia Coal Field," *Christian Century* 50 (Jan. 25, 1933): 117–119.

51. Transcript, "West Virginia" interview with Bettijane Burger, May 2, 1993.

52. Christine Kreiser, "I Wonder Whom God Will Hold Responsible?" *West Virginia History* 53 (1994) p.61–92.

53. Barney, "You Get What You Pay For," 34.

54. Fox, "West Virginia Coal Mines"; and Hoffman, *Eleanor Roosevelt and the Arthurdale Experiment,* 8.

55. Fox, "West Virginia Coal Mines."

56. James Myers, "Soft Coal and Hard Times," *Christian Century* 49 (Jan. 27, 1932): 116–118.

57. Barney, "You Get What You Pay For," 32.

58. Blanche Wiesen Cook, *Eleanor Roosevelt, Vol. 2: 1933–38* (New York: Viking Press, 1999), 32.

59. Barney, "You Get What You Pay For," 33.

60. "Sewickley Coal Is Premier Steam Fuel," *Black Diamond* 71 (Aug. 11, 1923): 185.

61. Barney, "You Get What You Pay For," 31.

Chapter 1: The Damnedest Cesspool of Human Misery

1. Film transcript, *West Virginia,* www.wvculture.org/history/wvmemory/filmtranscripts/wv.html.

2. Charles R. Joy, "In a West Virginia Coal Field," *Christian Century* 50 (Jan. 25, 1933): 117–119.

3. Sidney D. Lee, ". . . *And the Trees Cried*" (Morgantown, WV: self-published, 1991), 7.

4. Blanche Wiesen Cook, *Eleanor Roosevelt Vol. 2: 1933–38* (New York: Viking Press, 1999), 10; Phil Ross, "The Scotts Run Coalfield from the Great War to the Great Depression," *West Virginia History* 53 (1994): 21–42 also speaks to the absolute necessity for the coal operators to lower wage rates or reduce head count "to remain in business."

5. Ross, "The Scotts Run Coalfield," 21–42.

6. Amanda Griffith Penix, *Arthurdale* (Arthurdale, WV: Arthurdale Heritage, Inc., 2007), 13.

7. "Wonder Coal Field of West Virginia," *Black Diamond* 71 (Aug. 11, 1923): 180–181.

8. Ronald L. Lewis, "Scotts Run: America's Symbol of the Great Depression in the Coal Fields," in Bryan Ward, ed., *A New Deal for America* (Arthurdale, WV: Arthurdale Heritage, Inc., 1995), 10.

9. Ronald L. Lewis, "Scotts Run: An Introduction," *West Virginia History* 53 (1994).

10. Ross, "The Scotts Run Coalfield," 21–42.

11. "Wonder Coal Field of West Virginia."

12. Lewis, "Scotts Run: America's Symbol," 2.

13. I. C. White, "Morgantown's Wealth of Fuel," *Black Diamond* 71 (Aug. 11, 1923): 178–179.

14. Ross, "The Scotts Run Coalfield," 21–42.

15. Lewis, "Scotts Run: America's Symbol," 3.

16. White, "Morgantown's Wealth of Fuel."

17. "Sewickley Coal Is Premier Steam Fuel," *Black Diamond* 71 (Aug. 11, 1923): 185.

18. "Wonder Coal Field of West Virginia."

19. Ibid.

20. Lewis, "Scotts Run: America's Symbol," 3.

21. "West Virginia Output Shows Increase," *Black Diamond* 68 (Jan. 28, 1922): 85.

22. Earl L. Core, *The Monongalia Story: A Bicentennial History,* vol. 4 (Parsons, WV: McClain Printing, 1982), 456.

23. Ibid., 457.

24. Nancy Hoffman, *Eleanor Roosevelt and the Arthurdale Experiment* (North Haven, CT: Linnet Books, 2001), 4.

25. "West Virginia Output Shows Increase."

26. Lewis, "Scotts Run: America's Symbol," 5.

27. Ross, "The Scotts Run Coalfield," 21–42.

28. Ibid.

29. Millard Milburn Rice, "Footnote on Arthurdale," *Harper's Magazine* 180 (March 1940): 411–419.

30. Core, *The Monongalia Story*, 458.

31. Rice, "Footnote on Arthurdale," *Harper's Magazine*.

32. Malcolm Ross, "When Depression Blights a Great Area," *New York Times,* Jan. 31, 1932, Sec. 5, 6.

33. Lewis, "Scotts Run: America's Symbol," 9.

34. Phil Ross, "The Scotts Run Coalfield from the Great War to the Great Depression," *West Virginia History* 53 (1994).

35. James P. Johnson, *The Politics of Soft Coal* (Urbana: University of Illinois Press, 1937), 110.

36. "Calder Persists in Coal Control," *New York Times*, Nov. 22, 1920, 18.

37. Johnson, *The Politics of Soft Coal,* 111.

38. Ross, "The Scotts Run Coalfield," 21–42.

39. "West Virginia Output Shows Increase."

40. Lewis, "Scotts Run: America's Symbol," 3.

41. "West Virginia Output Shows Increase."

42. "Sewickley Coal Is Premier Steam Fuel."

43. Transcript, "West Virginia," WV History Film Project, www.wvculture .org/history/wvmemory/filmtranscripts/wv.html.

44. "Sewickley Coal Is Premier Steam Fuel."

45. Ross, "The Scotts Run Coalfield," 21–42; "Wonder Coal Field of West Virginia"; and Lewis, "Scotts Run: America's Symbol," 2.

46. "Wonder Coal Field of West Virginia."

47. Stephen Haid, "Arthurdale: An Experiment in Community Planning, 1933–47." PhD diss., West Virginia University, 1975, 4.

48. Ludwig von Mises, *Interventionism: An Economic Analysis* (Irvington-on-Hudson, NY: Foundation for Economic Education, 1998), 3.

49. Amity Shlaes, *The Forgotten Man: A New History of the Great Depression* (New York: HarperCollins, 2007), 38.

50. Ross, "The Scotts Run Coalfield," 21–42.

51. Niall Ferguson, *The Pity of War* (New York: Basic Books, 1999), 331.

52. Ross, "The Scotts Run Coalfield," 21–42.

53. Ibid.

54. Johnson, *The Politics of Soft Coal,* 118.

55. Ross, "The Scotts Run Coalfield," 21–42.

56. Ibid.

57. Lewis, "Scotts Run: American's Symbol," 10.

58. Jerry Bruce Thomas, *An Appalachian New Deal: West Virginia in the Great Depression* (Lexington: University Press of Kentucky, 1998), 99.

59. Ross, "The Scotts Run Coalfield," 21–42.

60. "What Will Happen in Anthracite Wages?" *Black Diamond* 68 (Jan. 7, 1922): 2.

61. Johnson, *The Politics of Soft Coal*, 119.

62. Ibid.

63. "Miner's Strike Leader Fears Tilt with I.W.W.," *Washington Post*, July 27, 1926, 12.

64. Johnson, *The Politics of Soft Coal*, 121.

65. Ibid., 120.

66. Ibid., 121.

67. Transcript, "West Virginia."

68. "Unionizing in West Virginia," *New Republic* 66 (Apr. 4, 1931): 289.

69. Ross, "The Scotts Run Coalfield," 21–42.

70. "General Strike Opens as Miners Celebrate," *Washington Post*, Apr. 2, 1925, 4.

71. Ross, "The Scotts Run Coalfield," 21–42.

72. Ibid.

73. Johnson, *The Politics of Soft Coal*, 120.

74. Lewis, "Scotts Run: American's Symbol," 11.

75. James Myers, "Rehabilitation in the Coal Fields," the *Christian Century* 49 (August 31, 1932), 1053–1055.

76. "Nine Miners Are Held after Colliery Fight," *Washington Post*, Nov. 29, 1924, 2.

77. Bureau of Labor Statistics, www.bls.gov/data/inflation_calculator.htm.

78. "Nine Miners Are Held after Colliery Fight."

79. Ross, "The Scotts Run Coalfield," 21–42.

80. "Dynamite Exploded at Open Shop Mine," *Washington Post*, Aug. 2, 1926, 3.

81. Howard Burton Lee, *Bloodletting in Appalachia: The Story of West Virginia's Four Major Mine Wars* (Morgantown, WV: West Virginia University, 1969), 153.

82. Connie P. Rice, *Our Monongalia: A History of African Americans in Monongalia County, West Virginia* (Terra Alta, WV: Headline Books, 1999), 109.

83. Lee, *Bloodletting in Appalachia,* 154.

84. Lee, ". . . And the Trees Cried," 79–80.

85. Johnson, *The Politics of Soft Coal*, 121.

86. Ross, "The Scotts Run Coalfield," 21–42.

87. Transcript, "West Virginia."

88. Ross, "When Depression Blights a Great Area."

89. Haid, "Arthurdale: An Experiment in Community Planning," 17.

90. Ross, "When Depression Blights a Great Area."

91. Ibid.

92. "Vetoing Mrs. Roosevelt's Pet Project," *Christian Century* 51 (Mar. 14, 1934): 348.

93. Haid, "Arthurdale: An Experiment in Community Planning," 4.

94. Louis Stark, "Fare Worst in Mines of West Virginia," *New York Times*, Nov. 29, 1931, N39.

95. "Pay Scales Divide West Virginia Pits," *New York Times*, Nov. 28, 1931, Books, 20.

96. Ibid., 20. If you really want to know, they were the Bethlehem Mines Corporation (43 cents), the Consolidation Coal Company (39 cents), the Jamison Coal and Coke Company (38 cents), and the New England Fuel and Transport (38 cents).

97. Ibid.

98. Haid, "Arthurdale: An Experiment in Community Planning," 13.

99. Ibid.

100. Cook, *Eleanor Roosevelt, Vol. 2*," 11.

101. Rice, "Footnote on Arthurdale," 411–419.

102. Cook, *Eleanor Roosevelt, Vol. 2*, 131.

103. Michael Byers, "Brave New Town: Revisiting Arthurdale, WV," *Preservation* (March/April 2006): 32–37.

104. Hoffman, *Eleanor Roosevelt and the Arthurdale Experiment*, 7.

105. Interview of Bob McLaughlin Sr. by son Bob McLaughlin Jr., November 2009, mark 6:20. (Mark is the time on the tape where the quote is located.)

106. Cook, *Eleanor Roosevelt, Vol. 2*, 131; and Joy, "In a West Virginia Coal Field," 117–119.

107. Haid, "Arthurdale: An Experiment in Community Planning," 3.

108. Ross, "When Depression Blights a Great Area."

109. Lee, ". . . And the Trees Cried," 7.

110. Ibid., 44–45.

111. Christine Kreiser, "I Wonder Whom God Will Hold Responsible?," *West Virginia History* 53 (1994): 61–92.

112. Hoffman, *Eleanor Roosevelt and the Arthurdale Experiment*, 2.

113. Lee, ". . . And the Trees Cried," 22.

114. Transcript, "West Virginia."

115. Haid, "Arthurdale: An Experiment in Community Planning," xii.

116. David E. Kyvig, *Daily Life in the United States, 1920–1940* (Chicago: Ivan R. Dee, 2002), 129.

117. Sandra Barney, "You Get What You Pay For: The Political Economy of Health Care Delivery on Scotts Run, 1920–1935," in Bryan Ward, ed., *A New Deal for America* (Arthurdale, WV: Arthurdale Heritage, Inc., 1995), 31.

118. Ross, "The Scotts Run Coalfield," 21–42.

119. Lee, ". . . And the Trees Cried," 22–23.

120. Clarence Pickett, *For More than Bread* (Boston: Little, Brown, 1953), 37.

121. Penix, *Arthurdale*, 16.

122. Kreiser, "I Wonder Whom God Will Hold Responsible?," 61–92.

123. Johnson, *The Politics of Soft Coal*, 120; see footnote 52 as well.

124. Joy, "In a West Virginia Coal Field," 117–119.

125. Penix, *Arthurdale*, 19.

126. Stark, "Fare Worst in Mines of West Virginia."

127. Ross, "When Depression Blights a Great Area."

128. Joy, "In a West Virginia Coal Field."

129. Lee, ". . . *And the Trees Cried*," 46.

130. Myers, "Soft Coal and Hard Times," 116–118; when looking at pictures of Scotts Run children, the lack of shoes is noticeable.

131. Haid, "Arthurdale: An Experiment in Community Planning," 18.

132. Myers, "Soft Coal and Hard Times," 116–118.

133. Ross, "When Depression Blights a Great Area."

134. Transcript, "West Virginia," interview with Bettijane Burger, May 2, 1993.

135. Ross, "When Depression Blights a Great Area."

136. Ibid.

137. Stark, "Fare Worst in Mines of West Virginia."

138. James S. Olson, "The Depths of the Great Depression," *West Virginia History* 38 (1977), 214–225.

139. Pickett, *For More than Bread,* 25.

140. Olson, "The Depths of the Great Depression," 214–225.

141. Ibid.

142. Ibid.

143. Lewis, "Scotts Run: American Symbol," 15.

144. Joy, "In a West Virginia Coal Field," 117–119.

145. James Myers, "Rehabilitation in the Coal Fields," *Christian Century* 49 (Aug. 31, 1932): 1053–1055).

146. Haid, "Arthurdale: An Experiment in Community Planning," 8.

147. Pickett, *For More than Bread,* 27.

148. Ibid., 31.

149. Lewis, "Scotts Run: American Symbol."

150. Haid, "Arthurdale: An Experiment in Community Planning," 6.

151. Lewis, "Scotts Run: American Symbol," 17.

152. Cook, *Eleanor Roosevelt, Vol. 2*, 17.

153. Kreiser, "I Wonder Whom God Will Hold Responsible?," 61–92.

154. Transcript, "West Virginia," interview with Bettijane Burger.

155. Penix, *Arthurdale*, 22.

156. Pamphlet, "The Shack Idea," www.wvculture.org/history/greatdepression/shack03.jpg.

157. Kreiser, "I Wonder Whom God Will Hold Responsible?," 61–92.

158. Ibid.

159. Ibid.

160. Transcript, "West Virginia," interview with Bettijane Burger; Kreiser, "I Wonder Whom God Will Hold Responsible?," 61–92.

161. Kreiser, "I Wonder Whom God Will Hold Responsible?," 61–92.

162. Ibid.

163. Ibid.

164. Ibid.

165. Ibid.

166. Transcript, "West Virginia," interview with Bettijane Burger.

167. Kreiser, "I Wonder Whom God Will Hold Responsible?," 61–92.

168. Transcript, "West Virginia," interview with Bettijane Burger.

169. Ibid.

170. Lewis, "Scotts Run: America's Symbol"; and Kreiser, "I Wonder Whom God Will Hold Responsible?," 61–92.

171. Pickett, *For More than Bread*, 31.

172. Ibid., v–vii.

173. Ibid., x.

174. Ross, "When Depression Blights a Great Area."

175. Pickett, *For More than Bread*, 26; and Haid, "Arthurdale: An Experiment in Community Planning," 19.

176. Pickett, *For More than Bread*, 19; and Mary Jones Hoxie, *Swords into Ploughshares: An Account of the AFSC* (Westport, CT: Greenwood Press, 1971), 224.

177. Hoxie, *Swords into Ploughshares*, 224.

178. Pickett, *For More than Bread*, 19.

179. Hoxie,. *Swords into Ploughshares*, 224–225; Haid, "Arthurdale: An Experiment in Community Planning"; and Pickett, *For More than Bread*, 20.

180. Hoxie, *Swords into Ploughshares*, 225.

181. Pickett, *For More than Bread*, 19.

182. Ibid., 21, 36.

183. Hoxie, *Swords into Ploughshares*, 226–227.

184. Stark, "Fare Worst in Mines of West Virginia."

185. Pickett, *For More than Bread*, 25.

186. Olson, "The Depths of the Great Depression," 214–225.

187. Pickett, *For More than Bread*, 22.

188. Hoxie, *Swords into Ploughshares*, 228.

189. Myers, "Rehabilitation in the Coal Fields," 1053–1055.

190. Hoxie, *Swords into Ploughshares*, 229.

191. Lewis, "Scotts Run: America's Symbol," 15.

192. Haid, "Arthurdale: An Experiment in Community Planning," 20.

193. Ibid.

194. Pickett, *For More than Bread*.

195. Myers, "Soft Coal and Hard Times," 116–118.

196. Pickett, *For More than Bread*.

197. Barney, "You Get What You Pay For," 34.

198. Hoxie, *Swords into Ploughshares*, 229.

199. Ibid., 234.

200. Haid, "Arthurdale: An Experiment in Community Planning," 21.

201. Ross, "When Depression Blights a Great Area."

202. Joy, "In a West Virginia Coal Field," 117–119.

203. Stark, "Fare Worst in Mines of West Virginia."

204. Barney, "You Get What You Pay For."

205. Ibid., 36.

206. Hoxie, *Swords into Ploughshares*, 233.

207. Haid, "Arthurdale: An Experiment in Community Planning," 9–11.

208. Pickett, *For More than Bread*, 35.

209. Hoxie, *Swords into Ploughshares*, 231.

210. Do they ever?

211. Ross, "When Depression Blights a Great Area."

212. Pickett, *For More than Bread*, 36.

213. Ibid., 29.

214. Ibid., x.

215. Myers, "Rehabilitation in the Coal Fields."

Chapter 2: The Angel of Arthurdale Arrives

1. Michael Byers, "Brave New Town: Revisiting Arthurdale, WV," *Preservation* (March/April 2006): 32–37.

2. Doris Faber, *The Life of Lorena Hickok* (New York: William Morrow, 1980), 142.

3. Ronald L. Lewis, "Scotts Run: America's Symbol of the Great Depression in the Coal Fields," in Bryan Ward, ed., *A New Deal for America* (Arthurdale, WV: Arthurdale Heritage, Inc., 1995), 10.

4. Thomas Coode and Dennis Fabbri, "The New Deal's Arthurdale Project in West Virginia," *West Virginia History* 36, no. 4 (1974–75): 292.

5. Bryan Ward, "Introduction," in Bryan Ward, ed., *A New Deal for America* (Arthurdale, WV: Arthurdale Heritage, Inc., 1995), iv.

6. Faber, *The Life of Lorena Hickok*, 143–144.

7. Blanche Wiesen Cook, *Eleanor Roosevelt, Vol. 2: 1933–38* (New York: Viking Press, 1999), 132.

8. Faber, *The Life of Lorena Hickok*, 144.

9. Lewis, "Scotts Run: America's Symbol," 14.

10. Amanda Griffith Penix, *Arthurdale* (Arthurdale, WV: Arthurdale Heritage, Inc., 2007), 9.

11. Cook, *Eleanor Roosevelt Vol. 2*, 11.

12. Phil Ross, "The Scotts Run Coalfield from the Great War to the Great Depression," *West Virginia History* 53 (1994): 21–42.

13. Lewis, "Scotts Run: America's Symbol."

14. Ibid.

15. Robert L. Reid, "Documenting Arthurdale: Looking at New Deal Photography," in Bryan Ward, ed., *A New Deal for America* (Arthurdale, WV: Arthurdale Heritage, Inc., 1995), 155.

16. Clarence Pickett, *For More than Bread* (Boston: Little, Brown, 1953), 40.

17. Cook, *Eleanor Roosevelt, Vol. 2*, 133.

18. James S. Olson, "The Depths of the Great Depression," *West Virginia History* 38 (1977): 214–225.

19. Pickett, *For More than Bread*, 29–30.

20. Christine Kreiser, "I Wonder Whom God Will Hold Responsible?," *West Virginia History* 53 (1994): 61–92.

21. Cook, *Eleanor Roosevelt, Vol. 2*, 131.

22. James Myers, "Rehabilitation in the Coal Fields," *Christian Century*, 49 (Aug. 31, 1932): 1053–1055.

23. Penix, *Arthurdale*, 23.

24. Pickett, *For More than Bread*, 45.

25. Rexford Tugwell, *The Battle for Democracy* (New York: Columbia University Press, 1935), 105.

26. Albert Shaw, "From New York to Idaho," *Review of Reviews* 64 (July–Dec. 1921): 179–80).

27. Ibid., 180.

28. Paul K. Conkin, *Tomorrow a New World, The New Deal Community Program* (Ithaca, NY: Cornell University Press, 1959), 22.

29. Ibid., 18.

30. R. W. Murchie, "Land Settlement as a Relief Measure," *Day and Hour Series #5,* University of Minnesota, 1933, 31–32.

31. Conkin, *Tomorrow a New World*, 28.

32. Ralph Borsodi, *This Ugly Civilization* (New York: Simon & Schuster, 1929), 221; and Conkin, *Tomorrow a New World*, 26.

33. Andrew Dodd, "Back to the Land: A Poem," *Literary Digest* 61 (June 14, 1919): 36.

34. Bolton Hall, *A Little Land and a Living* (New York: Arcadia Press, 1908), 41.

35. Conkin, *Tomorrow a New World*, 25.

36. Malcolm Cowley and Willard T. David, "How Far Back the Land?," *New Republic* 65 (Aug. 9, 1933): 336–338.

37. Conkin, *Tomorrow a New World*, 28.

38. Arthur Pound, "Land Ho!" *Atlantic Monthly* 151 (June 1933): 714.

39. Rexford Tugwell, "The Sources of New Deal Reformism," *Ethics* 64 (July 1954): 250.

40. Dodge, Henry Irving. "Back to the Land for Soldiers," *Country Gentleman* 84 (Feb. 15, 1919): 45.

41. *The Federalist Papers,* no. 6.

42. Paul Johnstone and Russell Lord, *A Place on Earth: A Critical Appraisal of Subsistence Homesteads* (Washington, DC: U.S. Dept. of Agriculture, Bureau of Agricultural Economics, 1942), 15.

43. Ibid., 14.

44. Conkin, *Tomorrow a New World*, 3.

45. Benjamin G. Rader, *The Academic Mind and Reform* (Lexington: University of Kentucky Press, 1966), 192–193.

46. Ibid., 4–8.

47. Ibid., 41.

48. Ibid., 29.

49. Conkin, *Tomorrow a New World*, 75.

50. Rader, *The Academic Mind and Reform.*

51. Conkin, *Tomorrow a New World*, 43.

52. James R. Kluger, *Turning on Water with a Shovel* (Albuquerque: University of New Mexico Press, 1992), 131.

53. Ibid., 1–11.

54. Ibid., 37.

55. Conkin, *Tomorrow a New World.*

56. Elwood Mead, *Helping Men Own Farms* (New York: Macmillan, 1920), 207.

57. Elwood Mead, "Government Aid and Direction in Land Settlement," *American Economic Review* 8, no. 1 Supp. (March 1918): 95.

58. Conkin, *Tomorrow a New World*, 55.

59. Ibid., 34.

60. Tugwell, "The Sources of New Deal Reformism," 266.

61. Franklin D. Roosevelt, "Growing Up by Plan," *Survey* 67, no. 9 (Feb. 1, 1932): 483.

62. Conkin, *Tomorrow a New World*, 34.

63. Roosevelt, "Growing Up by Plan," 506.

64. Holly Cowan, "Arthurdale." M.A. thesis, New York, Columbia University, 1968, 7.

65. Faber, *The Life of Lorena Hickok*, 151.

66. Johnstone and Lord, *A Place on Earth*, 20.

67. Ibid., 21.

68. Conkin, *Tomorrow a New World*, 73.

69. S. Robles art sketch from *Washington Post*, Oct. 20, 1934, www.nal.usda.gov/speccoll/collect/history/wilsonpg.htm.

70. M. L. Wilson, "Farm Relief and Allotment Plan," *Day and Hour Series #2,* University of Minnesota, 1933, 33–34.

71. Conkin, *Tomorrow a New World*, 81.

72. Johnstone, and Lord, *A Place on Earth*, 21.

73. Conkin, *Tomorrow a New World,* 73.

74. Rexford Tugwell, "Farm Relief and a Permanent Agriculture," *Annals of the American Academy of Political and Social Science* 142 (Mar. 1929): 275.

75. Amity Shlaes, *The Forgotten Man: A New History of the Great Depression* (New York: HarperCollins, 2007), 73.

76. Philip Hubert, Jr., *Liberty and a Living* (New York: G. P. Putnam's Sons, 1889), 370.

77. Hall, *A Little Land and a Living*, 69.

78. Shaw, "From New York to Idaho," 181.

79. Frederic C. Howe, *The Land and the Soldier* (New York: Charles Scribner's Sons, 1919), 11–12.

80. Pound, "Land Ho!" 721.

81. Cowan, "Arthurdale," 1.

82. Shlaes, *The Forgotten Man: A New History of the Great Depression* (New York: HarperCollins, 2007), 54.

83. Rexford Tugwell, "Resettling America: A Fourfold Plan," *New York Times*, July 28, 1935, SM5.

84. Conkin, *Tomorrow a New World*, 23.

85. Pound, "Land Ho!" 716.

86. www.npg.org/facts/us_historical_pops.htm, and Conkin, *Tomorrow a New World*, 23.

87. Pascal K. Whelpton, "The Extent, Character, and Future of the New Landward Movement." *Journal of Farm Economics* 15, no. 1 (Jan. 1933): 57.

88. Bolton Hall, *Three Acres and Liberty* (London, England: Macmillan, 1907), 3–4.

89. Pound, "Land Ho!"

90. Ibid., 714; and Cowan, "Arthurdale," 5.

91. Wilson, "Farm Relief and Allotment Plan," 50.

92. Conkin, *Tomorrow a New World*, 17; and M. L. Wilson, "The Place of Subsistence Homesteads in Our National Economy," *Journal of Farm Economics* 16, no. 1 (Jan. 1934): 76.

93. Borsodi, *This Ugly Civilization*, 310.

94. Ibid., 320.

95. Wilson, "The Place of Subsistence Homesteads in Our National Economy," 81.

96. Cowley and David, "How Far Back the Land?," 339.

97. Dodge, Henry Irving, "Back to the Land for Soldiers," *Country Gentleman* 84 (Feb. 15, 1919): 46.

98. Mead, "Government Aid and Direction in Land Settlement," 72.

99. Mead, *Helping Men Own Farms*, 198.

Chapter 3: The Definition of Insanity

1. Richard Ely, *Ground Under Our Feet: An Autobiography* (New York: Macmillan 1938), 96.

2. Paul K. Conkin, "Arthurdale Revisited," in Bryan Ward, ed., *A New Deal for America* (Arthurdale, WV: Arthurdale Heritage, Inc., 1995), 50.

3. Ludwig von Mises, *Theory and History* (Auburn, AL: Ludwig von Mises Institute, 1985), 160.

4. Frederic C. Howe, *The Land and the Soldier* (New York: Charles Scribner's Sons, 1919), 5–6.

5. Ralph Borsodi, *This Ugly Civilization* (New York: Simon & Schuster, 1929), 316.

6. Daniel R. Fusfeld, *The Economic Thought of Franklin D. Roosevelt and the Origins of the New Deal* (New York: Columbia University Press, 1954), 154.

7. Benjamin G. Rader, *The Academic Mind and Reform* (Lexington: University of Kentucky Press, 1966), 197–198.

8. Elwood Mead, *Helping Men Own Farms* (New York: Macmillan, 1920), 214.

9. William E. Smythe, "New Homestead Policy for America," *Review of Reviews* 65 (Jan.–Jun. 1922): 293.

10. James R. Kluger, *Turning on Water with a Shovel* (Albuquerque: University of New Mexico Press, 1992), 73.

11. Rexford Tugwell, "The Sources of New Deal Reformism," *Ethics* 64 (July 1954): 253.

12. Franklin D. Roosevelt, *The Public Papers and Addresses of Franklin D. Roosevelt* (New York: Random House, 1938), 193.

13. Richard Ely, *Ground under Our Feet: An Autobiography* (New York: Macmillan, 1938), 135; and Paul K. Conkin, *Tomorrow a New World: The New Deal Community Program* (Ithaca: Cornell University Press, 1959), 83.

14. Conkin, *Tomorrow a New World*, 3.

15. Ibid., 16.

16. M. L. Wilson, "The Place of Subsistence Homesteads in Our National Economy," *Journal of Farm Economics* 16, no. 1 (Jan. 1934): 79.

17. Bolton Hall, *A Little Land and a Living* (New York: Arcadia Press, 1908), 252–253.

18. M. L. Wilson, "Farm Relief and Allotment Plan," *Day and Hour Series #2,* University of Minnesota, 1933, 51.

19. Hall, *A Little Land and a Living*, 70–71.

20. Ralph Borsodi, *This Ugly Civilization* (New York: Simon & Schuster, 1929), 338.

21. Bolton Hall, *Three Acres and Liberty* (London, England: Macmillan, 1907), 20.

22. Franklin D. Roosevelt, "Growing Up by Plan," *The Survey* 67, no. 9 (Feb. 1, 1932): 484.

23. Wilson, "The Place of Subsistence Homesteads in Our National Economy," 79.

24. Elwood Mead, "Government Aid and Direction in Land Settlement," *American Economic Review* 8, no. 1 Supp. (March 1918): 81.

25. Elwood Mead, "The New Forty-Niners," *The Survey* 47, no. 18 (Jan. 28, 1922): 703.

26. Henry Irving Dodge, "Back to the Land for Soldiers," *Country Gentleman* 84 (Feb. 15, 1919): 5–13.

27. Conkin, "Arthurdale Revisited," 62.

28. Howe, *The Land and the Soldier*, 4–5.

29. Borsodi, *This Ugly Civilization,* 332–333.

30. Rexford Tugwell, *The Battle for Democracy* (New York: Columbia University Press, 1935), 123.

31. Paul Johnstone and Russell Lord, *A Place on Earth: A Critical Appraisal of Subsistence Homesteads* (Washington, DC: U.S. Dept. of Agriculture, Bureau of Agricultural Economics, 1942), 3.

32. Ibid., 35.

33. Wilson, "Farm Relief and Allotment Plan," 47.

34. Roosevelt, "Growing Up by Plan," 507.

35. Dodge, "Back to the Land for Soldiers," 4.

36. Wilson, "The Place of Subsistence Homesteads In Our National Economy."

37. Mead, "Government Aid and Direction in Land Settlement," 72.

38. Johnstone and Lord, *A Place on Earth*, 3.

39. Rexford Tugwell, "Farm Relief and a Permanent Agriculture," *Annals of the American Academy of Political and Social Science* 142 (Mar. 1929): 275.

40. Howe, *The Land and the Soldier*, 30.

41. Ibid., 28; Dodge, "Back to the Land for Soldiers," 46; and Hall, *Three Acres and Liberty*, 376.

42. Conkin, *Tomorrow a New World*, 71.

43. Wilson, "The Place of Subsistence Homesteads In Our National Economy," 77.

44. Borsodi, *This Ugly Civilization,* 49.

45. Tugwell, "Farm Relief and a Permanent Agriculture," 273.

46. Howe, *The Land and the Soldier*, 34.

47. Mead, "The New Forty-Niners," 703.

48. Howe, *The Land and the Soldier*, 88–90.

49. Clarence Pickett, *For More than Bread* (Boston: Little, Brown, 1953), 44.

50. Howe, *The Land and the Soldier*, 65–66.

51. Wilson, "The Place of Subsistence Homesteads in Our National Economy," 73.

52. Wilson, "Farm Relief and Allotment Plan," 40.

53. Wolfgang Schivelbusch, *Three New Deals* (New York: Metropolitan Books, 2006), 116.

54. R. W. Murchie, "Land Settlement as a Relief Measure," from *Day and Hour Series #5*, University of Minnesota, 1933, 27; Eleanor Roosevelt, "Subsistence Homesteads," *Forum* 91 (April 1934): 199–201; Wilson, "The Place of Subsistence Homesteads in Our National Economy," 78; and Wilson, "Farm Relief and Allotment Plan," 50–51.

55. Howe, *The Land and the Soldier*, 70.

56. Borsodi, *This Ugly Civilization*, 322.

57. Howe, *The Land and the Soldier*, 23.

58. Dodge, "Back to the Land for Soldiers," 4.

59. Rexford Tugwell, "Resettling America: A Fourfold Plan," *New York Times*, July 28, 1935, SM5).

60. Hoffman, *Eleanor Roosevelt and the Arthurdale Experiment*, 17.

61. Howe, *The Land and the Soldier*, 31.

62. Ibid., 24.

63. Ibid., 28.

64. Conkin, *Tomorrow a New World*, 34.

65. Johnstone and Lord, *A Place on Earth*, 3.

66. R. W. Murchie, "Land Settlement as a Relief Measure," from *Day and Hour Series #5* (University of Minnesota, 1933), 8.

67. E. Roosevelt, "Subsistence Homesteads," 199–201.

68. Roosevelt, *The Public Papers and Addresses of Franklin D. Roosevelt*, 193.

69. Conkin, *Tomorrow a New World*, 13.

70. Ibid., 19–20.

71. Henry S. Anderson, "The Little Landers' Land Colonies," *Agricultural History* 5, no. 4 (October 1931): 140–143.

72. Ibid., 144–146.

73. Ibid., 146–148.

74. Ibid., 149–150.

75. Conkin, *Tomorrow a New World*, 76–77.

76. M. L. Wilson, "The Fairway Farms Project," *Journal of Land and Public Utility Economics* 2 (1926): 156–159.

77. Deborah Kay Fitzgerald, *Every Farm a Factory: The Industrial Ideal in American Agriculture* (New Haven, CT: Yale University Press, 2003), 63.

78. Wilson, "The Fairway Farms Project."

79. Fitzgerald, *Every Farm a Factory*, 72.

80. Conkin, *Tomorrow a New World*, 77.

81. Mead, "The New Forty-Niners," 654–655.

82. Conkin, *Tomorrow a New World*, 47.

83. Ibid., 46–47.

84. Kluger, James R. *Turning on Water with a Shovel* (Albuquerque: University of New Mexico Press, 1992), 94.

85. Conkin, *Tomorrow a New World*, 43; and Kluger, *Turning on Water with a Shovel*, 85–86.

86. Conkin, *Tomorrow a New World*, 46.

87. Ibid., 46.

88. Mead, "The New Forty-Niners," 652.

89. Kluger, *Turning on Water with a Shovel*, 86–87.

90. Mead, "The New Forty-Niners," 653.

91. Ibid., 652.

92. Conkin, *Tomorrow a New World*, 46–47.

93. Mead, "Government Aid and Direction in Land Settlement," 79–80.

94. Conkin, *Tomorrow a New World*, 45; and Kluger, *Turning on Water with a Shovel*, 85–86.

95. Mead, "The New Forty-Niners," 655.

96. Ibid., 653.

97. Mead, *Helping Men Own Farms*, 9.

98. Mead, "The New Forty-Niners," 655; and Kluger, *Turning on Water with a Shovel*, 130.

99. Mead, "The New Forty-Niners."

100. Ibid., 656.

101. Conkin, *Tomorrow a New World*, 47.

102. Kluger, *Turning on Water with a Shovel*, 90–92.

103. Conkin, *Tomorrow a New World*, 47.

104. Mead, "The New Forty-Niners," 702.

105. Kluger, *Turning on Water with a Shovel*.

106. Mead, "The New Forty-Niners," 702.

107. Conkin, *Tomorrow a New World*, 48.

108. Mead, "The New Forty-Niners," 656–657.

109. Ibid., 702; and Conkin, *Tomorrow a New World*, 48.

110. Kluger, *Turning on Water with a Shovel*, 92–93.

111. Mead, "The New Forty-Niners," 658.

112. Ibid.

113. Kluger, *Turning on Water with a Shovel*, 88–89.

114. Mead, *Helping Men Own Farms*, 71.

115. Kluger, *Turning on Water with a Shovel*, 95.

116. Smythe, "New Homestead Policy for America." *Review of Reviews,* 293.

117. Kluger, *Turning on Water with a Shovel*; "What of the Colony Plan of Land Settlement?" *Agricultural Review* 18 (Apr. 1925): 16–17.

118. Kluger, *Turning on Water with a Shovel*, 98–99.

119. Though damaged, the painting was saved and now hangs in the University of California, Berkeley's Giannini Hall, part of the Agricultural Economics library.

120. "What of the Colony Plan of Land Settlement?" *Agricultural Review*.

121. Kluger, *Turning on Water with a Shovel*, 99–101.

122. Conkin, *Tomorrow a New World*, 48.

123. Kluger, *Turning on Water with a Shovel*, 101.

124. Conkin, *Tomorrow a New World*.

125. Wilson, "The Place of Subsistence Homesteads in Our National Economy," 81.

126. Frederic Booth-Tucker, "Farm Colonies of the Salvation Army," *Bulletin, U.S. Dept. of Commerce & Labor* 47I (Sept. 1903): 983–988.

127. Malcolm Cowley and Willard T. David, "How Far Back the Land?" *New Republic* 75 (Aug. 9, 1933): 336.

128. Ebenezer Howard, *Garden Cities of Tomorrow* (London, England: Swan Sonnenschein, 1902), 95.

129. Frederic C. Howe, *The Land and the Soldier* (New York: Charles Scribner's Sons, 1919), 9.

130. Conkin, *Tomorrow a New World*, 35.

131. Wilson, "Farm Relief and Allotment Plan," 37.

132. Tugwell, "Farm Relief and a Permanent Agriculture," 271.

133. Roosevelt, *The Public Papers and Addresses of Franklin D. Roosevelt*, 193.

134. Wilson, "Farm Relief and Allotment Plan," 48.

135. Borsodi, *This Ugly Civilization,* 334.

136. Johnstone and Lord, *A Place on Earth*, 38.

137. Conkin, *Tomorrow a New World*, 88.

138. Cowan, "Arthurdale," 9.

139. Johnstone and Lord, *A Place on Earth*, 36.

140. Ibid., 39.

Chapter 4: We Lucky Few

1. Kathleen Cullinan and Beth Spence, "Arthurdale: The New Deal Comes to Preston County," *Goldenseal* 7, no. 2 (Apr.–June 1981): 12.

2. John Lilly, "Weaver Dorothy Thompson," *Goldenseal* 29, no. 4 (Winter 2003): 12.

3. Amanda Griffith Penix, *Arthurdale* (Arthurdale, WV: Arthurdale Heritage, Inc., 2007), 34.

4. Cullinan and Spence, "Arthurdale: The New Deal Comes to Preston County," 20.

5. Ibid., 12.

6. Bryan Ward, "Introduction," in Ward, ed., *A New Deal for America* (Arthurdale, WV: Arthurdale Heritage, Inc., 1995), vi, gives the number as 180. Both Penix, *Arthurdale*, 8, and Paul K. Conkin, *Tomorrow a New World: The New Deal Community Program* (Ithaca, NY: Cornell University Press, 1959), 6–7, claim 99.

7. Cullinan and Spence, "Arthurdale: The New Deal Comes to Preston County," 12.

8. Wesley Stout, "The New Homesteaders," *Saturday Evening Post* (Aug. 4, 1934), 5.

9. "First Subsistence Homestead Project Formally Dedicated," *Washington Post*, Feb. 27, 1934, 11.

10. Wesley Stout, "The New Homesteaders," *Saturday Evening Post*, Aug. 4, 1934, 65.

11. Other federal notables attending were Nancy Cook, a friend of Eleanor Roosevelt put on the payroll as a "consultant"; F. M. Williams, the fourth assistant postmaster general; Clarence Pickett, working with M. L. Wilson; and two employees of the Department of the Interior, Clark T. Forman and Carl T. Taylor.

12. See Dianne Y. Ghirardo, *Building New Communities: New Deal America and Fascist Italy* (Princeton, NJ: Princeton University Press, 1989).

13. Conkin, *Tomorrow a New World*, 108.

14. Blanche Wiesen Cook, *Eleanor Roosevelt, Vol. 2: 1933–38* (New York: Viking Press, 1999), 136.

15. Ibid., 135.

16. Cited in Calvert L. Estill, "Blunders at Arthurdale," *Washington Post*, Aug. 12, 1934, SM1.

17. Bruce Beezer, "Arthurdale: An Experiment in Community Living," *West Virginia History* 36, no. 1 (1974/75): 19.

18. Ibid.

19. M. A. Glavin, "Reedsville Model for Homestead Plans," *Washington Post*, Mar. 11, 1934, B4.

20. Thomas Coode and Dennis Fabbri, "The New Deal's Arthurdale Project in West Virginia," *West Virginia History* 36, no. 4 (1974/75): 297.

21. Cook, *Eleanor Roosevelt, Vol. 2*, 137.

22. Amity Shlaes, *The Forgotten Man* (New York: HarperCollins, 2007), 155.

23. West Virginia University, Arthurdale Project Papers, West Virginia Regional and History Collection. A&M 2178/Folder 3.

24. Cook, *Eleanor Roosevelt, Vol. 2*, 135.

25. Ibid., 134.

26. Deanna Hornyak, "Arthurdale: Homesteading in West Virginia," *Now and Then* 13, no. 2 (Summer 1996): 27.

27. Cullinan and Spence, "Arthurdale: The New Deal Comes to Preston County," 9.

28. Stephen Haid, "Arthurdale: An Experiment in Community Planning, 1933–47." PhD diss., West Virginia University, 1975, 73.

29. Stout, "The New Homesteaders," 64.

30. Jerry Bruce Thomas, *An Appalachian New Deal: West Virginia in the Great Depression* (Lexington: University Press of Kentucky, 1998), 170–171.

31. Felix G. Robinson, "The Arthurdale Story," *Tableland Tales* 1 (Spring 1953–Summer 1954): 104.

32. Stout, "The New Homesteaders," 62.

33. Millard Milburn Rice, "Footnote on Arthurdale," *Harper's Magazine* 180 (Mar. 1940): 413.

34. Glavin, "Reedsville Model for Homestead Plans."

35. Rice, "Footnote on Arthurdale," 414.

36. Haid, "Arthurdale: An Experiment in Community Planning," 413.

37. Glavin, "Reedsville Model for Homestead Plans."

38. Cullinan and Spence, "Arthurdale: The New Deal Comes to Preston County," 9.

39. Shlaes, *The Forgotten Man*, 173.

40. Thomas, *An Appalachian New Deal*, 117.

41. Conkin, *Tomorrow a New World*, 118.

42. W. E. B. DuBois, *The Seventh Son: The Thought and Writings of W. E. B. DuBois Vol. 2* (New York: Random House, 1971), 245.

43. Holly Cowan, "Arthurdale." M.A. thesis, New York, Columbia University, 1968, 33.

44. Haid, "Arthurdale: An Experiment in Community Planning," 75.

45. West Virginia University, Arthurdale Project Papers, A&M 2178/Folder 1.

46. Tamara K. Hareven, *Eleanor Roosevelt: An American Conscience* (Chicago: Quadrangle Books, 1968), 95.

47. Haid, "Arthurdale: An Experiment in Community Planning," 76.

48. U.S. Dept. of the Interior, *Bulletin,* Division of Subsistence Homesteads (Washington, DC: 1935), 16; and Penix, *Arthurdale*, 29.

49. Interview with homesteader Elma Martin (C420, R569) West Virginia University Libraries, Morgantown, WV and Regional History Collection, mark 6:50.

50. Cowan, "Arthurdale," 33.

51. Haid, "Arthurdale: An Experiment in Community Planning," 78.

52. Nancy Hoffman, *Eleanor Roosevelt and the Arthurdale Experiment* (North Haven, CT: Linnet Books, 2001), 21.

53. Haid, "Arthurdale: An Experiment in Community Planning," 76–77.

54. West Virginia University, Arthurdale Project Papers, A&M 2178/Folder 6.

55. Haid, "Arthurdale: An Experiment in Community Planning," 78.

56. Hoffman, *Eleanor Roosevelt and the Arthurdale Experiment*, 22; and Connie P. Tivr, *Our Monongalia: A History of African Americans in Monongalia County, West Virginia* (Terra Alta, WV: Headline Books, 1999), 122.

57. Cowan, "Arthurdale," 35.

58. Hoffman, *Eleanor Roosevelt and the Arthurdale Experiment*, 22–23.

59. West Virginia University, Arthurdale Project Papers, A&M 2178/Folder 3.

60. Ghirardo, *Building New Communities*, 189.

61. Cowan, "Arthurdale," 34.

62. Ibid., 35.

63. Brian Q. Cannon, *Remaking the Agrarian Dream: New Deal Rural Resettlement in the Mountain West* (Albuquerque: University of New Mexico Press, 1996), 21.

64. Remarks by Jim McNelis, at Arthurdale Homestead Panel, July 9, 2009.

65. Interview with homesteader Bertie Swick (C420, R579), West Virginia University Libraries, Morgantown, WV, and Regional History Collection, mark 9:05.

66. Glavin, "Reedsville Model for Homestead Plans."

67. Interview with homesteaders Dan and Anna Houghton (C420, R571), West Virginia University Libraries, Morgantown, WV, and Regional History Collection, mark 21:00.

68. Cowan, "Arthurdale," 34.

69. Author interview with Ann Shannon, Feb. 7, 2010, mark 22:35.

70. Stephen Haid, "Arthurdale's Greatest Failure and Arthurdale's Greatest Success," in Bryan Ward, ed., *A New Deal for America* (Arthurdale, WV: Arthurdale Heritage, Inc., 1995), 85.

71. Interview with Ann Shannon, Feb. 7, 2010, with author, mark 3:15.

72. West Virginia University, Arthurdale Project Papers, A&M 2178/Folder 6.

73. West Virginia University, Arthurdale Project Papers, WA&M 2178/Folder 1.

74. Like John Cusack in *Say Anything*, but he used a boom box.

75. Jane Goldstrom, *Knoxville Borough: A History* (Pittsburgh, PA: Whortleberry Press, 1939), 57.

76. Ibid., 12.

77. Ibid., 48. Bushrod Grimes took to tennis like a fish to water, personally coaching his three daughters, of whom Frances, the middle one, was the most accomplished.

Chapter 5: "Spending Money . . . Like Drunken Sailors"

1. West Virginia University, Arthurdale Project Papers, West Virginia Regional and History Collection. A&M 2178/Folder 6.

2. Stephen Haid, "Arthurdale: An Experiment in Community Planning, 1933–47." PhD diss., West Virginia University, 1975, 113.

3. M. A. Glavin, "Reedsville Model for Homestead Plans," *Washington Post*, Mar. 11, 1934, B4.

4. West Virginia University, Arthurdale Project Papers, West Virginia Regional and History Collection, A&M 2178/Folder 6.

5. Calvert L. Estill, "Blunders at Arthurdale," *Washington Post*, Aug. 12, 1934, SM1.

6. Kathleen Cullinan and Beth Spence, "Arthurdale: The New Deal Comes to Preston County," *Goldenseal* 7, no. 7 (Apr.–June 1981): 10.

7. Thomas Coode and Dennis Fabbri, "The New Deal's Arthurdale Project in West Virginia," *West Virginia History* 36, no. 4 (1974/75): 296.

8. Amanda Griffith Penix, *Arthurdale* (Arthurdale, WV: Arthurdale Heritage, Inc., 2007), 40.

9. Estill, "Blunders at Arthurdale."

10. Ibid.

11. Wesley Stout, "The New Homesteaders," *Saturday Evening Post*, Aug. 4, 1934.

12. Cullinan and Spence, "Arthurdale: The New Deal Comes to Preston County," 11.

13. Tamara K. Hareven, *Eleanor Roosevelt: An American Conscience* (Chicago: Quadrangle Books, 1968), 96.

14. Stout, "The New Homesteaders," while Estill, "Blunders at Arthurdale," stated they were quartered in the Arthur mansion. Wherever they may have slept, there they were.

15. Coode and Fabbri, "The New Deal's Arthurdale Project in West Virginia," *West Virginia History* (1974/75, Vol.36/4, 296).

16. Haid, "Arthurdale: An Experiment in Community Planning, 88.

17. Coode and Fabbri, "The New Deal's Arthurdale Project in West Virginia."

18. Ibid., 298.

19. West Virginia University, Arthurdale Project Papers, West Virginia Regional and History Collection. A&M 2178/Folder 4.

20. Blanche Wiesen Cook, *Eleanor Roosevelt. Vol. 2: 1933–38* (New York: Viking Press, 1999), 136.

21. Ibid.; Estill, "Blunders at Arthurdale"; and Glavin, "Reedsville Model for Homestead Plans."

22. Glavin, "Reedsville Model for Homestead Plans."

23. Stout, "The New Homesteaders."

24. Glavin, "Reedsville Model for Homestead Plans."

25. Stout, "The New Homesteaders."

26. Penix, *Arthurdale*, 45.

27. Stout, "The New Homesteaders."

28. Lee A. Gladwin, "Arthurdale: Adventure into Utopia," *West Virginia History* 28, no. 4 (1967): 313.

29. Estill, "Blunders at Arthurdale."

30. Ibid.

31. Paul K. Conkin, *Tomorrow a New World: The New Deal Community Program.* Ithaca: Cornell University Press, 1959, 249.

32. Ibid., 245.

33. Penix, *Arthurdale*, 45.

34. Ibid.

35. Conkin, *Tomorrow a New World.*

36. Penix, *Arthurdale*, 46; and Jeanna S. Rymer, "Arthurdale: A Social Experiment in the 1930s," *West Virginia History* 46, no. 1 (1985–1986): 91.

37. Dianne Y. Ghirardo, *Building New Communities: New Deal America and Fascist Italy,* (Princeton, NJ: Princeton University Press, 1989), 161; and Conkin, *Tomorrow a New World*, 249.

38. U.S. Dept. of Interior, *Circular No.1* (Washington, DC: Division of Subsistence Homesteads 1933), 7.

39. Stout, "The New Homesteaders."

40. Holly Cowan, "Arthurdale," M.A. thesis, New York: Columbia University, 1968, 29.

41. M. L. Wilson, "The Place of Subsistence Homesteads in Our National Economy." *Journal of Farm Economics* 16, no. 1 (Jan. 1934): 81.

42. Elwood Mead, "Government Aid and Direction in Land Settlement," *American Economic Review* 8, no. 1 Supp. (Mar. 1918): 94.

43. Rexford Tugwell, *The Battle for Democracy* (New York: Columbia University Press, 1935), 115.

44. Clarence Pickett, *For More than Bread* (Boston: Little, Brown, 1953), 46.

45. Cowan, "Arthurdale," 26.

46. Cullinan and Spence, "Arthurdale: The New Deal Comes to Preston County," 10.

47. Penix, *Arthurdale*, 32.

48. Paul Johnstone and Russell Lord, *A Place on Earth: A Critical Appraisal of Subsistence Homesteads* (Washington, DC: U.S. Dept. of Agriculture, Bureau of Agricultural Economics, 1942), 30.

49. West Virginia University, Arthurdale Project Papers, A&M 2178/Folder 6.

50. Stout, "The New Homesteaders."

51. West Virginia University, Arthurdale Project Papers, A&M 2178/Folder 1.

52. Haid, "Arthurdale: An Experiment in Community Planning," 87.

53. Cullinan and Spence, "Arthurdale: The New Deal Comes to Preston County," 9.

54. Author interview with Robert McLaughlin Sr., 2009, mark 16:40. He remembers them using surplus World War I ambulances and trucks to transport the workman and schoolchildren back and forth to Arthurdale.

55. Stout, "The New Homesteaders."

56. Gladwin, "Arthurdale: Adventure into Utopia," 311–312.

57. Haid, "Arthurdale: An Experiment in Community Planning," 85.

58. Thomas, *An Appalachian New Deal*, 170; and Gladwin, "Arthurdale: Adventure into Utopia," 308.

59. Coode and Fabbri, "The New Deal's Arthurdale Project in West Virginia," 296.

60. Ibid., 298.

61. West Virginia University, Arthurdale Project Papers, A&M 2178/Folder 6.

62. Interview with homesteader Andy Wolfe, (C433, R720) WVU Libraries, Morgantown, WV and Regional History Collection, mark 9:00.

63. Gladwin, "Arthurdale: Adventure into Utopia," 313.

64. Cook, *Eleanor Roosevelt, Vol. 2*, 135.

65. Stout, "The New Homesteaders."

66. Conkin, *Tomorrow a New World*, 245.

67. U.S. Dept. of Interior, *Circular No.1* (Washington, DC: Division of Subsistence Homesteads, 1933), 11.

68. Johnstone and Lord, Russell, *A Place on Earth*, 51.

69. Cullinan and Spence, "Arthurdale: The New Deal Comes to Preston County," 10.

70. West Virginia University, Arthurdale Project Papers, A&M 1291.

71. Coode and Fabbri, "The New Deal's Arthurdale Project in West Virginia," 299.

72. West Virginia University, Arthurdale Project Papers, A&M 2178/Folder 6.

73. Ibid., Folder 1.

74. Ibid., Folder 3.

75. Stout, "The New Homesteaders."

76. Rymer, "Arthurdale: A Social Experiment in the 1930s," 91.

77. Estill, "Blunders at Arthurdale."

78. Ibid.; Conkin, *Tomorrow a New World*, 245; and Ghirardo, *Building New Communities*, 161.

79. Ghirardo, *Building New Communities*; and Stout, "The New Homesteaders."

80. Estill, "Blunders at Arthurdale."

81. Jerry Bruce Thomas, *An Appalachian New Deal: West Virginia in the Great Depression* (Lexington, KY: University Press of Kentucky, 1998), 171.

82. Conkin, *Tomorrow a New World*, 246.

83. West Virginia University, Arthurdale Project Papers, A&M 2178/Folder 6.

84. Stephen Haid, "Arthurdale's Greatest Failure and Arthurdale's Greatest Success," in *A New Deal for America*, ed. Bryan Ward (Arthurdale Heritage Inc, 1995), 82.

85. Nancy Hoffman, *Eleanor Roosevelt and the Arthurdale Experiment* (North Haven, CT: Linnet Books, 2001), 41.

86. Ibid.

87. Cullinan and Spence, "Arthurdale: The New Deal Comes to Preston County," 10.

88. Conkin, *Tomorrow a New World*, 250.

89. Felix G. Robinson, "The Arthurdale Story," *Tableland Tales* 1 (Spring 1953–Summer 1954): 100.

90. West Virginia University, Arthurdale Project Papers, A&M 2178/Folder 3.

91. Jim McNelis, "Jim McNelis Remembers," *Arthurdale Heritage Newsletter* (Jan./Apr./July 2000, 3 parts); and see also T. R. Carskadon, "Hull House in the Hills," *New Republic* 79 (Aug. 1, 1934): 312–314. There was a sign inside warning those visitors not to use the toilet—it was broken.

92. Interview with homesteader Joseph Roscoe (C433, R716), West Virginia University Libraries, Morgantown, WV, and Regional History Collection, mark 6:45.

93. Robert L. Reid, "Documenting Arthurdale: Looking At New Deal Photography," in Bryan Ward, ed., *A New Deal for America* (Arthurdale, WV: Arthurdale Heritage, Inc., 1995), 155–179.

94. Haid, "Arthurdale: An Experiment in Community Planning," 177.

95. West Virginia University, Arthurdale Project Papers, A&M 2178/Folder 6; and Carskadon, "Hull House in the Hills."

96. Carskadon, "Hull House in the Hills," 312.

97. Glavin, "Reedsville Model for Homestead Plans."

98. Author interview with Robert McLaughlin Sr., mark 33:00.

99. Interview with homesteader Andy Wolfe (C433, R720), West Virginia University Libraries, Morgantown, WV, and Regional History Collection, mark 14:38.

100. Author interview with Robert McLaughlin Sr., mark 35:00.

101. Wolfgang Schivelbusch, *Three New Deals* (New York: Metropolitan Books, 2006), 128.

102. Stout, "The New Homesteaders."

103. Ghirardo, *Building New Communities*, 163.

104. Haid, "Arthurdale: An Experiment in Community Planning," 100.

105. Rice, "Footnote on Arthurdale," 414.

106. Rymer, "Arthurdale: A Social Experiment in the 1930s," 90.

107. Ghirardo, *Building New Communities*, 177.

108. West Virginia University, Arthurdale Project Papers, A&M 2178/Folder 3.

109. Ghirardo, *Building New Communities*, 176.

110. Estill, "Blunders at Arthurdale."

111. Ibid.

112. Haid, "Arthurdale: An Experiment in Community Planning," 91.

113. Stout, "The New Homesteaders."

114. West Virginia University, Arthurdale Project Papers, A&M 1291.

115. Robert McLaughlin Jr. and Norma (Turner), "McLaughlin Family: SR-7," *Arthurdale Heritage Newsletter* (Spring/Summer 2007, two-part series); and Penix, *Arthurdale*, 40.

116. Stephen Haid, "Arthurdale's Greatest Failure and Arthurdale's Greatest Success," in Bryan Ward, ed., *A New Deal for America* (Arthurdale, WV: Arthurdale Heritage, Inc., 1995), 82–83; and Haid, "Arthurdale: An Experiment in Community Planning," 170.

117. West Virginia University, Arthurdale Project Papers, A&M 1291.

118. McLaughlin and Norma (Turner), "McLaughlin Family: SR-7."

119. Haid, "Arthurdale: An Experiment in Community Planning," 205.

120. Felix G. Robinson, "The Arthurdale Story," *Tableland Tales* 1 (Spring 1953–Summer 1954), 99.

121. Arthurdale Town Archives, *Records of Births at Arthurdale Health Clinic*, Arthurdale, WV.

122. Interview with homesteaders Alice and Warren Whittaker and Florence (Groves) Hovatter (C433, R723), West Virginia University Libraries, Morgantown, WV, and Regional History Collection, mark 35:47.

123. Hareven, *Eleanor Roosevelt: An American Conscience*, 110–111.

124. Carskadon, "Hull House in the Hills," 312.

125. Hareven, *Eleanor Roosevelt: An American Conscience*, 107.

126. Hoffman, *Eleanor Roosevelt and the Arthurdale Experiment*, 26–35; and Lois Scharf, "First Lady/First Homestead," in Ward, *A New Deal for America*, 103.

127. Hoffman, *Eleanor Roosevelt and the Arthurdale Experiment*, 36.

128. Scharf, "First Lady/First Homestead," 102–103.

129. We deserved a better president, while we are on the subject.

130. Robinson, "The Arthurdale Story," *Tableland Tales*, 99; and Scharf, "First Lady/First Homestead," 106.

131. Haid, "Arthurdale: An Experiment in Community Planning," 98.

132. Scharf, "First Lady/First Homestead," 108–109.

133. Ibid., 106.

134. Bruce Beezer, "Arthurdale: An Experiment in Community Living," *West Virginia History* 36, no. 1 (1974/75): 20.

135. Cook, *Eleanor Roosevelt, Vol. 2*, 141.

136. Gladwin, "Arthurdale: Adventure into Utopia," 313.

137. Haid, "Arthurdale: An Experiment in Community Planning," 204.

138. Ibid., 176.

Chapter 6: The Darkening of the Light

1. "Arthurdale Inn, Three Factories Sold," *New York Times* (June 16, 1946), 33.

2. Stephen Haid, "Arthurdale's Greatest Failure and Arthurdale's Greatest Success," in Bryan Ward, ed., *A New Deal for America* (Arthurdale, WV: Arthurdale Heritage, Inc., 1995), 82.

3. West Virginia University, Arthurdale Project Papers, West Virginia Regional and History Collection. A&M 1291, *Dominion News* (Oct. 3, 1934).

4. C. J. Maloney, "The Peculiar History of Arthurdale," Mises.org, Aug. 8, 2007, http://mises.org/daily/2645.

5. Haid, "Arthurdale's Greatest Failure and Arthurdale's Greatest Success," 92; and Nancy Hoffman, *Eleanor Roosevelt and the Arthurdale Experiment* (North Haven, CT, Linnet Books, 2001), 49.

6. Interview with homesteader Hilda Hendershot (C433, R718), West Virginia University Libraries, Morgantown, WV, and Regional History Collection, mark 27:40.

7. Paul K. Conkin, *Tomorrow a New World, The New Deal Community Program* (Ithaca, NY: Cornell University Press, 1959), 26.

8. Ibid., 99.

9. Paul K. Conkin, "Arthurdale Revisited: When Subsistence Farming Made Sense," in Ward, *A New Deal for America*, 64.

10. Stephen Haid, "Arthurdale: An Experiment in Community Planning, 1933–47." PhD diss., West Virginia University, 1975, 174.

11. College of Education, West Virginia University, "Report of the Survey of Arthurdale School," May 6, 1940, 5.

12. Dianne Y. Ghirardo, *Building New Communities: New Deal America and Fascist Italy* (Princeton, NJ: Princeton University Press, 1989), 174–175; and U.S. Dept. of the Interior, *Circular No. 1* (Washington, DC: Division of Subsistence Homesteads, 1933), 8.

13. U.S. Dept. of the Interior, *Bulletin* (Washington, DC: Division of Subsistence Homesteads, 1935), 18.

14. Haid, "Arthurdale's Greatest Failure and Arthurdale's Greatest Success," 84.

15. Amanda Griffith Penix, *Arthurdale* (Arthurdale, WV: Arthurdale Heritage, Inc., 2007), 35.

16. Haid, "Arthurdale's Greatest Failure and Arthurdale's Greatest Success," 85.

17. Ibid., 84–85.

18. Interview with homesteader Ralph Brown (C433, R722), West Virginia University Libraries, Morgantown, WV, and Regional History Collection, mark 10:40.

19. West Virginia University, Arthurdale Project Papers, West Virginia Regional and History Collection. A&M 2178/Folder 6.

20. Hall, Bolton. *Three Acres and Liberty*. London, England, The Macmillan Co., 1907, 12.

21. West Virginia University, Arthurdale Project Papers, A&M 2178.

22. Ghirardo, *Building New Communities*, 113.

23. Ibid., 114.

24. West Virginia University, Arthurdale Project Papers, A&M 2178/Folder 1. Letter, O. B. Smart to Charles Pynchon, July 19, 1934.

25. Ibid., Ltr C. E. Pynchon to "All Project Managers," Sept. 25, 1934.

26. Ibid., Folder 3. "Minutes to a Homesteaders Meeting," July 11, 1934.

27. Ibid., Folder 1 Ltr. C. E. Pynchon to G. M. Flynn.

28. Haid, "Arthurdale's Greatest Failure and Arthurdale's Greatest Success," 88.

29. Interview with homesteaders Jacob and Bertie Swick (C420, R579), West Virginia University Libraries, Morgantown, WV, and Regional History Collection, mark 11:35.

30. Stephen Haid, "Arthurdale: An Experiment in Community Planning, 1933–47." PhD diss., West Virginia University, 1975, 175.

31. College of Education, West Virginia University, "Report of the Survey of Arthurdale School," (May 6, 1940), 43.

32. Conkin, "Arthurdale Revisited," 61.

33. Haid, "Arthurdale's Greatest Failure and Arthurdale's Greatest Success," 85.

34. Author interview with Norma (Turner) McLaughlin, 2010, mark 11:50.

35. Author interview with Glenn Luzier, 2010, mark 23:15.

36. According to Norma (Turner) McLaughlin, her family continued to farm until 1953. Author interview with Norma (Turner) McLaughlin, 2010, mark 17:00.

37. Paul Johnstone and Russell Lord, *A Place on Earth: A Critical Appraisal of Subsistence Homesteads* (Washington, DC: U.S. Dept. of Agriculture, Bureau of Agricultural Economics, 1942), 187.

38. Conkin, "Arthurdale Revisited," 59.

39. Haid, "Arthurdale: An Experiment in Community Planning, 1933–47."

40. Haid, "Arthurdale's Greatest Failure and Arthurdale's Greatest Success," 70.

41. Wesley Stout, "The New Homesteaders," *Saturday Evening Post*, Aug. 4, 1934.

42. Johnstone and Lord, *A Place on Earth*, 1942, 190.

43. U.S. Dept. of the Interior, *Circular No. 1*, 8.

44. Conkin, *Tomorrow a New World*, 99.

45. M. A. Glavin, "Reedsville Model for Homestead Plans," *Washington Post*, Mar. 11, 1934, B4.

46. Lee A. Gladwin, "Arthurdale: Adventure into Utopia," *West Virginia History* 28, no. 4 (1967): 309.

47. "First Subsistence Homestead Project Formally Dedicated," *Washington Post*, Feb. 27, 1934, 11.

48. Haid, "Arthurdale's Greatest Failure and Arthurdale's Greatest Success," 67–68.

49. Haid, "Arthurdale: An Experiment in Community Planning," 125.

50. Tamara K. Hareven, *Eleanor Roosevelt: An American Conscience* (Chicago: Quadrangle Books, 1968), 102.

51. Ghirardo, *Building New Communities*, 116.

52. Haid, "Arthurdale: An Experiment in Community Planning," 140.

53. Gladwin, "Arthurdale: Adventure into Utopia," 312.

54. Thomas Coode and Dennis Fabbri, "The New Deal's Arthurdale Project in West Virginia," *West Virginia History* 36, no. 4 (1974/75): 303.

55. Penix, *Arthurdale*. 80. Thus $19,000 disappeared in a flash. If you ever wonder why the Great Depression lasted so long, wonder no more.

56. Haid, "Arthurdale: An Experiment in Community Planning," 130.

57. Gladwin, "Arthurdale: Adventure into Utopia," 314.

58. Michael Byers, "Brave New World: Revisiting Arthurdale, WV," *Preservation* (March/April 2006): 32–37.

59. Penix, *Arthurdale,* 80.

60. Millard Milburn Rice, "Footnote on Arthurdale," *Harper's Magazine* 180 (March 1940): 416.

61. Haid, "Arthurdale: An Experiment in Community Planning, 137.

62. Ibid., 137–139.

63. West Virginia University, Arthurdale Project Papers, A&M 2178/Folder 1. Ltr Bushrod Grimes to Raymond Kenny, June 22, 1939.

64. Haid, "Arthurdale: An Experiment in Community Planning," 143.

65. Julia Perry, Letter to Author, February 2010.

66. West Virginia University, Arthurdale Project Papers, A&M 2178/Folder 1. Ltr Bushrod Grimes to GM Flynn, Nov. 5, 1934.

67. Matthew Yeager, "Scotts Run: A Community in Transition." *West Virginia History* 53 (1994): 7–20.

68. Conkin, *Tomorrow a New World,* 248.

69. Ghirardo, *Building New Communities: New Deal America and Fascist Italy,* 136.

70. Haid, "Arthurdale: An Experiment in Community Planning," 225; and U.S. Dept. of the Interior, *Bulletin,* 16.

71. Haid, "Arthurdale: An Experiment in Community Planning," 221.

72. Byers, "Brave New World," 32–37; and U.S. Dept. of the Interior, *Bulletin,* 18.

73. Haid, "Arthurdale: An Experiment in Community Planning," 234.

74. Ibid., 309.

75. Ghirardo, *Building New Communities,* 132–133.

76. Haid, "Arthurdale: An Experiment in Community Planning," 224; and Conkin, *Tomorrow a New World,* 160.

77. Ghirardo, *Building New Communities,* 115.

78. Haid, "Arthurdale: An Experiment in Community Planning," 227.

79. Kathleen Cullinan and Beth Spence, "Arthurdale: The New Deal Comes to Preston County," *Goldenseal* 7, no. 2 (Apr.–June 1981): 14.

80. Haid, "Arthurdale: An Experiment in Community Planning," 229, 233.

81. Thomas Coode and Dennis Fabbri, "The New Deal's Arthurdale Project in West Virginia," *West Virginia History* 36, no. 4 (1974/75): 304.

82. Haid, "Arthurdale: An Experiment in Community Planning," 148.

83. Ibid., 252–254.

84. Interview with homesteader Hilda Hendershot (C433, R718), West Virginia University Libraries, Morgantown, WV, and Regional History Collection, mark 25:00.

85. Interview with homesteader Andy Wolfe (C433, R720), West Virginia University Libraries, Morgantown, WV, and Regional History Collection, mark 27:50.

86. Haid, "Arthurdale: An Experiment in Community Planning," 252–254.

87. Ibid., 222.

88. Jeanna S. Rymer, "Arthurdale: A Social Experiment in the 1930s," *West Virginia History* 46, no. 1 (1985–86): 99.

89. Haid, "Arthurdale: An Experiment in Community Planning," 249.

90. Interview with homesteader Hilda Hendershot, mark 9:15.

91. Haid, "Arthurdale: An Experiment in Community Planning."

92. Penix, *Arthurdale*, 84.

93. Conkin, *Tomorrow a New World*, 166.

94. Haid, "Arthurdale: An Experiment in Community Planning," 228–289.

95. Ibid., 235.

96. Ibid., 236.

97. Ibid., 238.

98. College of Education, West Virginia University, "Report of the Survey of Arthurdale School," May 6, 1940, 44.

99. Haid, "Arthurdale: An Experiment in Community Planning," 236.

100. Ibid., 237.

101. College of Education, West Virginia University, "Report of the Survey of Arthurdale School."

102. Haid, "Arthurdale: An Experiment in Community Planning," 237.

103. Ibid., 239–242.

104. Coode and Fabbri, "The New Deal's Arthurdale Project in West Virginia," 304.

105. Haid, "Arthurdale: An Experiment in Community Planning," 143–145.

106. "Business Hurt by New Deal," *Chicago Daily Tribune*, Dec. 30, 1939, 4.

107. Haid, "Arthurdale: An Experiment in Community Planning," 260, 317.

108. Frederic Booth-Tucker, "Farm Colonies of the Salvation Army," *Bulletin— U.S. Dept. of Commerce & Labor* 47I (Sept. 1903): 983–988.

109. Ghirardo, *Building New Communities*, 117.

110. Haid, "Arthurdale: An Experiment in Community Planning," 243.

111. "Arthurdale Inn, Three Factories Sold," *New York Times*, June 16, 1946, 33.

112. Hoffman, *Eleanor Roosevelt and the Arthurdale Experiment*, 75.

113. Ibid., 95.

114. Name and source withheld to protect the family's privacy, even if the head of the household from that time deserves no such courtesy. The source exists; look hard enough and you will find it.

115. Coode and Fabbri, "The New Deal's Arthurdale Project in West Virginia," 308.

116. Glenda (Stump) McLaughlin, "Joseph Harvey and Nellie Jane McLaughlin," in Marilee Hall, ed., "New Deal": Original Homesteaders of Arthurdale, WV (Arthurdale, WV: Arthurdale Heritage, Inc., 2009, 24.

117. Author interview with Linda (Honchell) McLaughlin, 2010, mark 7:30.

118. Author interview with Robert McLaughlin Sr., 2009, mark 30:30.

119. Ibid., mark 29:35.

120. Author interview with Linda (Honchell) McLaughlin.

121. Author interview with Glenda (Stump) McLaughlin, 2010, mark 7:15.

122. Author interview with Norma (Turner) McLaughlin, 2010, mark 24:35.

123. Ibid., mark 8:35.

124. Interview with homesteader Andy Wolfe (C433, R720), mark 22:40.

125. Deanna Hornyak, "Arthurdale: Homesteading in West Virginia," Now and Then 13, no. 2 (Summer 1996): 29; and Interview with homesteaders Edna and Robert Day (C433, R719), West Virginia University Libraries, Morgantown, WV, and Regional History Collection, mark 19:00.

126. Interview with homesteader Glenna Williams (C433, R725), West Virginia University Libraries, Morgantown, WV, and Regional History Collection, mark 54:15.

127. Interview with homesteader Andy Wolfe (C433, R720), mark 23:20 and FS, mark 12:30.

128. Conkin, Tomorrow a New World, 254.

129. Hoffman, Eleanor Roosevelt and the Arthurdale Experiment, 56.

130. Author interview with Dr. John Fullmer, 2010, marks 26:50 and 27:30.

131. College of Education, West Virginia University, "Report of the Survey of Arthurdale School," 77.

132. Interview with homesteaders Edna and Robert Day (C433, R719), mark 25:15.

133. College of Education, West Virginia University, "Report of the Survey of Arthurdale School," 52; see Svea Sauer, "The Doctor's Wife: My Life in Arthurdale," Arthurdale Heritage Newsletter (Fall 2007).

134. Conkin, Tomorrow a New World, 107.

135. Author interview with Norma (Turner) McLaughlin, mark 10:10.

136. Interview with homesteader Bill Watson (C433, R721), West Virginia University Libraries, Morgantown, WV, and Regional History Collection, mark 2:15.

137. Interview with homesteader Ralph Brown (C433, R722), West Virginia University Libraries, Morgantown, WV, and Regional History Collection, mark 16:15.

138. Author interview with Glenn Luzier, 2010, mark 33:00.

139. Ibid., mark 32:35.

140. Author interview with Dr. John Fullmer, mark 33:05.

141. Penix, *Arthurdale*, 72.

142. Sauer, "The Doctor's Wife."

143. Conkin, *Tomorrow a New World*, 197.

144. Haid, "Arthurdale: An Experiment in Community Planning," 255; and Sauer, "The Doctor's Wife."

145. Conkin, *Tomorrow a New World*.

146. College of Education, West Virginia University, "Report of the Survey of Arthurdale School," 75.

147. Haid, "Arthurdale: An Experiment in Community Planning."

148. Conkin, *Tomorrow a New World*," 254.

149. Rice, "Footnote on Arthurdale," 417.

150. Haid, "Arthurdale: An Experiment in Community Planning," 187.

151. U.S. Dept. of the Interior, *Bulletin*, 17.

152. Interview with homesteaders Alice and Warren Whittaker and Florence (Groves) Hovatter (C433, R723), mark 12:10.

153. Interview with homesteader Joseph Roscoe (C433, R716), West Virginia University Libraries, Morgantown, WV, and Regional History Collection, mark 12:10.

154. Robert A. Caro, *The Path to Power* (New York: Alfred A. Knopf, 1982), 360.

155. Conkin, *Tomorrow a New World,* 170.

156. Ghirardo, *Building New Communities*, 116.

157. Haid, "Arthurdale: An Experiment in Community Planning," 253.

158. Julia Perry, Letter to author.

159. West Virginia University, Arthurdale Project Papers, A&M 2178/Folder 1.

160. Author interviews with Glenn Luzier, mark, 24:40; and with Dr. John Fullmer, mark 26:25.

161. Haid, "Arthurdale's Greatest Failure and Arthurdale's Greatest Success," 81.

162. Ibid., 80.

163. Coode, and Fabbri, "The New Deal's Arthurdale Project in West Virginia," 305.

164. Haid, "Arthurdale's Greatest Failure and Arthurdale's Greatest Success," 81; and Haid, "Arthurdale: An Experiment in Community Planning," 147–148.

165. Conkin, *Tomorrow a New World*, 228.

166. Coode, and Fabbri, "The New Deal's Arthurdale Project in West Virginia."

167. Interview with homesteader Andy Wolfe (C433, R720), mark 9:20.

168. Interview with homesteaders Ruby and Maynard Weaver (C433, R728), West Virginia University Libraries, Morgantown, WV, and Regional History Collection, mark 9:40.

169. Conkin, *Tomorrow a New World*, 242.

170. Ibid., 186.

171. West Virginia University, Arthurdale Project Papers, A&M 1291.

172. Rice, "Footnote on Arthurdale," 418.

173. Coode, and Fabbri, "The New Deal's Arthurdale Project in West Virginia," 308.

174. Ibid., 306–307.

175. Ann Shannon (Bushrod Grimes's granddaughter), letter to Author, Feb. 14, 2010.

176. Conkin, *Tomorrow a New World*, 128.

177. Ibid., 118.

178. Haid, "Arthurdale's Greatest Failure and Arthurdale's Greatest Success," 89.

179. Rice, "Footnote on Arthurdale," 418.

Chapter 7: "A Human Experiment Station"

1. Lee A. Gladwin, "Arthurdale: Adventure Into Utopia," *West Virginia* History 28/4 (1967), 311 and Louis Howe Papers, 1934, FDRL.

2. *Report of the Administration of the FSA: 1939,* Printed Materials Collection, 18, FDRL.

3. Paul Johnstone and Russell Lord, *A Place on Earth: A Critical Appraisal of Subsistence Homesteads* (Washington, DC: U.S. Dept. of Agriculture, Bureau of Agricultural Economics, 1942), v.

4. Memorandum No. 732, Secretary Henry Wallace, U.S. Dept. of Agriculture, Sept. 1, 1937, Printed Materials Collection, FDRL.

5. *Progress Report #133*, U.S. Dept. of Agriculture, October 1940, Printed Materials Collection, FDRL.

6. Letter, Elsie Clapp to Eleanor Roosevelt, February 13, 1936, Eleanor Roosevelt Papers, FDRL.

7. Ibid.

8. Newspaper clip of *Washington Herald*, April 2, 1935, Rexford Tugwell Papers, FDRL.

9. Nancy Hoffman, *Eleanor Roosevelt and the Arthurdale Experiment* (North Haven, CT: Linnet Books, 2001), 25.

10. Memorandum, Division of Subsistence Homesteads, July 17, 1934, West Virginia University, Arthurdale Project Papers, West Virginia Regional and History Collection. A&M 2178/Folder 4.

11. Letter, H. W. MacGregor (Supervisor of Purchases, DSH) to F. O. Clark and Bushrod Grimes, August 20, 1934, West Virginia University, Arthurdale Project Papers, A&M 2178/Folder 1.

12. Letter C. E. Pynchon to All Project Managers, September 25, 1934, West Virginia University, Arthurdale Project Papers, A&M 2178/Folder 1.

13. Clarence Pickett, *For More than Bread* (Boston: Little, Brown, 1953), 44.

14. Henry Irving Dodge, "Back to the Land for Soldiers," *Country Gentleman* 84 (Feb. 15, 1919): 43.

15. Rexford G. Tugwell, "Farm Relief and a Permanent Agriculture," *Annals of the American Academy* 142 (March 1929): 279.

16. Stephen Haid, "Arthurdale: An Experiment in Community Planning, 1933–47." PhD diss., West Virginia University, 1975, 57.

17. Webster Powell and Harold Ware, "Planning for Permanent Poverty," *Harper's Magazine* 170 (Apr. 1935): 524.

18. Johnstone and Lord, *A Place on Earth*, 40–41.

19. Paul K. Conkin, *Tomorrow a New World: The New Deal Community Program* (Ithaca, NY: Cornell University Press, 1959), 105.

20. Ibid., 103, 124–125.

21. Johnstone and Lord, *A Place on Earth*, 48.

22. Conkin, *Tomorrow a New World,* 80.

23. Ibid., 94.

24. Johnstone and Lord, *A Place on Earth*, 42.

25. Blanche Wiesen Cook, *Eleanor Roosevelt, Vol. 2: 1933–38* (New York: Viking Press, 1999), frontispiece, quoting *New York Times*, December 29, 1933.

26. Author interview with Glenn Luzier, 2010, mark 35:15.

27. U.S. Dept. of the Interior, *Circular No.1* (Washington, DC: Division of Subsistence Homesteads, 1933), 6–7.

28. Ibid., 7.

29. Conkin, *Tomorrow a New World,* 111; and see Brian Q. Cannon, *Remaking the Agrarian Dream: New Deal Rural Resettlement in the Mountain West* (Albuquerque: University of New Mexico Press, 1996), 15–19, for discussion of the same.

30. Conkin, *Tomorrow a New World,* 120.

31. See Johnstone and Lord, *A Place on Earth*; Conkin, *Tomorrow a New World,* 119; and U.S. Dept. of the Interior, *Circular No.1*, 8, and addendum.

32. Johnstone and Lord, *A Place on Earth*, 48.

33. Haid, "Arthurdale: An Experiment in Community Planning," 340.

34. Cook, *Eleanor Roosevelt, Vol. 2*, 142.

35. See Official File 1568, Boxes 2, 3, and 4. FDRL.

36. Powell and Ware, "Planning for Permanent Poverty," 515.

37. Haid, "Arthurdale: An Experiment in Community Planning," 53.

38. Radio Broadcast Transcript, Colonel Louis Howe, September 29, 1934, Louis Howe Papers, FDRL.

39. Johnstone and Lord, *A Place on Earth*, 40.

40. U.S. Dept. of the Interior, *Bulletin*, 8–10.

41. Ibid., 6.

42. Conkin, *Tomorrow a New World,* 128–129.

43. Johnstone and Lord, *A Place on Earth*, 51.

44. Conkin, *Tomorrow a New World,* 147.

45. Ibid., 156, 178.

46. Dianne Y. Ghirardo, *Building New Communities: New Deal America and Fascist Italy* (Princeton, NJ: Princeton University Press, 1989), 118.

47. Conkin, *Tomorrow a New World,* 151.

48. Amanda Griffith Penix, *Arthurdale* (Arthurdale, WV: Arthurdale Heritage, Inc., 2007), 51.

49. Deanna Hornyak, "Arthurdale: Homesteading in West Virginia," *Now and Then* 13, no. 2 (Summer 1996): 29.

50. Annabelle Mayor, Interview transcript (late 1980s?), Arthurdale Heritage, Inc., 3.

51. Ibid., 6; and John Maxwell, "Learning by Doing: Teachers Remember Arthurdale School," *Goldenseal* 8, no. 1 (Spring 1982): 71; and Mary Wuenstel, "Participants in the Arthurdale Community School's Experiment

in Progressive Education from the Years 1934–1938 Recount Their Experiences," *Education* 122, no. 4 (2002): 766.

52. Hoxie, Mary Jones. *Swords into Ploughshares, An Account of the AFSC.* Westport, CT, Greenwood Press, 1971, 240 and see Michael Byers, "Brave New World: Revisiting Arthurdale, WV," *Preservation* (Mar./Apr. 2006): 32–37.

53. Byers, "Brave New World."

54. College of Education, West Virginia University, "Report of the Survey of Arthurdale School," Morgantown, WV, 1940, 74.

55. Ibid., 101–104.

56. Daniel Perlstein, "Community and Democracy in American Schools," *Teachers College Record* 97, no. 4 (Summer 1996): 634.

57. See Dodge, "Back to the Land for Soldiers," 46; and Ralph Borsodi, *This Ugly Civilization*, 326–327.

58. Conkin, *Tomorrow a New World*, 4.

59. Letter, Elsie Clapp to Eleanor Roosevelt, January 4, 1936, Eleanor Roosevelt Papers, FDRL.

60. Perlstein, "Community and Democracy in American Schools," 635.

61. Rexford G. Tugwell, "Social Objectives of Education." Manuscript, Columbia University, 1932, 104.

62. Ibid., 117.

63. Perlstein, "Community and Democracy in American Schools," 631.

64. Ibid., 637.

65. Letter, Clapp to Eleanor Roosevelt, January 4, 1936.

66. "Hush!" *Saturday Evening Post*, Apr. 3, 1937, 24.

67. Elsie Clapp, *Community Schools in Action* (New York: Arno Press, 1971), 89.

68. Ibid., 333.

69. College of Education, West Virginia University, "Report of the Survey of Arthurdale School," 5.

70. Sam Stack, "Elsie Ripley Clapp and the Arthurdale Schools," Paper presented at the annual meeting of the American Educational Research Association, Montreal, Canada, April 23, 1999, 27–28.

71. Interview with homesteader Jettie Eble (C433, R724) WVU Libraries, Morgantown, WV, and Regional History Collection.

72. Nancy Hoffman, *Eleanor Roosevelt and the Arthurdale Experiment* (North Haven, CT: Linnet Books, 2001), 64.

73. Stack, "Elsie Ripley Clapp and the Arthurdale Schools," 23.

74. Felix G. Robinson, "The Arthurdale Story," *Tableland Tales* 1 (Spring 1953–Summer 1954): 100.

75. Stack, "Elsie Ripley Clapp and the Arthurdale Schools," 2.

76. Ibid.

77. Ibid., 3–4.

78. Ibid., 6–7.

79. Haid, "Arthurdale: An Experiment in Community Planning," 274; and Stack, "Elsie Ripley Clapp and the Arthurdale Schools," 1, 15.

80. Interview with homesteader Jettie Eble (C433, R724), West Virginia University Libraries, Morgantown, WV, and Regional History Collection, mark 6:50.

81. Perlstein, "Community and Democracy in American Schools," 634.

82. Interview with homesteader Andy Wolfe (C433, R720), West Virginia University Libraries, Morgantown, WV, and Regional History Collection, mark 5:10.

83. Stuart Patterson, "Constructing Ideal Families in Ideal Communities: The Case of Arthurdale, West Virginia." Manuscript, Emory University, April 2002, 8.

84. College of Education, West Virginia University, "Report of the Survey of Arthurdale School," 17.

85. Haid, "Arthurdale: An Experiment in Community Planning," 276; and Stack, *Elsie Ripley Clapp and the Arthurdale Schools*, 25.

86. Tamara K. Hareven, *Eleanor Roosevelt: An American Conscience* (Chicago: Quadrangle Books, 1968), 100.

87. College of Education, West Virginia University, "Report of the Survey of Arthurdale School," 120.

88. Ibid., 101.

89. Interview with homesteader Richard Glass (C433, R726), West Virginia University Libraries, Morgantown, WV, and Regional History Collection, mark 5:00.

90. John Maxwell, "Learning By Doing: Teachers Remember Arthurdale School." *Goldenseal* 8, no. 1 (Spring 1982): 66; and College of Education, West Virginia University, "Report of the Survey of Arthurdale School," 104.

91. College of Education, West Virginia University, "Report of the Survey of Arthurdale School," 86, 106.

92. Haid, "Arthurdale: An Experiment in Community Planning," 292.

93. Hareven, *Eleanor Roosevelt: An American Conscience*, 100–101.

94. College of Education, West Virginia University, "Report of the Survey of Arthurdale School," 108.

95. Ibid., 2.

96. Ibid.

97. Ibid., 111.

98. Haid, "Arthurdale: An Experiment in Community Planning," 299; and College of Education, West Virginia University, "Report of the Survey of Arthurdale School," 4.

99. Haid, "Arthurdale: An Experiment in Community Planning."

100. College of Education, West Virginia University, "Report of the Survey of Arthurdale School," 115.

101. Ibid., 16.

102. Annabelle Mayor, Interview transcript, 3.

103. Interview with homesteaders Alice and Warren Whittaker & Florence (Groves) Hovatter, (C433, R723) West Virginia University Libraries, Morgantown, WV, and Regional History Collection, mark 6:15.

104. College of Education, West Virginia University, "Report of the Survey of Arthurdale School," 3, 19; Stack, "Elsie Ripley Clapp and the Arthurdale Schools," 27; and Perlstein, "Community and Democracy in American Schools," 633.

105. College of Education, West Virginia University, "Report of the Survey of Arthurdale School," 24.

106. Memorandum of E. Grant Nine, "Philosophy of the Arthurdale School," 1938, Eleanor Roosevelt Papers, FDRL; and see College of Education, West Virginia University, "Report of the Survey of Arthurdale School," 17, for comments by Nine.

107. College of Education, West Virginia University, "Report of the Survey of Arthurdale School," 16.

108. Perlstein, "Community and Democracy in American Schools," 636.

109. Letter, Elsie Clapp to Eleanor Roosevelt, January 4, 1936; and Patterson, "Constructing Ideal Families in Ideal Communities," 7.

110. Stuart Patterson, *Defining Memory*, ed. Amy K. Leven (Plymouth, England: AltaMira Press, 2007), 118.

111. Fullmer, Elizabeth, Interview transcript, June 25, 1987, Arthurdale Heritage, Inc., 15.

112. Stack, "Elsie Ripley Clapp and the Arthurdale Schools," 13–14.

113. Maxwell, "Learning by Doing," 69.

114. Ibid.; and Haid, "Arthurdale: An Experiment in Community Planning," 285–286.

115. College of Education, West Virginia University, "Report of the Survey of Arthurdale School," 3.

116. Ibid., 31.

117. Ibid., 84–89.

118. Ibid., 67.

119. Ibid., 7.

120. Patterson, "Constructing Ideal Families in Ideal Communities," 8.

121. College of Education, West Virginia University, "Report of the Survey of Arthurdale School," 59.

122. Bruce Beezer, "Arthurdale: An Experiment in Community Living," *West Virginia History* 36, no. 1 (1974/75): 33.

123. College of Education, West Virginia University, "Report of the Survey of Arthurdale School," 16.

124. Eleanor Roosevelt, *This I Remember* (New York: HarperCollins, 1949), 130.

125. Minutes of Homesteaders Club Meeting, February 26, 1936, West Virginia University, Arthurdale Project Papers, West Virginia Regional and History Collection. A&M 182.

126. James David, Interview transcript (early 1990s?), Arthurdale Heritage, Inc., 2.

127. See also interview with homesteaders Edna and Robert Day (C433, R719), West Virginia University Libraries, Morgantown, WV, and Regional History Collection, mark 5:00.

128. Interview with homesteader Jettie Eble (C433, R724), mark 4:10.

129. Robert McLaughlin Sr., interviewed by son Robert Jr. on behalf of author, 2009, mark 27:10.

130. Interview with homesteader Joseph Roscoe (C433, R716), West Virginia University Libraries, Morgantown, WV, and Regional History Collection, mark 6:30.

131. Letter from Dr. John Fullmer to author, March 30, 2010.

132. Author interview with Dr. John Fullmer, mark 18:25.

133. Letter, Elsie Clapp to Eleanor Roosevelt, August 16, 1936, Eleanor Roosevelt Papers, FDRL.

134. Letter, Eleanor Roosevelt to Elsie Clapp, January 8, 1937, Eleanor Roosevelt Papers, FDRL.

135. Haid, "Arthurdale: An Experiment in Community Planning," 297.

136. Haid, Stephen. "Arthurdale: An Experiment in Community Planning."

137. Johnstone and Lord, *A Place on Earth*, 42.

138. Memorandum to the Press, Department of the Interior, October 12, 1933, West Virginia University, Arthurdale Project Papers, West Virginia Regional and History Collection, A&M 2178/Folder 4.

139. College of Education, West Virginia University, "Report of the Survey of Arthurdale School," 11.

140. Johnstone and Lord, *A Place on Earth*, 46.

141. U.S. Dept. of the Interior, *Circular No. 1*, 5.

142. Conkin, *Tomorrow a New World,* 102.

143. Ghirardo, *Building New Communities*, 178.

144. Pickett, *For More than Bread,* 63.

145. Letter, Elsie Clapp to Eleanor Roosevelt, January 10, 1936, Eleanor Roosevelt Papers, FDRL.

146. Hoffman, *Eleanor Roosevelt and the Arthurdale Experiment*, 52; and Haid, "Arthurdale: An Experiment in Community Planning," 208.

147. Letter, J. O. Walker to Eleanor Roosevelt, May 24, 1939, Eleanor Roosevelt Papers, FDRL.

148. Letter, Anne Savage to J. O. Walker, May 30, 1939, Eleanor Roosevelt Papers, FDRL.

149. Report on James Lawrence, February 16, 1939, Eleanor Roosevelt Papers, FDRL.

150. Case History of Dallas Earl Riley, January 9, 1936, Eleanor Roosevelt Papers, FDRL.

151. Homestead Contract, June 4, 1934, blank copy, Louis Howe Papers, FDRL.

152. Haid, "Arthurdale: An Experiment in Community Planning," 197.

153. Holly Cowan, "Arthurdale," M.A. thesis, New York, Columbia University, 1968, 40.

154. Letter, Bushrod Grimes to M. L. Wilson, April 4, 1937, West Virginia University, Arthurdale Project Papers, West Virginia Regional and History Collection. A&M 2178/Folder 1.

155. Letter, Bushrod Grimes to O. B. Smart, September 10, 1934, West Virginia University, Arthurdale Project Papers, West Virginia Regional and History Collection. A&M 2178/Folder 1.

156. Letter, O. B. Smart to J. C. Sillenbeck and Bushrod Grimes, July 16, 1934, West Virginia University, Arthurdale Project Papers, West Virginia Regional and History Collection. A&M 2178/Folder 1.

157. M. L. Wilson, "How New Deal Agencies Are Affecting Family Life," *Journal of Home Economics* 27 (1935): 277.

158. Patterson, "Constructing Ideal Families in Ideal Communities," 6.

159. Dr. Edward Banfield, *Government Project* (Glencoe, IL: Free Press, 1951), 13.

160. Letter, Elsie Clapp to Eleanor Roosevelt, March 17, 1936, Eleanor Roosevelt Papers, FDRL.

161. Orval and Edith Pugh, Interview transcript, June 16, 1987, Arthurdale Heritage, Inc., 36.

162. Letter, Elsie Clapp to Eleanor Roosevelt, July 13, 1936, Eleanor Roosevelt Papers, FDRL.

163. Haid, "Arthurdale: An Experiment in Community Planning," 152.

164. Letter, Bernard Baruch to Elsie Clapp, January 15, 1936, Eleanor Roosevelt Papers, FDRL.

165. No author, Memorandum on Arthurdale, circa 1937, Eleanor Roosevelt Papers, FDRL.

166. Letter, J. O. Walker to W. W. Alexander, 1939, Eleanor Roosevelt Papers, FDRL.

167. Conkin, *Tomorrow a New World*, 31.

168. Millard Milburn Rice, "Footnote on Arthurdale," *Harper's Magazine* 180 (March 1940): 419.

169. Letter, E. G. Swift to M. L. Wilson, October 24, 1933. Franklin Delano Roosevelt Official Papers, OF-466e, FDRL.

170. M. L. Wilson, "The Place of Subsistence Homesteads in Our National Economy." *Journal of Farm Economics* 16, no. 1 (Jan. 1934): 84.

171. Letter, E. G. Swift to M. L. Wilson, October 24, 1933, Franklin Delano Roosevelt Official Papers, OF-466e, FDRL.

172. Conkin, *Tomorrow a New World,* 102.

173. Hornyak, "Arthurdale: Homesteading in West Virginia," 30.

174. Hoffman, *Eleanor Roosevelt and the Arthurdale Experiment*, 41.

175. Haid, "Arthurdale: An Experiment in Community Planning," 183.

176. Letter, Elsie Clapp to Eleanor Roosevelt, January 10, 1936.

177. Cowan, "Arthurdale," 40.

178. Legal Statement of Bushrod Grimes to Special Agent Shafor, PWA, October 18, 1934, 11–12, West Virginia University, Arthurdale Project Papers, West Virginia Regional and History Collection. A&M 2178/Folder 6.

179. Letter, Bushrod Grimes to M. L. Wilson, April 4, 1937.

180. "Arthurdale Inn, Three Factories Sold," *New York Times*, June 16, 1946, 33.

181. M. A. Glavin, "Reedsville Model for Homestead Plans," *Washington Post*, Mar. 11, 1934, B4.

182. Andy Wolfe, Interview transcript, June 11, 1987, Arthurdale Heritage, Inc., 4.

183. *Pittsburgh Sun Times*, March 1, 1935, by Frank C. Wardrop, West Virginia University, Arthurdale Project Papers, West Virginia Regional and History Collection. A&M 1291.

184. Rice, "Footnote on Arthurdale," 419.

185. Andy Wolfe, Interview transcript, 17.

186. Letter from a group of homesteader wives to Eleanor Roosevelt, October 18, 1933, West Virginia University, Arthurdale Project Papers, West Virginia Regional and History Collection. A&M 2178/Folder 1.

187. Haid, "Arthurdale: An Experiment in Community Planning," 185–186.

188. Letter, Homesteaders Club to J. O. Walker, October 30, 1940, Eleanor Roosevelt Papers, FDRL.

189. Cook, *Eleanor Roosevelt, Vol. 2*, 148.

190. Letter, Elsie Clapp to Eleanor Roosevelt, January 4, 1936.

191. "Homesteader's Wife," *Liberty*, January 2, 1937, 12–13.

192. College of Education, West Virginia University, "Report of the Survey of Arthurdale School," 57.

193. Ibid., 54.

194. Author interview with Dr. John Fullmer, mark 31:50.

195. Hoffman, *Eleanor Roosevelt and the Arthurdale Experiment*, 83.

196. Ibid., 85.

197. Hareven, *Eleanor Roosevelt*, 99.

198. Hoffman, *Eleanor Roosevelt and the Arthurdale Experiment*, 85.

199. M. L. Wilson, *Democracy Has Roots* (New York: Carrick & Evans, 1939), 177.

200. Rice, "Footnote on Arthurdale," 419.

201. Ibid., 415.

202. College of Education, West Virginia University, "Report of the Survey of Arthurdale School," 12.

Chapter 8: At Long Last, Arcadia

1. William Fulton, "Cut Rate Utopia Just a Mudhole to Homesteader," *Chicago Daily Tribune* (March 10, 1942), 1.

2. Ibid.

3. Stephen Haid, "Arthurdale: An Experiment in Community Planning, 1933–47." PhD diss., West Virginia University, 1975, 308.

4. William Fulton, "Meddling by U.S. Blamed in Mess at Arthurdale," *Chicago Tribune*, March 13, 1942, 7; and Paul K. Conkin, *Tomorrow a New World: The New Deal Community Program* (Ithaca, NY: Cornell University Press, 1959), 226.

5. Fulton, "Cut Rate Utopia Just a Mudhole to Homesteader."

6. Interview with homesteader Richard Glass (C433, R726), West Virginia University Libraries, Morgantown, WV and Regional History Collection, mark 11:50.

7. Interview with homesteaders Alice and Warren Whittaker and Florence (Groves) Hovatter (C433, R723), West Virginia University Libraries, Morgantown, WV, and Regional History Collection, mark 15:20.

8. Kathleen Cullinan and Beth Spence, "Arthurdale: The New Deal Comes to Preston County," *Goldenseal* 7, no. 2 (Apr./June 1981): 19.

9. Fulton, "Meddling by U.S. Blamed in Mess at Arthurdale"; and Conkin, *Tomorrow a New World*, 332.

10. Haid, "Arthurdale: An Experiment in Community Planning," 312.

11. Ibid., 313.

12. Amanda Griffith Penix, *Arthurdale* (Arthurdale, WV, Arthurdale Heritage, Inc., 2007), 117.

13. *Final Cost and Expenditure Survey*, Department of Agriculture, Farm Security Administration, October 31, 1937, Eleanor Roosevelt Papers, FDRL.

14. W. T. Frazier, *Records Relating to the History of the FSA, Vol. 1.*(1942) Records Group 96, National Archives, College Park, MD.

15. Haid, "Arthurdale: An Experiment in Community Planning," 312.

16. "Another 'Human Engineering' Job Jolts Taxpayers," *Chicago Daily Tribune*, Mar. 13, 1942, 7.

17. http://data.bls.gov/cgi-bin/cpicalc.pl.

18. Fulton, "Meddling by U.S. Blamed in Mess at Arthurdale"; and Conkin, *Tomorrow a New World*, 230.

19. Paul Johnstone and Russell Lord, *A Place on Earth: A Critical Appraisal of Subsistence Homesteads* (Washington, DC: U.S. Dept. of Agriculture, Bureau of Agricultural Economics, 1942), 195.

20. Haid, "Arthurdale: An Experiment in Community Planning," 113.

21. Fulton, "Meddling by U.S. Blamed in Mess at Arthurdale"; and Conkin, *Tomorrow a New World*, 219.

22. Fulton, "Meddling by U.S. Blamed in Mess at Arthurdale"; and Conkin, *Tomorrow a New World*, 231.

23. Interview with homesteaders Alice and Warren Whittaker and Florence (Groves) Hovatter (C433, R723), mark 14:10.

24. Interview with homesteader Bertie Swick (C420, R579), West Virginia University Libraries, Morgantown, WV, and Regional History Collection, mark 14:33.

25. Andy Wolfe, Interview transcript, June 11, 1987, Arthurdale Heritage, Inc., 14.

26. Letter, Raymond Kenny to O. C. Brown, May 29, 1941, Eleanor Roosevelt Papers, FDRL.

27. Interview with homesteaders Alice and Warren Whittaker and Florence (Groves) Hovatter (C433, R723), mark 14:10.

28. Haid, "Arthurdale: An Experiment in Community Planning," 322.

29. Interview with homesteader Andy Wolfe (C433, R720), West Virginia University Libraries, Morgantown, WV, and Regional History Collection, mark 12:30.

30. Film transcript, *West Virginia*, www.wvculture.org/history/wvmemory/filmtranscripts/wv.html.

31. Author interview with Dr. John Fullmer, mark 45:05.

32. Fulton, "Cut Rate Utopia Just a Mudhole to Homesteader."

33. Interview with homesteaders Edna and Robert Day (C433, R719) West Virginia University Libraries, Morgantown, WV and Regional History Collection, mark 12:15.

34. *Report on the Arthurdale Development,* May 11, 1936, Eleanor Roosevelt Papers, FDRL.

35. Letter, Elsie Clapp to Eleanor Roosevelt, March 17, 1936, Eleanor Roosevelt Papers, FDRL.

36. M. A. Glavin, "Reedsville Model for Homestead Plans," *Washington Post*, Mar. 11, 1934, B4.

37. Interview with homesteader Bertie Swick (C420, R579), mark 12:10.

38. Author interview with Glenda (Stump) McLaughlin, 2010, mark 21:15.

39. Perry, Julia, Letter to author, February 2010.

40. Interview with homesteaders Alice and Warren Whittaker and Florence (Groves) Hovatter (C433, R723), mark 3:55.

41. Interview with homesteader Joseph Roscoe (C433, R716), West Virginia University Libraries, Morgantown, WV, and Regional History Collection, mark 1:10.

42. Interview with homesteader Andy Wolfe, (C433, R720), mark 34:56; and Interview with homesteader Richard Glass, (C433, R726), mark 6:10.

43. Fulton, "Meddling by U.S. Blamed in Mess at Arthurdale"; and Conkin, *Tomorrow a New World*, 40.

44. Donna Hale, "Edson and Gertrude McClain," in Marilee Hall, ed., "*New Deal": Original Homesteaders of Arthurdale, WV* (Arthurdale, WV: Arthurdale Heritage, Inc., 2009), 23.

45. Orval and Edith Pugh, Interview transcript, June 16, 1987, Arthurdale Heritage, Inc., 34.

46. Interview with homesteader Ralph Brown (C433, R722), West Virginia University Libraries, Morgantown, WV, and Regional History Collection, mark 26:50.

47. Interview with homesteader Andy Wolfe (C433, R720), mark 18:40; and interview with homesteaders Alice and Warren Whittaker and Florence (Groves) Hovatter (C433, R723), mark 19:10.

48. Author interview with Dr. John Fullmer, mark 6:50.

49. Interview with homesteader Ellen Estep (C433, R717), West Virginia University Libraries, Morgantown, WV, and Regional History Collection, mark 7:15.

50. Author interview with Norma (Turner) McLaughlin, mark 34:40.

51. Birdie Swick, Interview transcript, June 15, 1987, Arthurdale Heritage, Inc., 10.

52. Interview with homesteaders Alice and Warren Whittaker and Florence (Groves) Hovatter (C433, R723) WVU Libraries, Morgantown, WV and Regional History Collection, mark 1:50.

53. Interview with homesteader Hilda Hendershot (C433, R718), West Virginia University Libraries, Morgantown, WV, and Regional History Collection, mark 22:00.

54. Author interview with Larry McLaughlin, 2010, mark 11:20.

55. Pamphlet, "Dedication of the Community Presbyterian Church, Arthurdale, WV," Eleanor Roosevelt Papers, FDRL.

56. Visitor pamphlet, Hospice Center, Arthurdale, WV.

57. Eleanor (Harvey) DeGolyer, Interview transcript, no date, Arthurdale Heritage, Inc., 8.

58. Jim McNelis, Letter to author, March 2010.

59. Ibid.

60. James David, Interview transcript, no date, Arthurdale Heritage, Inc., 3.

61. John Maxwell, "Learning by Doing: Teachers Remember Arthurdale School," *Goldenseal* 8, no. 1 (Spring 1982): 70.

62. U.S. Dept. of Interior, *Bulletin,* Division of Subsistence Homesteads (Washington, DC, 1935), 20.

63. Michael Byers, "Brave New Town: Revisiting Arthurdale, WV," *Preservation* (Mar./Apr. 2006): 32–37.

64. Penix, *Arthurdale*, 123.

65. Interview with homesteader Elma Martin (C420, R569), West Virginia University Libraries, Morgantown, WV, and Regional History Collection, mark 39:30.

66. Mary Meek Atkeson, "Too Many Hopes," *Country Gentleman* 105 (Dec. 1935): 39.

Epilogue: To the Victor, the Spoils

1. Robert Higgs, "Government and the Economy," *The Independent Review* (April 20, 2005), 1.

2. Stephen Haid, "Arthurdale: An Experiment in Community Planning, 1933–47." PhD diss., West Virginia University, 1975, 40.

3. "Passing of a Great Illusion," *Nation's Business* 30 (Apr. 1942): 66.

4. Paul Johnstone and Russell Lord, *A Place on Earth: A Critical Appraisal of Subsistence Homesteads* (Washington, DC: U.S. Dept. of Agriculture, Bureau of Agricultural Economics, 1942), 184.

5. Ibid., 177.

6. Ebenezer Howard, *Garden Cities of Tomorrow* (London, England: Swan Sonnenschein, 1902), 95.

7. R. W. Murchie, "Land Settlement as a Relief Measure," from *Day and Hour Series #5,* University of Minnesota, 1933, 15.

8. Johnstone and Lord, *A Place on Earth*, 31.

9. Ibid., 179.

10. Millard Milburn Rice, "Footnote on Arthurdale," *Harper's Magazine* 180 (March 1940): 411–419.

11. Franklin D. Roosevelt, *The Public Papers and Addresses of Franklin D. Roosevelt* (New York: Random House, 1938), 193.

12. Kathleen Cullinan and Beth Spence, "Arthurdale: The New Deal Comes to Preston County," *Goldenseal* 7, no. 2 (Apr./June 1981): 8.

13. Michael Byers, "Brave New Town: Revisiting Arthurdale, WV." *Preservation* (March/April 2006), 32–37.

14. "What of the Colony Plan of Land Settlement?" *Agricultural Review* 18 (Apr. 1925): 16–17.

15. Rexford Tugwell, "The Sources of New Deal Reformism," *Ethics* 64 (July 1954): 257.

16. Frederic C. Howe, *The Land and the Soldier* (New York: Charles Scribner's Sons, 1919), 4–5.

17. Ralph Borsodi, *This Ugly Civilization* (New York: Simon & Schuster, 1929), 332–333.

18. Millard Milburn Rice, "The Fuller Life at Reedsville," *Nation's Business* 24 (May 1936): 24.

19. Letter, Millard M. Rice to B. Grimes, November 20, 1939, West Virginia University, Arthurdale Project Papers, West Virginia Regional and History Collection. A&M 2178/Folder 1.

20. Bruce Beezer, "Arthurdale: An Experiment in Community Living," *West Virginia History* 36, no. 1 (1974/75): 32.

21. M. L. Wilson, speech to American Farm Economic Association, December 27, 1933, West Virginia University, Arthurdale Project Papers, West Virginia Regional and History Collection. A&M 2178/Folder 3.

22. Rexford Tugwell, "The Resettlement Idea," *Agricultural History* 33 (Oct. 1959): 161–163.

23. Oren Stephens, "FSA Fights for Life," *Harper's Magazine* 176 (1942–1943): 482–483.

24. M. L. Wilson, "How New Deal Agencies Are Affecting Family Life," *Journal of Home Economics* 27 (1935): 275–279.

25. *Arthurdale: A Partial Pattern for the New American Way of Life*, 1937, prepared for President Roosevelt, West Virginia University, Rare Books Collection, 2.

26. Wilson, "How New Deal Agencies Are Affecting Family Life"; Ralph Borsodi, "Dayton, Ohio, Makes Social History," *Nation* 136 (1933): 448; Borsodi, *This Ugly Civilization*, 313; and Wilson, "The Place of Subsistence Homesteads in Our National Economy," 84.

27. M. L. Wilson, "Farm Relief and Allotment Plan," from *Day and Hour Series #2*, University of Minnesota, 1933, 49.

28. Jeanna S. Rymer, "Arthurdale: A Social Experiment in the 1930s," *West Virginia History* 46, no. 1 (1985–1986): 100.

29. *Report of the Survey of Arthurdale School*, West Virginia University College of Education, Morgantown, WV, 1940, 43.

30. M. A. Glavin, "Reedsville Model for Homestead Plans," *Washington Post*, Mar. 11, 1934, B4.

31. Johnstone and Lord, *A Place on Earth*, 181.

32. Ibid.

33. Interview with homesteaders Dan and Anna Houghton, (C420, R571), West Virginia University Libraries, Morgantown, WV, and Regional History Collection, mark 28:30.

34. Letter, Bushrod Grimes to O. B. Smart, September 10, 1934, West Virginia University, Arthurdale Project Papers, West Virginia Regional and History Collection. A&M 2178/Folder 1.

35. Murchie, "Land Settlement as a Relief Measure," 15.

36. Memo, George Beecher (Arthurdale school staff), July 15, 1935, Eleanor Roosevelt Papers, FDRL.

37. Fred W. Perkins, "Check Election Returns From Arthurdale," *Pittsburgh Press*, Nov. 1, 1944, 2.

38. Elwood Mead, "Government Aid and Direction in Land Settlement," *American Economic Review* 8, no. 1 Supp. (Mar. 1918): 84.

39. Letter, J. O. Walker to Eleanor Roosevelt, January 25, 1937, OF-2700, Franklin Delano Roosevelt Papers, FDRL.

40. Tugwell, "The Resettlement Idea," 161–163.

41. Jane Goldstrom, *Knoxville Borough: A History* (Pittsburgh, PA: Whortleberry Press, 1939), 12.

42. "Should Honor City Builder," *Bulletin Index*, Jan. 15, 1916.

43. Ibid.

44. Goldstrom, *Knoxville Borough*, 12–13.

45. Amanda Griffith Penix, *Arthurdale* (Arthurdale, WV: Arthurdale Heritage, Inc., 2007), 150.

46. West Virginia University, Arthurdale Project Papers, West Virginia Regional and History Collection. A&M 1291.

47. Tamara K. Hareven, *Eleanor Roosevelt: An American Conscience* (Chicago: Quadrangle Books, 1968), 109.

48. Dianne Y. Ghirardo, *Building New Communities: New Deal America and Fascist Italy* (Princeton, NJ: Princeton University Press, 1989), 9–13.

49. Wilson, "How New Deal Agencies Are Affecting Family Life," 274.

50. Haid, "Arthurdale: An Experiment in Community Planning," 98.

51. Holly Cowan, "Arthurdale," M.A. thesis, New York, Columbia University, 1968, 53.

52. Howard, *Garden Cities of Tomorrow*, 97.

53. Christine Kreiser, "I Wonder Whom God Will Hold Responsible?" *West Virginia History* 53 (1994): 61–92.

54. T. R. Carskadon, "Hull House in the Hills," *New Republic*, 79 (Aug. 1, 1934).

55. "Arthurdale," *Chicago Daily Tribune*, March 5, 1942, 14.

56. Daniel Perlstein, "Community and Democracy in American Schools," *Teachers College Record* 97, no. 4 (Summer 1996): 626.

57. Mary Meek Atkeson, "Too Many Hopes," *Country Gentleman* 105 (Dec. 1935): 38.

58. Perkins, "Check Election Returns from Arthurdale."

59. William Fulton, "Meddling by U.S. Blamed in Mess at Arthurdale," *Chicago Tribune*, Mar. 13, 1942, 7; and Paul K. Conkin, *Tomorrow a New World: The New Deal Community Program* (Ithaca, NY: Cornell University Press, 1959), 213.

60. Letter, Elsie Clapp to Eleanor Roosevelt, January 4, 1936, Eleanor Roosevelt Papers, FDRL.

61. Sam Stack, "Elsie Ripley Clapp and the Arthurdale Schools." Paper presented at the annual meeting of the American Educational Research Association, Montreal, Canada, April 23, 1999, 26.

62. Cullinan and Spence, "Arthurdale: The New Deal Comes to Preston County," 9.

63. Johnstone and Lord, *A Place on Earth*, 191.

64. Wilson, "Farm Relief and Allotment Plan," 31.

65. Wilson, "How New Deal Agencies Are Affecting Family Life," 276.

66. Johnstone and Lord, *A Place on Earth*, 53.

67. *Dominion News*, Oct. 3, 1934, West Virginia University, Arthurdale Project Papers, West Virginia Regional and History Collection. A&M 1291.

68. Rice, "The Fuller Life at Reedsville," 87.

69. Louis M. Hacker, "Plowing the Farmer Under," *Harper's Magazine* 169 (1934): 72–73; Clarence Pickett, *For More than Bread* (Boston: Little, Brown, 1953), 37; Blanche Wiesen Cook, *Eleanor Roosevelt, Vol. 2: 1933–38* (New York: Viking Press, 1999), 28; Sandra Barney, "You Get What You Pay For: The Political Economy of Health Care Delivery on Scotts Run, 1920–1935," in Bryan Ward, ed., *A New Deal for America* (Arthurdale, WV: Arthurdale Heritage, Inc., 1995), 28; and Rice, "Footnote on Arthurdale," 418.

70. Fulton, "Meddling by U.S. Blamed in Mess at Arthurdale"; and Conkin, *Tomorrow a New World*, 38.

71. Philip M. Glick, "The Federal Subsistence Homestead Program," *Yale Law Journal* 44(1935): 1330, note 18.

72. Fulton, "Meddling by U.S. Blamed in Mess at Arthurdale"; and Conkin, *Tomorrow a New World*, 38.

73. Lee A. Gladwin, "Arthurdale: Adventure into Utopia," *West Virginia History* 28, no. 4 (1967): 314.

74. Oren Stephens, "FSA Fights for Life," 482.

75. Johnstone and Lord, *A Place on Earth*, 181–183.

76. Beezer, "Arthurdale: An Experiment in Community Living," 30.

77. Johnstone & Lord, *A Place On Earth*, 196.

78. Cullinan and Spence, "Arthurdale: The New Deal Comes to Preston County," 9.

79. Fulton, "Meddling by U.S. Blamed in Mess at Arthurdale"; and Conkin, *Tomorrow a New World*, 38.

80. Wilson, "How New Deal Agencies Are Affecting Family Life," 275.

81. Ibid., 278.

82. Eleanor Roosevelt, *This I Remember* (New York: HarperCollins, 1949), 131.

83. Haid, "Arthurdale: An Experiment in Community Planning," 2.

84. "Is Reedsville Communistic?" *Literary Digest* 117 (Apr. 21, 1934): 45.

85. Pickett, *For More than Bread*, 40.

86. Glavin, "Reedsville Model for Homestead Plans."

87. Brian Q. Cannon, *Remaking the Agrarian Dream: New Deal Rural Resettlement in the Mountain West*, 1.

88. Webster Powell and Harold Ware, "Planning for Permanent Poverty," *Harper's Magazine* 170 (Apr. 1935): 513.

89. Wilson, speech to American Farm Economic Association.

90. Wilson, "How New Deal Agencies Are Affecting Family Life," 275.

91. U.S. Dept. of the Interior, *Bulletin* (Washington, DC: Division of Subsistence Homesteads, 1935), 21.

92. Wilson, "How New Deal Agencies Are Affecting Family Life," 280.

93. Fulton, "Meddling by U.S. Blamed in Mess at Arthurdale"; and Conkin, *Tomorrow a New World*, 106.

94. Johnstone and Lord, *A Place on Earth*, 37.

95. George S. Wehrwein, "Appraisal of Resettlement," *Journal of Farm Economics* 19 (1937): 195.

96. Nancy Hoffman, *Eleanor Roosevelt and the Arthurdale Experiment* (North Haven, CT: Linnet Books, 2001), 16; and Powell and Ware, "Planning for Permanent Poverty," 523.

97. Franklin D. Roosevelt, "Growing Up by Plan," *Survey* 67, no. 9 (Feb. 1, 1932): 484.

98. Pickett, *For More than Bread*, 46.

99. Congressional Record, 73rd Congress, 2nd Session, Feb. 28, 1934, 3493.

100. Wilson, "Farm Relief and Allotment Plan," 55.

101. Memo, Attorney General's Office to Louis Howe, Sept. 11, 1933, Louis Howe Papers, FDRL.

102. Fulton, "Meddling by U.S. Blamed in Mess at Arthurdale"; and Conkin, *Tomorrow a New World*, 130.

103. Memo to Louis Howe, 1933, Louis Howe Papers, FDRL.

104. Tugwell, "The Resettlement Idea," 164.

105. Elwood Mead, "The New Forty-Niners," *Survey* 47, no. 18 (Jan. 28, 1922): 654.

106. "Dr. Wirt's Testimony on His 'Brain Trust' Revolt Charges," *Washington Post*, Apr. 11, 1934, 2.

107. Malcolm Ross, "When Depression Blights a Great Area," *New York Times*, Jan. 31, 1932, Sec. 5, 6.

108. Barack Obama, "Renewing American Leadership," *Foreign Affairs* 86, no. 4 (2007): 2–16.

109. Thomas E. Ricks, *Fiasco* (New York: Penguin Press, 2006), 424.

110. Johnstone and Lord, *A Place on Earth*, 194.

111. "Arthurdale," *Chicago Daily Tribune*, Mar. 5, 1942, 14.

112. Rexford Tugwell, *The Battle for Democracy* (New York: Columbia University Press, 1935), 123.

Bibliography

This bibliography consists of every source I consulted in my research. Although every single source did not contribute directly to the book, taken as a whole, they were each and every one necessary for its completion. Of particular importance to anyone looking to dive deep into Arthurdale or the New Deal program that created it, Paul Conkin's *Tomorrow a New World* is like the Beatles catalog to music—utterly indispensable and the best starting point for both the lay reader and the professional.

For the historian, the National Archives at College Park, Maryland, yield much information regarding the subsistence homesteads project in all its various organizational states. For a treasure chest's worth of Arthurdale specific primary sources, FDR's Library in Hyde Park, New York, and West Virginia University's West Virginia and Regional History Collection are incomparable.

If any researcher/reader has any questions regarding sources, please feel free to contact me at peloponny1@aol.com.

Newspapers

Arthurdale Heritage Newsletter
Chicago Daily Tribune
Chicago Tribune
New York Times
Pittsburgh Press
Roanoke Times
Washington Post

Magazines/Journals

Agricultural Engineering
Agricultural History
Agricultural Review
American City
American Economic Review
American Historical Review
American Mercury
Annals of the American Academy of Political & Social Science
Atlantic Monthly
Black Diamond
Bulletin Index
BusinessWeek
Charities
Christian Century
Country Gentleman
Craftsman
Current History
Education
Ethics
Forum
Free America
Goldenseal
Harper's Magazine
Independent Review

Journal of Farm Economics
Journal of Land and Public Utility Economics
Journal of Home Economics
Journal of Politics
Ladies' Home Journal
Liberty
Literary Digest
Nation
Nation's Business
New Republic
Now & Then
Popular Mechanics
Preservation
Review of Reviews
Rotarian
Saturday Evening Post
Scientific American
South Atlantic Quarterly
Sunset Magazine
Survey
Survey Graphic
Tableland Trails
Teachers College Record
West Virginia History
Western Political Quarterly
Yale Law Journal

Pamphlets/Bulletins

A Brief History of the Arthurdale Inn, handout by Hospice Care, current owners of Arthurdale Inn, no date.

Charm School News, www.wvculture.org/history/greatdepression/shack02.jpg.

Elijah—the Mountain Choir Festival Association. Arthurdale, WV, Souvenir Program, August 1947.

"The 50th Anniversary of the Homesteading of Arthurdale, WV," ed. Jettie and Charles Eble, Arthurdale Heritage, Inc., 1984.

"'New Deal': Original Homesteaders of Arthurdale, West Virginia," Part 1, ed. Marilee Hall. Arthurdale Heritage, Inc., 2009.

"A Primer on the New Deal: What It Means to You," ed. Dr. E. E. Lewis. New York: American Education Press, 1933.

The Shack Idea, www.wvculture.org/history/greatdepression/shack03 .jpg.

Students Follow Christ to a Stable, www.wvculture.org/history/ greatdepression/shack01.jpg.

"The 25th Anniversary of Arthurdale Heritage Inc.," ed. Marilee Hall, Arthurdale Heritage, Inc., 2010.

Archives

Arthurdale Town Archives, Arthurdale, West Virginia.

Arthurdale Project Papers/Bushrod Grimes Papers, West Virginia and Regional History Collection, WVU, Morgantown, West Virginia.

Louis McHenry Howe Papers, Franklin D. Roosevelt Library, Hyde Park, New York (FDRL).

Eleanor Roosevelt Papers, FDRL.

Franklin D. Roosevelt Papers, FDRL.

Printed Materials Collection, FDRL.

Records of the Farmers Home Administration, Records Group 96, National Archives, College Park, MD.

Records of the Office of the Secretary of the Interior, Records Group 48, National Archives, College Park, MD.

Records of the Public Housing Administration, Records Group 196, National Archives, College Park, MD.

Rexford Guy Tugwell Papers, FDRL.

Government Reports

Arthurdale: A Partial Pattern for the New American Way of Life, 1937, written on behalf of President Franklin Delano Roosevelt.

Booth-Tucker, Frederick. "Farm Colonies of the Salvation Army," *Bulletin* (U.S. Dept. of Commerce and Labor) 48 (1903): 1001–1003.

Division of Subsistence Homesteads: Bulletin (U.S. Dept. of the Interior). 1935.

Division of Subsistence Homesteads: Circular No. 1 (U.S. Dept. of the Interior). 1933.

Paul Johnstone and Russell Lord. *A Place on Earth: A Critical Appraisal of Subsistence Homesteads*. Washington, DC: U.S. Dept. of Agriculture, Bureau of Agricultural Economics, 1942.

Staff of the College of Education, West Virginia University. *Report of the Survey of Arthurdale School*, 1940.

Wilson, M. L. "Farmers in a Changing World." *Yearbook 1727* (U.S. Dept. of Agriculture), 1941.

Unpublished Manuscripts

Cowen, Holly. "Arthurdale." Master's thesis, Columbia University, 1968.

Haid, Stephen. "Arthurdale: An Experiment in Community Planning, 1933–47." PhD diss., West Virginia University, 1975.

Patterson, Stuart. "Constructing Ideal Families in Ideal Communities: The Case of Arthurdale, West Virginia," Apr. 2002.

Stack, Sam. "Elsie Ripley Clapp and the Arthurdale Schools," Apr. 1999.

Tugwell, Rexford G. "Social Objectives of Education," Columbia University, 1932.

Interviews Conducted with Author
from Fall 2009 to Spring 2010

Dr. John Fullmer
Linda (McLaughlin) Honchell
Glenn Luzier
Larry McLaughlin
Robert McLaughlin Sr.
James McNelis
Julia Perry

Ann Shannon
Glenda (McLaughlin) Stump
Norma (McLaughlin) Turner

Interviews Conducted by Arthurdale Heritage Inc. from Late 1980s to Early 1990s

Ralph Brown
James David
Edna and Robert Day
Eleanor (Harvey) DeGolyer
Henry and Thurla Donahue
Jettie Eble
Ellen Estep
Elizabeth Fullmer
Richard Glass
Charles and Hilda Hendershot
Anna and Dan Houghton
Deanna Hornyak
Glenn Luzier
Elma Martin
Annabelle Mayor
Lucille Smith Myers
Orval and Edith Pugh
Hugh Radcliff
Herman Reber
Joseph Roscoe
Jacob and Bertie Swick
Bill Watson
Maynard and Ruby Weaver
Oscar Whipkey
Alice and Warren Whittaker (with Florence (Groves) Hovatter)
Glenna Williams
Andy Wolfe
Carolyn Zinn

Multimedia

Arthurdale: A First Lady's Legacy. West Virginia Public Broadcasting, WNPB, 1988.

Film Transcript, *West Virginia*, www.wvculture.org/history/wvmemory/ filmtranscripts/wv.html.

Books

Baker, O. E. *Agriculture in Modern Life.* New York: Harper & Brothers, 1939.

Banfield, Dr. Edward. *Government Project.* Glencoe, IL: Free Press, 1951.

Bastiat, Frederic. *Selected Essays in Political Economy.* Irvington-on-Hudson, NY: Foundation for Economic Education, 1995.

Belloc, Hilaire. *The Servile State.* New York: Henry Holt & Co., 1946.

Borsodi, Ralph. *This Ugly Civilization.* New York: Simon & Schuster, 1929.

Borsodi, Ralph. *Flight from the City.* New York: Harper & Brothers, 1933.

Cannon, Brian Q. *Remaking the Agrarian Dream: New Deal Rural Resettlement in the Mountain West*, Albuquerque: University of New Mexico Press, 1996.

Clapp, Elsie. *Community Schools in Action.* New York: Arno Press, 1971.

Conkin, Paul K. *Tomorrow a New World: The New Deal Community Program.* Ithaca, NY: Cornell University Press, 1959.

Conkin, Paul K. *The New Deal.* New York: Thomas Y. Crowell Co., 1971.

Cook, Blanche Wiesen. *Eleanor Roosevelt, Vol. 2: 1933–38.* New York: Viking Press, 1999.

Core, Earl L. *The Monongalia Story: A Bicentennial History, Vol. 4.* Parsons, WV: McClain Printing, 1982.

DuBois, W. E. B. *The Seventh Son: The Thought and Writings of W. E. B. DuBois Vol. 2.* New York: Random House, 1971.

Ely, Richard. *Outlines of Economics*, 6th ed. New York: Macmillan, 1937.

Ely, Richard. *Ground Under Our Feet: An Autobiography.* New York: Macmillan, 1938.

Faber, Doris. *The Life of Lorena Hickok.* New York: William Morrow, 1980.

Ferguson, Niall. *The Pity of War.* New York: Basic Books, 1999.

Fitzgerald, Deborah Kay. *Every Farm a Factory: The Industrial Ideal in American Agriculture.* New Haven, CT: Yale University Press, 2003.

Ford, Henry. *Today and Tomorrow.* Garden City, NY: Doubleday, 1926.

Fusfeld, Daniel R. *The Economic Thought of Franklin D. Roosevelt and the Origins of the New Deal.* New York: Columbia University Press, 1954.

Ghirardo, Dianne Y. *Building New Communities: New Deal America and Fascist Italy.* Princeton, NJ: Princeton University Press, 1989.

Goldstrom, Jane. *Knoxville Borough: A History.* Pittsburgh, PA: Whortleberry Press, 1939.

Hall, Bolton. *Three Acres and Liberty.* London, England: Macmillan, 1907.

Hall, Bolton. *A Little Land and a Living.* New York: Arcadia Press, 1908.

Hareven, Tamara K. *Eleanor Roosevelt: An American Conscience.* Chicago: Quadrangle Books, 1968.

Haskell, H. J. *The New Deal in Old Rome.* Auburn, AL: Ludwig von Mises Institute, 2009.

Hoffman, Nancy. *Eleanor Roosevelt and the Arthurdale Experiment.* North Haven, CT: Linnet Books, 2001.

Hopkins, Harry L. *Spending to Save.* New York: Norton, 1936.

Howard, Ebenezer. *Garden Cities of Tomorrow.* London, England: Swan Sonnenschein, 1902.

Howe, Frederic C. *The Land and the Soldier.* New York: Charles Scribner's Sons, 1919.

Hoxie, Mary Jones. *Swords into Ploughshares; An Account of the AFSC.* Westport, CT: Greenwood Press, 1971.

Hubert, Philip Jr., *Liberty and a Living* (New York: G. P. Putnam's Sons, 1889).

Johnson, James P. *The Politics of Soft Coal.* Urbana: University of Illinois Press, 1937.

Kluger, James R. *Turning on Water with a Shovel.* Albuquerque: University of New Mexico Press, 1992.

Kyvig, David E. *Daily Life in the United States, 1920–1940*. Chicago: Ivan R. Dee, 2002.

Lee, Sidney D. *". . . And the Trees Cried."* Morgantown, WV: Author, 1991.

Lee, Howard Burton. *Bloodletting in Appalachia: The Story of West Virginia's Four Major Mine Wars*. Morgantown: West Virginia University Press, 1969.

Little, Richard and Margaret. *Arthurdale—Its History, Its Lessons for Today*. Morgantown, WV: WVU Foundation, Inc., 1976.

Mead, Elwood. *Helping Men Own Farms*. New York: Macmillan, 1920.

Murchie, R. W. *Land Settlement as a Relief Measure*. From *Day and Hour Series* #5. Minneapolis: University of Minnesota, 1933.

Murphy, Robert P. *The Politically Incorrect Guide to the Great Depression and the New Deal*. Washington, DC: Regnery, 2009.

Newell, Clayton R. *Lee vs. McClellan: The First Campaign*. Washington, DC: Regnery, 1996.

Preston County, West Virginia, History. Kingwood, WV: Preston County Historical Society, 1979.

Patterson, Stuart. *Defining Memory*, ed. Amy K. Leven. Plymouth, England: AltaMira Press, 2007.

Penix, Amanda Griffith. *Arthurdale*. Arthurdale, WV: Arthurdale Heritage, Inc., 2007.

Pickett, Clarence. *For More than Bread*. Boston: Little, Brown, 1953.

Rader, Benjamin G. *The Academic Mind and Reform*. Lexington: University of Kentucky Press, 1966.

Rice, Connie P. *Our Monongalia: A History of African Americans in Monongalia County, West Virginia*. Terra Alta, WV: Headline Books, 1999.

Roosevelt, Eleanor. *This I Remember*. New York: HarperCollins, 1949.

Roosevelt, Franklin D. *My Friends, 28 Famous Speeches*. Buffalo, NY: Foster & Stewart, 1945.

Roosevelt, Franklin D. *The Public Papers and Addresses of Franklin D. Roosevelt*. New York: Random House, 1938.

Schivelbusch, Wolfgang. *Three New Deals*. New York: Metropolitan Books, 2006.

Shlaes, Amity. *The Forgotten Man*. New York: HarperCollins, 2007.

Thomas, Jerry Bruce. *An Appalachian New Deal: West Virginia in the Great Depression.* Lexington: University Press of Kentucky, 1998.

Tugwell, Rexford. *The Battle for Democracy.* New York: Columbia University Press, 1935.

Tugwell, Rexford. *The Democratic Roosevelt.* Garden City, NY: Doubleday, 1957.

von Mises, Ludwig. *Interventionism: An Economic Analysis.* Irvington-on-Hudson, NY: Foundation for Economic Education, 1998.

Ward, Bryan, ed. *A New Deal for America.* Arthurdale, WV: Arthurdale Heritage, Inc., 1995.

Wilson, M. L. *Democracy Has Roots.* New York: Carrick & Evans, 1939.

Wilson, M. L. *Farm Relief and Allotment Plan.* In *Day and Hour Series* #2, Minneapolis: University of Minnesota, 1933.

Young, William and Nancy. *The 1930s.* Westport, CT: Greenwood Press, 2002.

About the Author

C. J. Maloney lives and works in New York City. He earned his M.B.A. at NYU Stern School of Business.

Index